STRUGGLE FOR THE HEARTLAND

GREAT CAMPAIGNS OF THE CIVIL WAR

SERIES EDITORS

Anne J. Bailey
Georgia College &
State University

Brooks D. Simpson
Arizona State University

STEPHEN D. ENGLE

Struggle for the Heartland

The Campaigns from Fort Henry to Corinth

University of Nebraska Press
Lincoln and London

© 2001 by the University of Nebraska Press
Manufactured in the United States of America
⊗
Library of Congress Cataloging-in-Publication Data
Engle, Stephen Douglas.
Struggle for the heartland : the campaigns from
Fort Henry to Corinth / Stephen D. Engle.
p. cm.—(Great campaigns of the Civil War)
Includes bibliographical references (p.) and index.
ISBN 0-8032-1818-4 (cloth : alk. paper)
1. United States—History—Civil War, 1861–1865—Campaigns.
2. Tennessee—History—Civil War, 1861–1865—Campaigns.
3. Kentucky—History—Civil War, 1861–1865—Campaigns.
4. Mississippi–History–Civil War, 1861–1865—Campaigns.
5. Alabama—History—Civil War, 1861–1865—Campaigns.
6. United States—History—Civil War, 1861–1865—Social aspects.
I. Title.   II. Series.
E470.E54 2001
973.7'3—dc21
2001027326

For Taylor and Claire

Contents

Illustrations

Maps

Series Editors' Introduction

Americans remain fascinated by the Civil War. Movies, television, and video—even computer software—have augmented the ever-expanding list of books on the war. Although it stands to reason that a large portion of recent work concentrates on military aspects of the conflict, historians have expanded our scope of inquiry to include civilians, especially women; the destruction of slavery and the evolving understanding of what freedom meant to millions of former slaves; and an even greater emphasis on the experiences of the common soldier on both sides. Other studies have demonstrated the interrelationships of war, politics, and policy and how civilians' concerns back home influenced both soldiers and politicians. Although one cannot fully comprehend this central event in American history without understanding that military operations were fundamental in determining the course and outcome of the war, it is time for students of battles and campaigns to incorporate nonmilitary themes in their accounts. The most pressing challenge facing Civil War scholarship today is the integration of various perspectives and emphases into a new narrative that explains not only what happened, why, and how, but also why it mattered.

The series Great Campaigns of the Civil War offers readers concise syntheses of the major campaigns of the war, reflecting the findings of recent scholarship. The series points to new ways of viewing military campaigns by looking beyond the battlefield and the headquarters tent to the wider political and social context within which these campaigns unfolded; it also shows how campaigns and battles left their imprint on many Americans, from presidents and generals down to privates and civilians. The ends and means of waging war reflect larger political objectives and priorities as well as social values. Historians may continue to debate among themselves as to which of these campaigns constituted true turning points, but each of the campaigns treated in this series contributed to shaping the course of the conflict, opening opportunities, and eliminating alternatives.

In this volume Stephen D. Engle reminds us of the importance of the western theater to the overall war effort in early 1862. As the conflict unfolded in Virginia, Americans tended to overlook the campaigns in the Confederate heartland, but decisions concerning this region had a profound influence on hundreds of thousands of people and on the subsequent events along the Mississippi River. Scholars have long acknowledged that Jefferson Davis often slighted the West and that he failed to recognize its immediate importance, even though Tennessee, a state with over a million people, ranked only behind Virginia in total population. Abraham Lincoln understood that occupying this region was essential to his overall strategy, and the campaigns from Fort Henry to Corinth provided the groundwork for eventual control of this vital area of the South. Yet the fighting in the heartland gave rise to significant challenges for both sides. Lincoln had to confront the problems of occupying large areas of the Confederacy and controlling a hostile slaveholding population, while Davis relinquished control of the Tennessee and Cumberland Rivers and the important railroad junctions at Nashville and Corinth. Professor Engle aptly shows us the geographic and strategic importance of the Confederate losses in these campaigns as well as the social and political implications for civilians. The decisions made by Richmond and Washington in the early months of 1862 would have dramatic consequences in the balance of power in the western theater and ultimately affect the course of the war.

Acknowledgments

This book was conceived by the editors of Great Campaigns of the Civil War, Anne J. Bailey and Brooks Simpson, and I am grateful to them for inviting me to contribute this volume to the series. While on a Fulbright fellowship in the Netherlands, Brooks took the time to share his thoughts with me about the organization of the following narrative, which reflects much of that discussion. The manuscript benefited greatly by colleagues kind enough to read, make suggestions, and recommend revisions. Benjamin Franklin Cooling reviewed part of the initial manuscript as a favor and was quite helpful in forcing me to rethink some conceptual aspects of the work. David Coles also read and made suggestions along the way. Larry Daniel proved once again why he is sought after as a reader. Like Cooling, his careful eye and judicious comments certainly made this a better book. Anne Bailey was an honest but gentle critic and encouraging throughout the process.

I also want to thank the folks at *Harpweek* who graciously extended permission to use and forwarded to me copies of original illustrations for this volume. Rob Kennedy especially deserves recognition for locating these most appropriate figures.

I would be remiss if I did not thank my departmental colleagues who have been supportive over the years. Former chair of the department John O'Sullivan, who passed away last September, was one of those who supported everything about my teaching and research. Not simply a scholar of tremendous intellectual substance, John had many gifts, perhaps the most important of which was making persons around him feel as though they were better for having known him.

Finally, I am blessed to have tremendous support from my wife and children. Stephanie continues to support my work in countless ways. Again, she read the entire manuscript and made her usual helpful suggestions. My children, Taylor and Claire, continue to be sources of distractions of the best kind, and I thank them.

Introduction

In 1861 Harvard-educated Manning Ferguson Force suspended a promising legal career in Ohio to serve in the Union army. Although a native of Washington DC, his experience as a soldier began in September 1861 as a major in the Twentieth Ohio Volunteer Infantry, eventually rising to the rank of brigadier general and leading a brigade in Maj. Gen. William T. Sherman's March to the Sea. He participated in the battles of Fort Donelson, Shiloh, the sieges of Corinth and Vicksburg, and the captures of Jackson, Mississippi; Atlanta; and Savannah. In 1892 he was awarded the Medal of Honor for his role in the battle of Atlanta. He mustered out of the service in January 1866 and returned to his law practice.

In 1882, nearly two decades after the war, Force contracted with the prominent New York publishing company Charles Scribner's Sons to write a volume in their Campaigns of the Civil War series. Up to that time, no extensive history of the military campaigns had been written, and it was the aim of Scribner's to compile a dozen volumes that would become the standard history of the war. The subject of Force's volume was the campaign from Fort Henry on the Tennessee River to Corinth, Mississippi, in early 1862. A reviewer at the time commented that his treatment was purely military and required some effort on the part of the reader to keep up with the "rapidly passing facts pointed out in such profusion."[1]

It is not surprising that Force conceptualized this campaign in the West around a framework of activity that began in February and ended essentially in late May. The drive from Fort Henry to Corinth was the first of the great struggles for occupation during the Civil War. Neither is it surprising that his volume was purely a military history. At the time, it was still necessary to set the record straight as to what actually transpired on the battlefield during those months, and Force was well suited to write such a volume. His was a campaign narrative that typified a preference for isolating military operations from the broader political, social, and economic aims of the warring parties. The attempt to study battles and campaigns exclusive of these larger considerations allowed historians of the pre–World War II era to analyze the significance of combat for strictly military reasons, and this characterized much of the Civil War scholarship of the period.

Still, the notion of studying the military operations in the West outside the larger political and social context in which these battles were fought diminishes the significance of the campaign's broader implications for the war itself. Although *Struggle for the Heartland* develops a narrative within the same time period as Force used, the narrative itself is a synthesis of scholarly secondary works framed around several themes exploring some key relationships of the war and society in early 1862. Several fine scholars, including Benjamin Franklin Cooling and Larry Daniel, have already examined the battles of Forts Henry and Donelson and Shiloh, respectively, and both have done an excellent job of placing the battles themselves within political and social contexts. Still, except for general histories of the war, few works consider these campaigns together, and those that do fail to adequately analyze them in connection to these larger issues. This study attempts to bring the early military campaigns in Kentucky, Tennessee, northern Mississippi, and northern Alabama into their proper social and political context. The twin rivers campaign, which commenced in early February and culminated in the capture of Fort Henry on the Tennessee River and Fort Donelson on the Cumberland River, facilitating the capture and occupation of Nashville and Corinth, was vital because of where it occurred as much as when it occurred.

The divided loyalties of the entire Upper South were no better reflected than in Kentucky and Tennessee. Nowhere would the Union's advance south more severely test the viability of Washington's political war aims than the penetration of the Confederate heartland along the Cumberland and Tennessee Rivers. In the slave states, extending the Federal olive branch was easily done to pro-Union citizens, who desired protection from their neighbors, but it was an altogether different matter to extend it to people who supported the Confederacy. The subsequent campaign toward the railroad junction at Corinth, Mississippi, a move that was interrupted by the battle of Shiloh in April 1862, added significantly to the region's geographic and strategic as well as its social and political importance. Though the Union was successful in seizing territory and cities, it was the location and nature of its occupation forces' experience that prompted a change in Northern attitudes, not only among commanders and soldiers stationed south but also among politicians in Washington and the various states, toward what they hoped to achieve. Just as the occupation of pro-Confederate and proslavery regions of Tennessee would alter Union aims, so too did it affect the sentiments toward reunion among the residents the Federals hoped to bring back.

As communities both north and south of the Ohio River went to war, these campaigns forced soldiers to rethink some of their previous conclusions about their enemies. Northern armies represented a newly forged and mobile community of citizens that had never experienced life, in any substantive way, beyond their hometowns. Campaigning through the Southern heartland provided soldiers with not only military impressions and circumstances but also new political and social situations that left indelible impressions on them, forcing these men to react to the realities of marching through and, for some, occupying the South. These experiences also left their imprint on Northerners elsewhere, from the president down to the lowliest private and civilian.

Therefore, it is necessary to understand the wider political and social context within which these campaigns unfolded. The ends and means of waging this war reflected larger political objectives and priorities as well as social values. In his recent work, *Shiloh: The Battle that Changed the Civil War,* Larry Daniel correctly asserts that the battle of Shiloh "cannot be viewed apart from the dynamics that occurred in the White House in Washington DC, and the Executive Mansion in Richmond."[2] I take the view that the same applies for the series of actions that commenced with the Fort Henry expedition and concluded with the capture of Corinth. Benjamin Franklin Cooling has demonstrated in his work *Fort Donelson's Legacy: War and Society in Kentucky and Tennessee, 1862–1863,* that beyond the fact that these campaigns were characterized by exploiting the rivers, the aftermath of Fort Donelson's capture formed an important legacy highlighting the "confluence of war and society." This convergence must be seen as a significant development in the war and helped shape Union policy, command relations, civil-military relations, and, ultimately, reconstruction aims.[3]

Part of placing this portion of the war in its proper context requires the redefinition of the Confederate "heartland," as Thomas Connelly so appropriately named the region of Tennessee, north-central Alabama, north-central Georgia, and northeast Mississippi. Of course, it is understood that this region was linked by its economic relationships to areas to the north such as Kentucky and those states above the Ohio River between the Appalachian Mountains and the Mississippi River. Nevertheless, the physical heart of the Confederacy was indeed the irregularly shaped region Connelly conceived.

An exploration of the prewar economic relationships and political allegiances formed in this larger American heartland, however, provides credible justification for why its residents were so divided when it came to choosing sides in the Civil War. Of course, some may take issue with this reconfiguration, but when seen in the context of antebellum economic relationships and political allegiances, the shared market and political activities of people on both sides of the Ohio River must be considered as significant influences in determining loyalty in the region as a whole. The firing on Fort Sumter provided the stimulus for people in those states contemplating secession to choose sides based largely on these established associations as well as the projected political aims of both national governments. The complex interplay of locality and loyalty, therefore, became crucial factors in this region.

Another dimension to these campaigns that warrants examination is the relationships between the commanders on each side. The winter and spring campaigns in the West reflected the inability of the high command, at least in the North, to subordinate military desires to political considerations. Maj. Gen. Henry Halleck and Maj. Gen. Don Carlos Buell, the principal Union commanders in the West, repeatedly failed to cooperate when President Abraham Lincoln desired to get their armies moving. Once the Union high command realized that the Cumberland, Tennessee, and Mississippi Rivers were the surest way to Union success and the armies commenced moving, these generals themselves failed to encourage productive relationships, which precluded them from effectively harnessing the strengths of their forces and seizing important strategic opportunities sooner. Interestingly, at a time when departmental commanders refused to cooperate, Halleck's and Buell's subordinates provided the necessary sense of initiative to risk battle and occupy strategic points.

Confederate president Jefferson Davis failed to see beyond the need of protecting Richmond during this period in the war, which revealed the West's apparent unimportance to the Confederacy during these first months of fighting. He gave Gen. Albert Sidney Johnston the authority for directing the war in this vast region between the Appalachians and the

Mississippi (and beyond) without allowing him the resources necessary to do his job well. Despite the relatively small sizes of Johnston's armies, they still proved as unmanageable as those in the East. Besides, he had to contend with the personalities and attitudes of P. G. T. Beauregard, Braxton Bragg, Leonidas Polk, Gideon J. Pillow, and John B. Floyd. Ulysses S. Grant's capture of Fort Donelson in February 1862 was more than just a decisive military victory; it placed the Union army in a position to demoralize the Southern populace in a region known for its many vital resources. With Nashville uncovered, Johnston was forced to fall back and establish a new defensive line from Memphis through Corinth to Chattanooga that, like his original positions, lacked natural defensive barriers. Worse, this redeployment left the region drained by the Tennessee and Cumberland Rivers in Union hands, crippling Confederate logistics.

Though Southern woes increased with the defeat at Pea Ridge, Arkansas, in March 1862, Union forces were unable to exploit their opportunities and instead allowed Johnston time to rally and reinforce his demoralized command. The Confederate concentration at Corinth and the subsequent battle of Shiloh symbolized the effort by a powerful North to amass its western forces against the courageous but inadequate intensity of the Confederacy hoping to reverse several months of defeat in the West. After Shiloh, the Union had yet another opportunity to catch and defeat the Confederate western army, but instead Halleck advanced slowly for nearly two months over twenty-five miles of inhospitable terrain to Corinth, and the Rebels eventually escaped. If there was ever a more anticipated battle that never came, Corinth was most certainly it. Still, after the capture of the northern Mississippi railroad hamlet, never again was the Confederacy able to restore the balance of power in the subtheater of Middle and West Tennessee.

Beyond the battlefield, the campaigns are also significant when considering the larger implications for restoring the captured regions of the Confederacy to the Union and how the relationship between civil and military authorities complicated the wishes of the Lincoln administration. These campaigns highlight the Federal attempt to initiate a process of reconstruction in a region where it was least desired. Certainly, commanders could shape and direct popular attitudes and uprisings by the attitudes they took in local activities, as Cooling has argued, but nowhere did these issues magnify the larger political and social considerations of the war than in the Confederate heartland.[4]

Of course, how the Union engaged in occupation and how the Confed-

eracy fared on the battlefield had as much to do with civilian resistance
and willingness to fight as it did with political and moral concerns over
the institution of slavery. Confederate defeat afforded the opportunity
for politicians and military commanders alike to come to grips with
the consequences of successful military penetration and occupation of
a significant yet deeply conflicted region. The fact that slavery was deeply
entrenched there gave tremendous substance to the strife between civilians and Unions troops—a conflict that sometimes spawned guerrilla
or irregular activity that engulfed people of the Southern heartland.
Once Grant captured Fort Donelson and Buell seized Nashville, both
warned against guerrillas forming in their rear and attempted to eliminate
secessionist intimidation and nurture any reported Unionist sentiment.
Consequently, the Federal presence caused a redefinition of the war with
regard to protection of one's domain. As Rebel forces retreated south,
shattering Confederate invincibility as Johnston's troops proved incapable
of preserving the citizens' guarantees of peace, liberty, and property,
people searched for other means to defend themselves. Thus, after the
fall of Donelson and the Union victory at Shiloh, the struggle became
more acutely a people's war, as civilians began to engage not only in overt
irregular activities but also in more silent efforts to undermine Unionism
in the occupied region precisely because the Confederate army had failed
to adequately protect them and their homeland. Thus, the war in the
West became two-dimensional, for as the Union and Confederate armies
fought one brand of war to gain territory and defeat one another, the
residents and Union soldiers fought a different kind of war to maintain
supremacy in the occupied zones.[5]

These campaigns would test the Lincoln administration's initial assessment that the Union could be restored without trampling the rights and
civil guarantees of Southern noncombatants. The capture of Nashville
in late February 1862 and the appointment of Andrew Johnson as Tennessee's military governor marked a turning point in how the Union
sought to deal with the captured South. Lincoln would have preferred
to commence his efforts in East Tennessee, where Union sentiment ran
high and slavery was not entrenched. But the loss of Fort Henry and Fort
Donelson, which led to the surrender of the Tennessee capital, forced
him to begin reconstruction in Middle Tennessee, where Confederate
sentiment was dominant and slaves were more numerous than anywhere
else in the state. Making Johnson a symbol of Union efforts to extend
to loyal Tennesseans the civil guarantees of a republican government

also signaled a turning point in the war for those who refused to be reconstructed. This juncture would provide the experiences necessary for the Federals to learn that if Southerners would not yield to half-hearted military campaigns with limited goals, then perhaps more-severe operations with broader goals would have to be undertaken.

Finally, like the confluence of the Ohio and Mississippi Rivers, these campaigns of early 1862 highlighted the societal reactions to military occupation as well as the political ambitions of the president and Congress for conceptualizing and managing the war's aims and the process of reconstruction. The relationship between the nature of the war as a whole and the conduct of the armies in this region is significant in that these operations helped bring about the departure from a philosophy of conducting a limited war for limited goals while bringing about the acceptance of broader political desires with more aggressive military conduct. Still, the cumulative effect of the fighting from Fort Henry to Corinth on the Southern countryside provided the regions inhabitants with the experience of the disintegration of their institutions such as slavery and inaugurated a process of social change that fundamentally altered their lives.

In referring to the battle of Shiloh as the "battle that changed the Civil War," Larry Daniel might just as well have been talking about the entire journey started first on the rivers in February and ending at an obscure railroad junction in northern Mississippi in late May. To be sure, readers will find in this volume not a new story, but rather an old one broadened to include social and political dimensions relevant to why Charles Scribner identified this continuous operation as one of the "Great Campaigns of the Civil War."

STRUGGLE FOR THE HEARTLAND

CHAPTER ONE

Rivers, Valleys, and Armies

"It was one of the weaknesses of the Confederacy in the West," wrote Allan Nevins in his seminal work *The War for the Union*, "that the two rivers, the Tennessee and Cumberland, reached inland from the North toward its center. . . . A mere glance at the map would seem to reveal that the Tennessee-Cumberland river system offered the North a heaven-sent opportunity to thrust a harpoon into the very bowels of the Confederacy."[1]

Referring to the rivers' strategic importance during the Civil War was hardly news to Kentuckians and Tennesseans, who had known for generations of their tremendous unifying social significance in forging economic relationships between people with vast differences. These Middle Americans could never have imagined that anything about these rivers would have created weaknesses, particularly since they were the reason for prosperous interior cities such as Nashville. Then again, they could not have imagined a Civil War that turned what was otherwise a lifeline for so many into something that threatened the region's security. Though Northerners and Southerners were late to fully appreciate the significance of the Cumberland and Tennessee Rivers as strategic channels, by late 1861 it had become clear that these waterways held the key to winning the early war in the West. For the Confederacy, to hold them was to maintain control of the vital artery of economic, and now military, traffic, to lose them meant changes of profound and irreparable economic and social significance.

Although not many generations had passed since opening the land west of the Appalachians for settlement, the Cumberland and Tennessee Rivers and their tributaries had been instrumental in developing ties among otherwise isolated and fragmented populations. Though they traversed a physically diverse landscape, the rivers provided a means by which to forge commercial relationships between people and places that shaped a political culture of divergent ideological interests into a regional unity. The fundamental economic characteristic of this western culture was its relative self-sufficiency, typical of hearty and industrious farmers and reflective of Jeffersonian principles based on the acquisition of land. Although roads and turnpikes offered a means to reach markets at great distances, when it came to transporting grain or livestock, these routes proved slow, difficult to traverse, and expensive. The prohibitive costs of hauling agricultural goods overland to markets outside the region made the rivers vital to agricultural self-sufficiency, particularly among interior communities. These communities were economically linked through local networks of rural market exchanges, and the rivers played a major role in fostering these connections. Shared market experiences cultivated a sense of common social and political interests as well.[2]

The Cumberland and Tennessee both descended out of the Great Smoky Mountains and flowed west through the Kentucky, Tennessee, and northern Alabama and Mississippi landscapes before heading north, ultimately emptying into the Ohio River. Long before railroads pushed into the region, keelboats, flatboats, and later steamboats had provided the means to tap into the Upper South interior, connecting people and goods to the downriver markets at Chattanooga, Nashville, Decatur, and Florence. Northbound riverboats carried Southern prosperity in the form of staples and commodities from the upper Cumberland and Tennessee Valleys downstream past Nashville, Clarksville, and Florence. South-bound steamboats loaded with produce from Northern farms navigated upstream year round to Nashville and Florence, carrying goods from Cincinnati, Louisville, and St. Louis. Although shipping became the chief means of transporting goods in the region, river passage could be difficult as sandbars, narrow gorges, and the Muscle Shoals of Alabama forced boatmen to unload their cargos, transport it overland for some distance, and then reload their freight and continue on water. Still, the combined influence of rivers and roads swelled the volume and significance of western trade.[3]

Like the Tennessee and Cumberland Rivers, both the Mississippi and Ohio Rivers, to some degree, also had a unifying influence in the region. Indeed, some Midwesterners thought that the Mississippi River, "the Father of Waters," flowed into the Ohio River as it curved south around Cairo, Illinois. These important waterways were symbols of the nation.

Anyone who had spent time along the Mississippi would have agreed with William T. Sherman, who recognized the river's vast importance, that the Mississippi was the "Spinal column of America."[4]

Despite the growing divide between the North and South, the states encompassing these rivers shared common social interests and associations resulting from the population's use of common highways and markets. The Mississippi-Ohio River system had also conditioned how people communicated, traded, and survived in the Upper South, creating ties of blood and experience between these Southerners and residents of the Old Northwest. Rivers such as the Wabash and the Illinois, which stretched well back into the interior and flowed south, mirrored several other streams that drained nearly every state north of the Ohio. This connected Missouri, southeastern Iowa, and Minnesota to Ohio, Indiana, and New Orleans.[5] Thus, such national rivers were reflective of "a bond of Union made by nature itself," as South Carolina senator James H. Hammond remarked.[6] When the war came, however, a divided nation could no longer share these waterways. As Sherman noted: "Should the Ohio River become a Boundary between the two new Combinations [Union and Confederacy], then will begin a new change. The extreme South will look on Kentucky & Tennessee as the North."[7]

For decades before the railroad, Ohio and Mississippi were the major arteries of transportation for the Midwest to other regions of the country. This produced a river tradition and nationalism that transcended region and benefited westerners, southerners, and easterners. Throughout the "great secession winter" of 1860–61, this tradition remained unchanged. Though the Ohio River was essentially the natural extension of the Mason-Dixon line, it was far less important than the barriers that separated Northerners and Southerners in the West from other sections. Because of the nature of their location—Illinois, Indiana, Ohio, and Michigan composed the Northern "heartland"—Midwesterners' chief dilemma was the maintenance of friendly relations throughout the country. "Heartlanders," whether Confederate or Union, had grown dependent upon one another during the prewar decades. The conflict threatened to sever the bonds of profitable intercourse as Southern states began to question their loyalties during the secession winter. After the formation of the Confederacy in February 1861, the *New Albany Daily Ledger,* which hailed from the Indiana town on the Ohio River, editorialized that "there is no great and fertile . . . region . . . embracing Kentucky, Missouri and a large portion of Ohio, Indiana and Illinois, whose people are not to any considerable extent effected by the ultraism of either of the extremes, who would in the event of the convulsion of the Republic, be drawn together by ties of commerce, neighborhood and general coincidence of views and interest."[8]

Like all Midwestern governors concerned about the foreign domination of such a vital commercial artery, Illinois governor Richard Yates echoed the sentiment of the *Daily Ledger*, arguing: *"There is no division of sentiment in this section. . . .* The Northwest will be a unit in maintaining its rights to a free and unobstructed use of the Mississippi river throughout its entire course."[9] Therefore, the real line of demarcation was not only the Ohio River that ran east and west but also the Allegheny Mountains that ran north and south. Indeed, what added to the significance of the Ohio River was not only that it skirted slave and free states but also that it joined the Mississippi. In many respects this union of rivers helped make the Confederate heartland a commercial appendage of the North. "The Power which controls the Ohio and the Mississippi," wrote Sherman to Salmon P. Chase, "will ultimately control this continent."[10]

By the Civil War, railroads, like the rivers, had forged relationships between people and places in the Midwestern heartland. Though the river system channeled western goods south to the port of New Orleans and the force of this commercial habit was still influential, the construction of railroads helped break this dependency. The immediate impact resulted in a community of commercial interests between the upper and lower Midwestern heartland. As they penetrated land-locked areas, railroads played an enormous role in creating an interior network with river cities and provided more opportunities for otherwise isolated farmers. The cumulative effect during the prewar decades expanded the market range of western produce and shifted trade routes from north-south to east-west. This change not only redirected economic traffic but also realigned political allegiances. Upper South residents reacted to this by developing an internal commerce cultivated from the region's interior streams, establishing cities and towns linked by rail and river. Residents engaged in the commercial sector of agriculture north of the Ohio responded by developing closer ties to surrounding towns and by centralizing in the urban areas the manufacturing elements needed to increase agricultural production. Consequently, by 1860 the Old Northwest, engaged largely in economic specialization and characterized by social diversification, was as urbanized as the Northeast had been in 1830. Railroads, therefore, like rivers, consumed the attention of residents of the northern heartland.[11]

These iron routes, by 1860 competing strongly with water-born traffic,

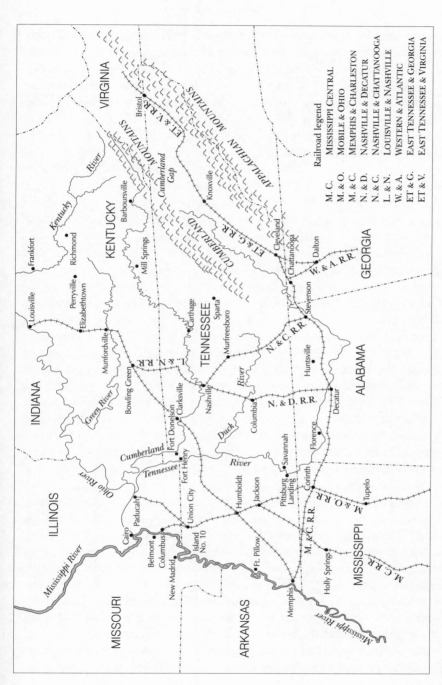

The Upper Heartland

Railroad legend

M. C.   MISSISSIPPI CENTRAL
M. & O.   MOBILE & OHIO
M. & C.   MEMPHIS & CHARLESTON
N. & D.   NASHVILLE & DECATUR
N. & C.   NASHVILLE & CHATTANOOGA
L. & N.   LOUISVILLE & NASHVILLE
W. & A.   WESTERN & ATLANTIC
ET & G.   EAST TENNESSEE & GEORGIA
ET & V.   EAST TENNESSEE & VIRGINIA

encouraged inland communities to develop internal trade. This released most Midwesterners from their dependence on Southern markets. Communities in isolated places sprang up overnight along the vast stretches of rails as had happened along the rivers decades before. Still, the great mass of people living on isolated farms were not keen on railroads and continued to rely on rivers for economic exchange. Many still failed to appreciate the significance of the great transportation change and continued to regard the commerce of the rivers as of the highest importance to them simply because it had been a way of life. Consequently, the growth of railroads in the North had not been matched by an iron-rail system in the South. Moreover, in times of peace, railroads offered distinct advantages in transporting goods, but in war, rivers afforded the safest and most effective means to transport armies and supplies.[12]

Several railroads played a prominent role in redirecting the market economy's shift. The Louisville-Nashville-Decatur Railroad stretched from northern Kentucky to northern Alabama and linked the Tennessee capital to the Ohio River. The fact that it crossed the Green, Cumberland, Duck, and Tennessee Rivers made it all the more vital a link in the internal trade, though also more vulnerable to significant destruction. The Memphis and Charleston stretched east from the Mississippi River though the mountains of Tennessee and Chattanooga before branching north to Virginia and east to Charleston. The Mobile and Ohio Railroad fanned out from Columbus through Corinth and south to Mobile. The Virginia and Tennessee, perhaps the most important railway in the South, however, threaded Tennessee and crossing into Virginia near Cumberland Gap. Like the cities through which rivers flowed, the railroad spawned an economic interdependence, and the flow of rail traffic helped shape the region's political culture.[13]

Cities of the Middle West connected by turnpike, river, and rail, particularly Louisville, St. Louis, Cincinnati, Nashville, Knoxville, Memphis, and Chattanooga, established powerful commercial interests that proved quite influential during the secession winter. Legislative leaders were preoccupied by attempting to alleviate the economic fears of Midwesterners who were particularly concerned when the closure of the prosperous intravalley trade seemed likely. Many regional businessmen traded profitably from the initial escalation in the purchase of war material, despite the fact that much of the profit came from trade with the South. Economically, the people were unified through their common means of livelihood. Nearly all of them were directly or indirectly dependent upon agriculture, and thus the importance of commerce was significant as politicians sought to secure uninterrupted routes of transportation and favorable treatment for their products. This increased the favorable relationships the Midwest shared with the East.[14]

The changes in the marketplace resulting from the more deliberate use of rivers and railroads made the Upper South particularly suspect as an area in which the defense of slavery was less prominent than farther south. Because these were not cotton states, slavery played a lesser role in their economy. Support for the institution in Kentucky and East Tennessee, both as an economic investment and a means of racial control, was eroding as in other Border States, many excess slaves being sold to Lower South planters. Because wheat was either replacing or competing with tobacco as the region's major cash crop and urban centers were shifting to manufacturing, in which employers preferred immigrant laborers to slaves, it became clear that slavery was giving way to free labor. Georgia senator Alfred Iverson alluded to this realization, concluding during the secession crisis that the "border States can get along without slavery." He argued, "Their soil and climate are appropriate to white labor; they can live and flourish without African slavery; the cotton States cannot."[15]

Although slavery in the Upper South played only a minimal role in the commercial life of the people, residents in slave states did not believe the institution was immoral, which diminished immediate prospects for emancipation. Furthermore, they resented the North trying to determine questions of morality for them. Because of the deterioration of slavery in the borderland, particularly in its urban centers, secessionists came to believe that Republicans would, through their control of federal patronage, organize a free-labor party throughout the South. These secessionists concluded that such a political movement would derive its strength from the nonslaveholding poor, especially in the Upper South, where the conditions for a free-labor victory were most favorable. The New Orleans–based *De Bow's Review* editorialized that those poor nonslaveholders harbored *"a feeling of deep-rooted jealousy and prejudice, of painful antagonism, if not hostility, to the institution of negro slavery, that threatens the most serious consequences, the moment Black-republicanism becomes triumphant in the Union."*[16]

The conclusions of the secessionists, however, presumed that the economic argument of free-labor ideology appealed to nonslaveholders who were resentful toward planters as representatives of an unrepublican aristocracy. This group constituted a tangible nucleus of borderland civilians anticipating both protection by the Federal army and perhaps the opportunity to join the Republican Party. Still, Upper South whites were fervently devoted to traditional republican ideals. An honorable self-identity constituted economic and social freedom in society, and slavery represented the debasement of those who lost their freedom. Many Southerners perceived the threat to representative government as essentially a Northern challenge to their social order, property interests, and racial controls. Upper South residents shared this perception, but not to the degree as those whites in the "black belt" and other regions. Because of the absence of slavery in the mountains, specifically the Appalachians, white culture was much more connected there than in the plantation regions. Thus, where the potential of free labor had been greatest in the South, so too was the desire to withdraw from the Union the weakest.[17]

Because of the rivers, railroads, and erosion of slavery, Kentuckians and Tennesseans did not see themselves linked in meaningful ways with residents of the Deep South. Though sharing a sympathy for the institution of slavery, they were bound culturally, economically, and even through blood with citizens of Virginia, North Carolina, and those states north of the Ohio River rather than those south of the Memphis and Charleston Railroad. The interplay of loyalty and locality proved especially crucial in the heartland. "There were at least three Tennessees," wrote Avery Craven, "with Knoxville, Nashville, and Memphis at their centers."[18] Such a divergent landscape caused East Tennessean William G. Brownlow, a Knoxville Unionist, to characterize his section of the state as the "Switzerland of America."[19]

Like Tennessee, the bluegrass region of middle Kentucky, where slaves were more numerous, differed considerably from both the mountainous area in the east and the rolling hills nearer the Mississippi River, where there were fewer slaves. Southern Illinois, Indiana, and Ohio were merely appendages of Kentucky. Kinship in the Midwest frequently reflected family journeys westward from the Alleghenies into the Midwest river basins, and the political boundaries now drawn by the Civil War separated those genealogical ties. Abraham Lincoln's family travel from Kentucky to Indiana and ultimately to Illinois was typical of thousands of such migrations. His marriage to Mary Todd, also a Kentuckian, revealed the extended bonds between the people of the Midwest and the Upper South.[20]

The outbreak of the war in the heartland changed waterways and railroads from commercial into strategic links and the Upper South into the nation's most prized region. The Ohio, Mississippi, Tennessee, and Cumberland Rivers that before had symbolized a regional identity now became military lines of invasion. "We are much obliged to the Tennessee," wrote Sherman, "for I am never easy with a railroad which takes a whole army to guard, each foot of rail being essential to the whole; whereas they can't stop the Tennessee and each boat can make its own game."[21]

The culture of the region was confronted with reconciling the interplay of locality and loyalty. What were once the South's greatest strengths in forging a vibrant Midwestern heartland economy now had become one of the Confederacy's weaknesses. The fact that the Mississippi and the Ohio threaded through was considerably more significant in light of the fact that they also formed a wall around the Confederacy to eastern Kentucky and Tennessee. This made its sister waterways extremely important to Northerners and Southerners. The Cumberland River reached inland from the north to Nashville and made the Tennessee capital all the more valuable to the Union and vulnerable to invasion. The Tennessee, however, curved deeper into the Southern landscape, traversing all of northern Alabama before heading north and emptying into the Ohio River at Paducah. Corinth, Mississippi; and Florence and Decatur, Alabama, could all be reached by water; in winter when high water allowed, boats could steam all the way to Stevenson and Chattanooga. This meant that at any of those towns, the Memphis and Charleston Railroad, the Confederacy's east-west lifeline, could be severed.[22]

What gave the Confederate heartland added logistical and economic prominence was its standing as the South's primary source for the production of war materials. Its munitions capacity was unsurpassed in the Confederacy. Nashville and Memphis instantly became home to numerous machine shops, foundries, and ordnance works, which supplied the army with manufactured powder, weapons, and equipment. The mountains of East Tennessee and northern Alabama contained important copper and saltpeter regions, vital for the manufactured gunpowder. The heartland ranked second behind the Shenandoah Valley of Virginia in supplying livestock, particularly horses and mules, for the Confederacy; Tennessee alone supplied more mules than any other state. Outside of the Union, the region became the Confederacy's largest manufacturer of pig iron; iron blooms; and bar, sheet, and railroad iron, all of which employed thousands of slaves. Indeed, as Thomas Connelly put it, "the entire Heartland seemed a maze of such small but critical installations."[23]

The Midwestern region was not only important for its economic prominence, both north and south, but also for its wealth of manpower. Lincoln's summons for volunteers to suppress the rebellion after the fall of Fort Sumter brought quick responses in the states west of the Alleghenies. Governor Richard Yates declared that his Illinoisans burned with "patriotism and all parties show the same alacrity to stand by the Government and the laws of the country. Our people will wade through seas of blood before they will see a single star or a solitary stripe erased from the glorious flag of our Union." Not to be outdone, Ohio governor William Dennison pledged that his state would furnish the largest number of volunteers for Lincoln's army. Kentucky governor Beriah Magoffin, however, a fire-eating secessionist, replied that "Kentucky will furnish no troops for the wicked purpose of subduing her sister Southern States." Still, some seventy-five thousand Kentuckians fought for the Union, while twenty-five thousand joined the Confederacy. Tennessee governor Isham G. Harris, a radical proslavery lawyer, informed Lincoln that his state would raise fifty thousand men, if necessary, to defend the rights of Southerners. Like Kentucky, however, Tennessee would also supply both sides with troops. Clearly, the advent of war had drawn unavoidable lines of loyalty in a region that was characterized by a maze of shared market activities.[24]

Within days of the fall of Sumter, even militarily inexperienced Midwestern governors recognized the incalculable strategic importance of the rivers and their cities. Cairo, Columbus, Paducah, Memphis, Louisville, and Cincinnati now held even more significance as military centers, and governors sent militia groups to seize control. Governors Dennison, Yates, and Oliver P. Morton of Indiana established posts to prevent the shipment of arms and military supplies to states that were not completely supportive of the Union. Governor Yates's Illinois was in a particularly troublesome situation with regard to its lower counties, a region nicknamed "Little Egypt." More than any other region, southern Illinois resembled the Bluegrass State in its economic and social makeup. At the confluence of the Ohio and the Mississippi Rivers, Cairo attracted considerable attention, though it was generally regarded as a dirty river city. Once considered the gateway to downriver traffic, the small river city now stood as a tiny Gibraltar, an effective place to enforce the embargo cutting off nearly all of the trade of western Kentucky and Tennessee coming down to St. Louis, from Louisville or Nashville. Wisconsin governor Alexander Randall wired Lincoln that it was a matter of "absolute necessity not only for the Northern border States but for all the Northwestern States, to be able to control the business and commerce of the Ohio River." Lincoln concurred with Yates that sending a militia force to Cairo to keep all of Illinois in the Union was wise.[25] Still, the question remained as to who governed the rivers that bordered the now separate nations.

The troops sent out of military necessity to Cairo and nearby Camp Defiance, however, aroused serious complaints among the people of Kentucky, who were trying to maintain political neutrality and continue to trade both north and south using the rivers. Initially, the problems of divided loyalties redirected river traffic to railroads, and in many cases cargo passed through or wound up in Louisville. Lincoln, realizing the Bluegrass State's delicate position, took control of the regulation of trade and relaxed the Union's embargo, which allowed for an immense trade to grow almost overnight in Kentucky. Louisville merchants prospered greatly from the shift in trade, even though the political elections in the summer of 1861 allowed the Lincoln administration to prohibit commercial intercourse with the insurrectionary states. Not recognizing the advantages to the Confederacy and intent on Northerners receiving little cotton, Tennessee's Isham Harris placed an embargo on the South's most precious product as well as some other staples. He intercepted northbound trains carrying commodities and agricultural goods, and when that failed he simply ordered the seizure of a portion of the rolling stock on the railroad in that part of his state, which ironically hurt farmers in Middle Tennessee. This also angered and alienated the people of Kentucky from the Confederacy and played well in Lincoln's favor. The president responded by tightening restrictions on the Southern trade, which delighted loyal Kentuckians.[26]

The competition in the marketplace combined with the political contest to gain a balance of power in the region affected states north of the Ohio just as it had affected those south of the river. What many came to believe was a war about defense of community and institutions quickly became a contest over governmental authority as it pertained to economic regulation, particularly along the rivers. Both sides linked political and social issues with economics, which helped obscure the line between military necessity and civilian practicality. Inevitably, civil-military issues became linked to political, social, and economic matters.

This inevitable combination inspired Union and Confederate governors to marshal their citizens into the military to seize both the economic and military balance of power in the region and to mobilize popular opinion behind the cause that would link war and society. Important as they were, however, economic disruptions were not the issues from which recruiters drew rhetoric to inspire citizens to fight. Their message was more substantive and significantly more profound. Throughout the war's inaugural summer, telegrams and newspapers cast the war as a threat to individualism or nationalism, depending on whether one was north or south of the Ohio River. Governors north of the Ohio such as Indiana's Morton implored Lincoln to create a military department of the West, create rules for stopping trade with the South, and emphasize military operations in the Mississippi Valley above all other theaters of war. These leaders wanted Lincoln to secure Kentucky for the Union by occupying Louisville, Covington, Newport, and Columbus. Morton epitomized the intense conviction of the justice of the cause. He was a natural-born leader whose organizational ability was unsurpassed by other Midwestern governors. His sheer force and determination transformed Indiana's administration and made it an efficient agency in carrying on the war and a model for mobilizing other Northern states.

Governors south of the Ohio such as Harris and Magoffin ignored Lincoln's call for troops and instead urged Jefferson Davis to neutralize the Unionist elements in their states. Harris not only had sided with the Confederacy but also had turned over the provisional Army of Tennessee, which comprised some seventy regiments. The Confederacy had fortified Island No. 10, a position in the Mississippi River just below the Kentucky-Tennessee line; begun to strengthen Fort Henry on the Tennessee River and Fort Donelson on the Cumberland; and established Camp Boone in eastern Tennessee. Whatever liberty and security Kentuckians thought they could enjoy by proclaiming neutrality seemed eminently vulnerable to the desires of both Federal and Confederate authorities who hoped to retain the balance of power in the region.[27]

As Lincoln and Davis thought of rules or strategies by which to fight a war in or around Kentucky, the business of recruiting, equipping, and training the residents of the borderland and Midwest consumed most of their attention. Before governors could think of tapping their states' armories or arsenals, they had to seize them, repair existing munitions factories, or build facilities from scratch. The summer and fall of 1861 witnessed the chaos of mobilization for a war that no one had prepared to fight. Teachers, farmers, political leaders, and professionals from every community eagerly anticipated mustering into the army and to defend themselves, their communities, and their governments in the earnest crusade to preserve liberty.

Because the western armies on both sides comprised soldiers from regions with similar geographical features, it was not surprising that they were socially and economically homogenous. The men largely came from occupations associated with agriculture; many had simply tilled the soil. They lived in small rural communities that were generally governed by the commercial activity of the residents. Northern soldiers in the armies of the Ohio and the Tennessee were recruited in rural townships where farmers produced grains such as wheat, barley, oats, and corn. Such economic activity produced an agricultural cycle that developed similar social patterns and institutions, reinforcing ties among residents. When going to war, many of these citizens simply exchanged plowshares for swords and formed a new military community that became mobile while retaining that cooperative spirit. Although inexperienced in travel and new to both the cultures they would contact and the landscapes through which they would campaign, these soldiers formed opinions reflective of both previously held notions about Southerners or Northerners and what they experienced in the field, in camp, or in garrison.[28]

This was the context in which the war in the West was fought, and it was complicated by the fact that the heartland residents south of the Ohio fought in both Union and Confederate armies. In many ways the Old Northwest was to the Union what the heartland was to the Confederacy. Not only were these regions that bordered the Ohio River important economically but also for their vital sources of manpower. Though Kentucky's neutrality initially stalled formal enlistments into either army in that state, large segments of Tennessee's manpower had been nearly drained by the Confederacy during the summer of 1861. As Governor Morton looked south to Kentucky for support, so too did Governor Harris look north to the Bluegrass State for defense. Too strategically vital to stay out of the war for long—a view shared by both governments—Kentucky remained uneasily neutral as both presidents steered a middle course in dealing with their native state. One correspondent perceptively, though metaphorically, articulated Kentucky's dubious nonalignment. "When the corn is between the mill-stones," he editorialized, "when it is a question of meal or grain, of grinding or not grinding, you can not be counted out; you must be meal or corn."[29]

More significant to the problems of mobilization was the search for competent leaders. Both the Union and Confederate high command was comprised of an eclectic group of officers ranging from those who had held high rank in the "old army" to those who had never seen a military force. Though Lincoln and Davis shared a native state and some military experience, they had little else in common. Davis had several military friends, and his soft spot for appointing them to commands for which their authority exceeded their ability became one of his greatest liabilities. Lincoln had no military friends, which, as it turned out, benefited the Union cause. Neither man had much help making strategic decisions when it came to the war beyond the Appalachian Mountains. Davis's first order of business in the West was to secure the Mississippi River and position an army in the Upper South so as to respect Kentucky's neutrality. Still, he needed to strategically place what forces he could to invade the Bluegrass State once the neutrality ended. He needed to arrange the defenses of the nation and required competent leaders with which to do it. Davis recognized he would be forced to do much with the little resources and with the lack of real leadership available. Still, he was better in devising strategy than choosing commanders, simply because the closer the friend the less reliable was his judgment. Though frontier defense on the banks of the Ohio River made better sense strategically, Davis clearly identified the crucial points in the West but placed them in unreliable hands, a reflection of one of his greatest weaknesses.[30]

To defend the northern tier of the Mississippi Valley near the confluence of the Ohio and Mississippi Rivers, Davis appointed North Carolinian Leonidas Polk. Polk was a graduate of West Point and had roomed with Davis there. But Polk resigned from the army upon graduation and entered the ministry, eventually becoming a bishop in the Episcopal Church. When the war came, however, Davis, out of necessity and friendship and against his better military judgment, gave his friend a top Confederate command along the central portion of the Mississippi and assigned him the task of fortifying the Mississippi Valley. Polk was a charismatic and persuasive man who had assumed an important military role, but whose authority far exceeded his ability. Davis had also concluded in the summer that native Kentuckian turned Texan Albert Sidney Johnston was the more logical choice to command the West. Johnston was also a presidential friend, and a man Davis considered perhaps the greatest living soldier. Still, until Johnston determined to participate in the contest, Davis would have to rely on Polk to handle the concentration along the Mississippi River.[31]

Polk arrived in Memphis in mid-July and found Gideon J. Pillow in command of the city. Pillow hailed from Tennessee's rich plantation district around Columbia and was a former lawyer who had been appointed a brigadier general of volunteers by his former law partner, President James K. Polk, during the Mexican War. Although he returned to practice afterward, when the Civil War broke out Governor Harris appointed him major general and named him the senior commander of Tennessee forces. When Leonidas Polk arrived, however, Pillow was outraged to find that Governor Harris intended the Confederate officer to assume sole command of his forces and the state. The command change made Pillow a subordinate and reduced him in rank to a brigadier. Pillow chafed at being in such a position and as a result resented Polk. Because Pillow was a political appointee, Davis had to be careful not to insult pro-Confederate Tennesseans by demoting him nor offend other officers by according the lawyer too high a rank or too prominent a position for someone with little military experience. Moreover, his undistinguished military background and proven flare for lacking judgment produced considerable disapproval over the appointment, and the Tennessean attracted as many critics as he did advocates.[32]

While Polk and Pillow, who managed to cooperate despite their obvious animosity for one another, contemplated what to do about idle Kentucky, Albert Sidney Johnston, having decided to join the Confederacy, was slowly making his way across the continent from Los Angeles to Richmond. At fifty-eight years of age, Johnston was a refined man whose charm was matched by his fame as a veteran of the old army. News of Fort Sumter's fall incited him to head east and secure a place in the Confederate army. Though Lincoln, recognizing his military prominence, had offered Johnston a high command in the Union army, the Texan declined. Although he regretted secession, like Robert E. Lee, he could not bear arms against his native people. Davis immediately gave him a full general's commission. The president had just the place for a commander with Johnston's talents and gave him command of the entire West, which included the Confederate states of Tennessee, Arkansas, the western part of Mississippi, and the border states of Kentucky, Missouri, and Kansas, as well as the Indian Territory. "I had hoped and expected that I had others who would prove Generals," Davis later said, "But I knew that I had *one*—and that was Sidney Johnston."[33]

It was clear to Davis that Johnston would better serve the West given the incompetence of its initial commander. No longer could Polk be entrusted with such a vitally strategic region. It seemed to be a consensus among the high political and military command that Johnston was the man for the entire western command. The fact that he was a native Kentuckian was also a valuable dimension to his appointment. "It was not without a severe struggle," Davis remarked at the time, that he sent his friend away from Richmond to the West.[34] Still, Johnston inherited some problems he failed to correct, foreshadowing his own downfall as a commander.

If Lincoln felt, as he surmised privately to his Illinois friend Orville Browning, that to lose Kentucky was to lose "the whole game," there was good reason for it. Neither side could afford to lose the state. Its large reservoir of manpower, livestock, and slaves along with its strategic position all combined to make the Bluegrass State extremely valuable for both governments. Still, when Davis appointed Johnston to command the entire West, Kentucky's importance had not yet been fully realized in Richmond. The Confederate president had conceived a policy that recognized Kentucky's neutrality. Johnston and Davis agreed that Confederate strategy in the Upper South underscored the importance of Kentucky and the Ohio and Mississippi Rivers, but Davis expected Johnston to direct most of his attention west of the Mississippi. A Confederate Kentucky would provide a base for Southern invasions of Illinois, Indiana, and Ohio and secure the Virginia and Tennessee Railroad through the Allegheny Mountains. It would also shield Nashville and the food producing region of Tennessee's heartland, effectively blockade the Ohio River, and deprive the Federals of any feasible base for a large-scale offensive in the Mississippi Valley. As Davis had done for months, Johnston immediately turned his attention to whether he should advance his line into the still unaligned state in an effort to secure it for the Confederacy or dispose his forces to defend Tennessee.[35]

Kentuckians were bitterly divided in their loyalties to either the Union or the Confederacy, and the state's officials tried to remain neutral, hoping citizens would not take up arms to support either cause. During the summer, however, both sides were recruiting actively in Kentucky. By early August, former navy lieutenant turned army officer William Nelson, nicknamed "Bull" for his overwhelming size, strength, and ungovernable attitude, established Union Camp Dick Robinson in the Bluegrass State. Within a week almost four thousand men were there. Polk knew as well as anyone that Kentucky needed very careful and special attention. Federal troops had already appeared at the small Mississippi River hamlet of Belmont, Missouri, just across from Columbus, Kentucky, and an easy target for Confederate artillery posted on the Kentucky side.[36]

As much as Polk wanted Johnston to command the West, he could not wait to seize Columbus, the only valuable river position between Cairo and Memphis. While he was in Richmond ministering to the troops, Polk had stressed to Davis the importance of seizing as much of the Mississippi River as possible. In early September, fearing a Union invasion, Polk sent Pillow to occupy the Kentucky hamlet, situated on the northern terminus of the Mobile and Ohio Railroad. Polk had blundered by taking Columbus, and as an afterthought, he might just as well have secured his blunder by taking Paducah thirty miles east at the confluence of the Tennessee and Ohio Rivers. But he did not move east, and Davis ordered him to withdraw to Tennessee immediately, arguing that the general had acted without orders. Federal forces reacted by moving troops to Paducah and relocating Union headquarters under Brig. Gen. Robert Anderson, who had been raising volunteers from western Virginia and Kentucky, from Cincinnati to Louisville. Naturally, Midwestern governors, waiting to see what would become of the neutral state, were alarmed by these actions. Indiana governor Morton declared to Secretary of War Simon Cameron, "war in Kentucky has commenced."[37]

The Confederate move to Columbus and the Federal occupation of Paducah changed the war's focus. Until September the war beyond the Appalachians had been waged mainly in Missouri, as Governor Claiborne Jackson actively attempted to take his state out of the Union. While Confederate authorities had been preoccupied with what to do about a neutral Kentucky, Johnston could now develop plans uninhibited by such conditions thanks to Polk. On his way to Nashville, Johnston passed through Knoxville and ordered Brig. Gen. Felix Zollicoffer, a journalist turned politician in command of the troubled East Tennessee region who had been suppressing Unionists there, to prepare an advance. Zollicoffer found it difficult to cultivate support in East Tennessee for the Confederate cause, and Johnston ordered him to move his forces into southeastern Kentucky to guard the Cumberland Gap through the mountains to Virginia.[38]

When he arrived at Nashville, Johnston conferred with Governor Harris and decided that Kentucky neutrality was a thing of the past. With Zollicoffer anchoring the right flank of his several-hundred-mile-long line and Polk anchoring his left flank at Columbus, the only likely path of Union invasion was over the railroad from Louisville to Nashville. To seize Bowling Green, Kentucky, on the Louisville-Nashville Railroad, Johnston sent a force under a Kentucky West Pointer, Brig. Gen. Simon Bolivar Buckner. Offered general-officer commissions by both the Union and the Confederacy, Buckner had refused all until Federal troops entered

Kentucky. Still, he had only a small command, some thirty thousand men, to carry out the grand orchestration along the western line. On September 22, 1861, Johnston published a formal proclamation that rationalized his purposes in entering the state. He reasoned that the Confederate army was in Kentucky because of the prior Federal invasion, and he pledged to depart from the state provided the Federals also withdrew.[39]

The truth was that Johnston's forces had begun to strengthen their position in Kentucky, hoping to hold on long enough for Confederate authorities to send reinforcements and for pro-Southern leaders in the state to rally its citizens to the Confederate cause. In the meantime, the Cumberland and Tennessee Rivers remained neglected. While he waited, the seventy-thousand-man Confederate line that stretched from the Appalachians to the western border of Arkansas, an expanse of more than five hundred miles, was beginning to feel the weight of the war. In the weeks to come, Brig. Gen. William J. Hardee would be ordered to reinforce Bowling Green. Still, the Confederacy had a problem. Davis had originally ordered Polk to defend both banks of the Mississippi and the area extending to the Tennessee River. Though perhaps unimportant at the time, this delineation was nonetheless significant as Polk was not responsible for the Tennessee or Cumberland Rivers. Holding on to the Mississippi River was only effective if the Cumberland and Tennessee could be covered by the same force. As the weeks passed, the fact that the twin rivers and their defenses went unattended became increasingly important as the Federals discovered this was the way to the very heart of the Confederacy.[40]

The end of Kentucky's neutrality came at a time when the Union high command was undergoing significant changes both in the West and in Washington. Brig. Gen. Robert Anderson, a proslavery Kentuckian and West Point graduate completely loyal to the Union who had been in command at Fort Sumter, had been the likely choice to head the Department of Kentucky, which in August 1861 merged into the Department of the Cumberland. Failing health and the pressure of the developing situation forced Lincoln to replace him with William T. Sherman, Anderson's second in command. Sherman too was a West Point graduate and had fought in the Mexican War. He had resigned from the army in 1853 and went into business and law, failing at both. In 1859 he was appointed superintendent of the Louisiana Military Seminary. At the outbreak of the war, however, he was living in St. Louis, where he volunteered for the military. Sherman understood fully the importance of Kentucky to the Union and had attempted, though unsuccessfully, to raise troops and supplies to defend Louisville. His want of resources, lack of confidence in the volunteers, and evaluation that Kentuckians were by and large sympathetic to the Confederacy caused him to insist that he needed an army of at least two hundred thousand men. His estimates got him into trouble, and newspapers reported he was insane. Nevertheless, Sherman was convinced that Johnston was preparing to strike for Louisville and the line of the Ohio River and that his force and the Union cause were in danger.[41]

Across the Mississippi River at St. Louis, Brig. Gen. John C. Fremont, the celebrated "Pathfinder" and antislavery politician, commanded about thirty-six thousand Federal soldiers distributed throughout Missouri, Illinois, and Kentucky. Fremont had been the target of severe criticism after the Union disaster at the battle of Wilson's Creek in August. Later, when he declared martial law and issued an emancipation proclamation, it became clear he had proved more a liability than an asset in the West. Fremont had decided to invade the Deep South by first securing Missouri, which had been racked by guerrilla warfare. Brig. Gen. John Pope, a native Kentuckian who had graduated from West Point in 1842, had tried to bring Missouri under Federal control north of St. Louis, and Fremont wanted to protect the southern portion of the Mississippi River in his department by strengthening Cairo, Illinois. For this task he selected an unassuming, somewhat colorless brigadier general named Ulysses S. Grant.[42]

Grant had been cast a failure and had been forced out of the army during the 1850s because of his weakness for liquor. His life in the prewar decade had been one failure after another, and by the commencement of the war, even his military ability was suspect. Grant now held a brigadier's commission only because his Galena, Illinois, congressman, Elihu B. Washburne, was influential in Washington. Still, everybody in the old army seemed to like Grant, though few had much confidence in him. Grant had impressed Fremont, who put him in charge at Cairo, a command that revealed Grant's finest attributes: his cast-iron determination and persistence. After seizing Paducah, Grant brigaded his command and worked tirelessly to keep the troops busy drilling, building fortifications and bridges, and scouting outposts. In November, when Fremont thought that the Confederates were sending troops to southwestern Missouri, he ordered Grant to make a demonstration against Belmont, the steamboat landing just across the river from Columbus, Kentucky. The truth was, however, that the Confederates had not intended to send troops west. Grant nonetheless saw a chance for action. On November 7 he found it along the Mississippi River, but by the end of the day had to fight his way out in the face of a numerically superior enemy force. Though the battle had little impact except to depress the spirits of the North and encourage those of the South, it indicated that the Federals were going to make use of the rivers.[43]

About the same time that Grant was steaming back north after almost being captured by Polk, Maj. Gen. George B. McClellan had assumed the general-in-chief post at Washington. McClellan was among the most sought-after military minds during the war's first summer. The Philadelphia native was a brilliant engineer, having graduated second in the West Point class of 1846. After serving in the Mexican War he returned to his alma mater to teach. In the mid-1850s, McClellan was dispatched to study European armies, which gave him invaluable experience. In 1857, however, he resigned his commission and became chief engineer and vice president of the Illinois Central Railroad. Despite his civilian success, McClellan was delighted to return to the military. After the Union debacle at First Bull Run and in light of his own military success in West Virginia, "Little Mac" was tapped to better organize and train the army defending the nation's capital. From there he actively worked for General in Chief Winfield Scott's retirement in hopes of assuming that position himself, which he did in early November 1861 at the age of thirty-five.[44]

It took McClellan less than a week to realize that the command situation in the West needed to be changed. Though he never acknowledged that operations there were more vital than in the East, he certainly realized the importance of Kentucky. Fremont, Anderson, and Sherman, none of whom had impressed McClellan, were liabilities in an extremely sensitive region. Fremont's proclamation, Anderson's physical health, and Sherman's emotional temperament convinced him that the Union command in the West needed someone who personified stability and could bring administrative and organizational order to the departments. He chose two of the most professional and thoroughly military men. Maj. Gen. Henry W. Halleck, a somewhat overbearing military intellectual who rivaled McClellan for the post of general in chief, was tapped to replace Fremont. Known as "Old Brains," Halleck had been the favorite of Winfield Scott for the Washington job, but McClellan's early victories had caught Lincoln's attention. Halleck's jealousy for having been thus passed over, however, flared up against McClellan's friends, namely Brig. Gen. Don

Carlos Buell. Still, McClellan wanted Halleck as far west as possible, since according to the editor of *Harper's Weekly,* the "country expects great things of General Halleck. His past record and his physiognomy encourage the belief that these expectations will not be disappointed."[45]

When McClellan sent Halleck to command the Department of the Missouri, he also sent General Buell to command the newly designated Department of the Ohio. McClellan had a great fondness for Buell, as did many of his regular-army colleagues, who considered the commander "brilliant." A conscientious, methodical soldier with a strong body, Buell had a firm commitment to fighting a limited war for limited goals. Besides his military qualifications, he had owned slaves, which would endear him to Kentucky planters. Buell replaced Sherman, who had grown completely despondent over the situation in Kentucky and Tennessee. *New York Herald* correspondent Henry Villard remembered that Sherman's earlier appraisal of the need for two hundred thousand troops had "startled the Secretary [of War] and excited doubts as to the state of the General's mind."[46] Either to keep him away from Washington or to burden Halleck, McClellan sent Sherman to Missouri. Buell assumed command of the newly designated Army of the Ohio, little more than a collection of regiments, and kept Louisville as his base.

Though the change in the Federal western commands helped bring order to Louisville and alleviate McClellan's and Lincoln's fears for the West, it did not help one important area—East Tennessee. More than any other region, Lincoln wanted the East Tennessee highlands and its residents in Union hands, but Buell had even less use for the thrust at Cumberland Gap than Sherman had had. McClellan himself had proposed to march down through southwestern Virginia at the conclusion of his West Virginia campaign with arms for the people, but he was transferred before those plans were developed. Like Halleck, Buell spent the remainder of 1861 getting his troops thoroughly trained, disciplined, and outfitted and keeping quiet. Campaigning down the historic Wilderness Road to Knoxville did not appeal to him. The trouble was that East Tennessee was hard to reach since its inhospitable landscape was an almost impenetrable network of peaks, valleys, and forests, which the approach of winter made all the worse. Still, the region represented something significantly vital to Lincoln, a solid nucleus of Southern Unionists. When Buell had sent some regiments in that direction in December, it was simply a gesture to assuage the president. Neither McClellan nor Lincoln could budge Buell from this position.[47]

The Union commanders who actually attempted to move the war in the West before the end of the year were Halleck's and Buell's subordinates. Grant had tried but failed at Belmont, and Brig. Gen. George H. Thomas showed considerable vigor in taking on an offensive into East Tennessee, but Buell, like Sherman, kept a tight reign on his most trusted subordinate. As a Virginia native, Thomas had chosen between conflicting loyalties to side with the Union. He had been ordered west from the Army of the Potomac in mid-September to command Camp Dick Robinson in Kentucky. Constantly besieged by Tennessee politicians such as Andrew Johnson and Horace Maynard for an offensive operation into their state, Thomas had taken some initiative to advance into the region. His command made it to Somerset, Kentucky, by November, which encouraged the pro-Union residents of East Tennessee to rise up and rebel in anticipation of the Federal troops' arrival. But Sherman and Buell had stifled this campaign, and Thomas spent the better part of the winter caught between the political dictates of civilian authority and the military feasibility of commencing such an operation.[48]

The search for competent leaders was accompanied by the discussion of some broad conceptions of the nature and conduct of the war. It was the people of the borderland Lincoln had most in mind when he tried to restrict the impact of war on civilians during the first year. This point harmonized nicely with McClellan's conception of the type of war that should be waged, a limited war without much bloodshed. It was no accident that the general in chief appointed officers who thought like he did regarding the nature of the rebellion. He embraced a policy of conciliation, and his departmental appointees both shared this attitude. "Little Mac" argued that Union forces were not merely to defeat the Confederacy's armies but "to display such an overwhelming strength, as will convince all our antagonists, especially those of the governing aristocratic class, of the utter impossibility of resistance. By thoroughly defeating their armies, taking their strong places, and pursuing a rigidly protective policy as to private property and unarmed persons, and a lenient course as to common soldiers, we may well hope for the permanent restoration of a peaceful Union."[49]

Because McClellan considered politics subordinate to military strategy, he sought to fashion political and military decisions as inseparable components in carrying out wartime operations. In the West he advised that a strong movement be made on the Mississippi and that the Rebels be driven out of Missouri. Once Kentucky joined the Union cause, a column should move into and liberate loyal East Tennessee and secure the railroads leading from Memphis to the East. The occupation of this region and its railroads, he concluded, "would go far towards determining the evacuation of Virginia by the rebels."[50]

This strategy was conceived in the context of the administration's initial understanding of the war. It confirmed that Lincoln and McClellan believed the bulk of the Southern population was apparently misguided and, if given the opportunity by the Federal army, would break from its supposedly weak loyalty to the secessionist politicians. Moreover, the Union would have to organize and position itself in such a way as to convince the governing aristocratic class that resistance to its forces was futile. Thus, to attract those Southerners who resisted secession back into the Union, Federal armies could not afford to be driven out of regions once occupied. They would have to remain in control of large territories for long periods of time if they were to be successful in enticing significant portions of the Southern populations into the Union. In the meantime, the army would impose a lenient policy designed to protect the civil liberties of noncombatants and hopefully not drive them to openly support the rebellion. Any departure from this conception, McClellan feared, would result in a much-strengthened Confederacy and change the character of Union war aims.[51]

Conciliation had its opponents from the very beginning of the war. By attempting to create an atmosphere for a more harmonious peace, military success became more difficult to achieve. Still, it was the experience of instituting a policy of conciliation that forced the Union to subsequently depart from it. Until political leaders came to believe that this dimension of military and political strategy needed modifying, Federal commanders would exercise considerable independence in managing affairs. Given the overwhelming size and chaos of departments, Lincoln thought it wise to allow commanders independence. The president himself added to the decentralized system of decision making by routinely avoiding to commit himself to any definite doctrine, which allowed generals and politicians alike considerable latitude in pursuing any policy they deemed most effective. This had huge ramifications, particularly in the sensitive Border States in the Upper South. Even before McClellan assumed the duties of general in chief, Federal commanders such as Fremont had attempted to invoke martial law and free slaves. The way policymakers had initially conceived the war played a significant role in how the war was waged west of the Alleghenies, particularly with regard to slavery, civilian property, and whether or not there was indeed a tangible nucleus of Union support in the region. In no other place and at no other time during the conflict did these issues play such a crucial role in how commanders conducted campaigns.[52]

Determining how the war would be waged was as dependent on political concerns as it was on military factors. It was necessary for the Federal government to proceed with caution against secessionists, thus placing much of the early responsibility for leadership in the war to the states. An overaggressive policy would prove disastrous, and thus commanders were kept on a tight leash when it came to slavery, civilian property, and constitutional rights. Union armies were to be seen as extending the guarantees of republican government with every mile they marched into the South. One of the most important features of the war in the West for both armies was not only the relationship between civilian and military authorities but also how that relationship affected campaigns and vice-versa. While Johnston and Davis contemplated the best defensive strategy for maintaining a line that stretched some three hundred miles with fewer than seventy thousand troops, Lincoln, McClellan, Halleck, and Buell considered the best offensive strategy for occupying regions while fighting a limited war.[53]

For Confederate policymakers, the war was easily defined. The Union's usurpation of power had increasingly diminished the liberty of the Southerners. Therefore, in republican fashion, the formation of the Confederacy represented evidence that individual rights had lost its prominence in shaping national political policy. The Confederacy represented a more conservative form of republicanism, and disunion, many secessionists believed, was an attempt to preserve the fruits of the founding fathers. Thus, the need for government authorities to compose a war plan seemed entwined with why the Southern states left the Union and how they might go about preserving their independence. Arriving at a unified military plan beyond the obvious need for defense was perplexing in a region that sought to protect the rights of states. In fact, according to historian Emory Thomas, "many people then and now have accused Davis and his generals of having no strategy at all."[54]

Still, the Confederacy developed clearly defined military strategies for the struggle. President Davis was bent on waging a conventional war, on defending the Upper South as well as the coastal regions, and on taking the offensive in the enemy's country. In assuming the defensive, though, a strategy of reaction rather than action, adjusting Davis's military movements to what he pictured the Federals doing, generally defined Confederate operations. This responsive mentality harmonized with the Confederacy's efforts to secure foreign aid. Though it was important to win battles on Union soil, it was more important to maintain the integrity of the Southern nation in order to attract and sustain formal international recognition.[55]

For Union policymakers, however, the result of what they hoped to accomplish shifted throughout the early part of the war. Initially, they understood the war to be a simple rebellion led by a small but influential group of secessionists who saw the events of the 1850s as reflective of a departure from initial Jeffersonian republican principles. These ideological, or interpretive, differences combined with economic divergence culminated in a nation's attempt to reconcile nationalism to an industrial world centered on wage labor, not slavery. The rural nature of the South gave reason to believe that residents felt passionately about their land and could easily envision their farms and homes destroyed, their town squares filled with armies, and their communities turned upside down by a war they feared would be fought on their soil.[56]

The war came abruptly for the people of the borderland. Residents understood the diametrically opposed feelings of both North and South on the subject of slavery. They watched with some misgivings the increasing bitterness of the controversy from the time it first arose. Still, in a region where residents' differences over the institution of slavery were polarized early, the war also manifested the sense of social and economic community forged by the very things that now sought to divide the natural barriers. When the fighting commenced, citizens in the region displayed a natural hesitancy to take sides, and for good reason. When the issue was defined in terms of union or disunion, states cast their lot with the North, since the generation-old economic allegiances with Union states had helped shape political allegiances. Because of the geographic location, its residents had tended to be nationalistic and the controversy over slavery had been subordinated to other concerns.[57]

Still, although the residents of the heartland had shared a common political, social, and cultural heritage, when they chose sides and conceived of the enemy, Northerners and Southerners alike depicted one another as evil. Illinoisan Charles W. Wills, who was stationed at Cairo, confided, "I want to fight the rest of my life if necessary, and die before we recognize them as anything but Rebels and traitors who must be humbled."[58]

Besides the delicate handling of political aims, civilians, and property as the armies moved south, the war in the winter and spring of 1862 would be fought along the very rivers that had given the region an identity. Commanders unfamiliar with the terrain, both geographic and political, were going to have to rely on experience as much as established military theory as their guide, even when these conflicted. Too, the Confederates' defensive circumstances would be much more difficult than taking the offensive. Although Columbus, Kentucky, had high bluffs along the Mississippi, an army could still threaten the city if other streams afforded alternative invasion routes. Anyone looking at a map was sure to figure out that the Cumberland River or the Tennessee River afforded such avenues. An invading army, however, would have to hold and move beyond Paducah at the confluence of the Tennessee and the Ohio. This could be done by overland march, though not as easily. As these campaigns unfolded, heartlanders along the rivers would soon experience war. The presence of Union soldiers significantly affected the economic and social lives of Southerners whether they were loyal to the Union or not. As the region came under increasing Federal occupation, Southern civilians would have to reshape and reconstitute their economic and social relationships. As for the Northern occupiers, their experience as guardians of Union republicanism in regions of open secessionism would influence substantially Federal policies for its armies' conduct, civilian property, and slavery. In many respects, the war in the Upper South threatened the same communal ties that had been such an identifiable strength of borderland residents. Nowhere was this more true than in the struggle for the nation's heartland.[59]

CHAPTER TWO

Politics, Planning, and Procrastination

Although the military inertia of the winter carried over into the new year of 1862, the war had entered a new phase for the Federals. Their defeat at Bull Run and the Balls Bluff fiasco in mid-October 1861 disgusted Union legislators, particularly the Radical Republicans, who waited anxiously for months to reconvene Congress and begin to redirect the administration's war aims. Throughout the fall of 1861, Lincoln had allowed Union commanders considerable latitude in conducting the war, simply because he had limited the boundaries of the conflict by resisting attempts at property confiscation and emancipation. In his December message to Congress, the president warned legislators that his policy for suppressing the insurrection was crafted to avoid it becoming a violent and remorseless revolutionary struggle. He argued that tremendous changes would accompany a destructive war. Unless the conflict was restricted to a struggle of armies and not societies, the fruits of victory would be difficult to digest. Still, an impatient and unforgiving public grew increasingly tired of inactivity.[1]

The fact that Lincoln's generals had been conducting the war practically independent of civilian desires and had proven unsuccessful in achieving a victory in the previous months was the subject of much debate during the war's first winter. Thus, when legislators met for the second session of Congress in early December, Radical Republicans sought not only to redefine the Union's war aims but also to get the war moving by pressuring Lincoln to play a more decided role in military affairs. Consequently, the Republican majority, frustrated by mounting expenses and the failure of Union armies to advance, decided to take charge in hopes of bringing the conflict to an end. At the very least, this meant winning the great victory that Lincoln and his generals had failed to produce. At the most, it meant in the eyes of abolitionist leaders such as Frederick Douglass that Union armies "must meet them [the enemy], defeat them, and conquer them."[2]

In an attempt to make military commanders accountable to Congress, legislative leaders created the Joint Committee on the Conduct of the War. The committee's initial purpose was to get generals to fight the enemy rather than just manage troops. By securing an understanding that the government would run the war and the professional soldiers would run the government's armies, Republicans hoped to overcome the annoyingly slow prosecution of military campaigns. They also hoped to abandon the dominant Union policy of conciliation and targeted confiscation and the abolition of slavery as primary wartime goals, pressuring Lincoln to embrace these aims. Radical leaders such as Pennsylvania representative Thaddeus Stevens did not share Lincoln's fear of a revolution brought by emancipation. The Northern press picked up on this pressure and change of attitude. "Slowly but surely," wrote the editor of the *New York Independent*, "the Administration is drifting into the right attitude toward slavery."[3]

Although the Union army had yet to achieve a major victory, it would be easy to imagine that the Northern war machine was capable of eliminating slavery and confiscating property had the people and the Lincoln administration considered these essential preconditions for reconstruction. Moreover, getting civil and military leaders to accept emancipation and confiscation as wartime objectives in 1861 proved troublesome. As conservative Democrats, neither George McClellan, Henry Halleck, nor Don Carlos Buell considered these measures desirable aims because either would turn a limited insurrection into an outright revolution. Like Lincoln, they resisted making war against the Southern populace because it seemed unnecessary. In fact, they came to believe that doing so would excessively burden their military campaigns. Besides, it was Lincoln's policy to carry out the laws of the Constitution while conducting military operations.[4]

In the absence of any specific directives from Washington, Federal commanders hoped to eliminate the logistical and supply problems created by fugitive slaves by excluding them from camp. This they hoped would also sway masters to reaffirm loyalty to the Union and keep the army from settling debates over the peculiar institution. Though this solution naturally complicated matters, it was supported by Lincoln and some members in Congress. Moreover, a departure from the "soft" war position might severely weaken the Union's efforts in wooing back the majority of those who had not supported secession. Still, wartime demands severely hindered the administration's commitment to put down the rebellion without interfering with slavery. As the Federal army and navy penetrated the Confederacy, commanders recognized the burden that the war placed on slave labor; the longer the Northern army occupied Southern soil, the more it disrupted the slave-master relationship, which in turn disrupted the Confederate war effort. Of course, for commanders such as Halleck, Buell, and McClellan who had no toleration for abolitionists, the prosecution of the war under Lincoln's initial conception suited them fine. Over time, however, civil and military leaders would have to reach a compromise solution if for no other reason than to protect runaways and to pacify radicals.[5]

Turbulent though it was, the opening of the second session of the Thirty-seventh Congress reflected the political course legislators sought to take in handling armies. Though the Union was waging what amounted to three wars against the Confederacy—one each in Virginia, Kentucky, and Missouri—its high command had yet to attempt any significant coordinating movement. McClellan had done nothing with the Army of the Potomac, and Buell and Halleck appeared to be too busy preparing their armies to actually use them. Congressional politicians sought to assert themselves as the sole proprietors of the nation's civilian armies precisely because commanders apparently kept these forces too idle for an eager Northern populace. Republicans came to believe that the immobility resulted from the lack of coordination between military authorities in any of those states and their insensitivity toward political urgency. Politicians eager to suppress the rebellion urged the president to get the obstinate generals in the West to move by launching offensive campaigns, particularly in regions where there was significant Union sentiment. Lincoln, however, was apprehensive about performing the role of the military commander; that is, his role as commander in chief. Meanwhile, Halleck and Buell remained preoccupied with the organizational and administrative aspects of their departments.[6]

Besides complaining that the approach of winter precluded any serious movement overland, Buell and Halleck reasoned to Lincoln that the primary difficulty in launching such offensives was that their armies were simply not ready to move. Discipline among the soldiers, they argued, remained poor, and the lack of clothing, arms, finances, and equipment of every sort convinced them that more time was necessary to overcome these deficiencies. In addition, both commanders were frustrated by the large numbers of fugitive slaves appearing almost daily in their camps. Halleck also had to deal with overcoming the corruption in his department left over from John C. Fremont and an emotionally distraught William T. Sherman. Consequently, in both western departments there were more internal difficulties to conquer than enemy forces in the field.[7]

Besides lacking the mental aggressiveness to overcome these weaknesses, neither Buell nor Halleck could agree on where they should strike first. From a map it was clear that the most significant avenue open to Federal forces was along the rivers that traversed the Confederate heartland. But Lincoln wanted East Tennessee liberated, and McClellan kept Buell's attention on that region and the political urgency of relieving its pro-Union loyalists. The general in chief argued that the relief of East Tennessee offered not only political significance and protection to Southern Unionists but also the opportunity to cut the vital Virginia and Tennessee Railroad. The two generals had shaped a strategy before Buell left for Louisville that emphasized a move through Cumberland Gap and down to Knoxville. After surveying the possible routes, however, Buell considered Nashville a better base than the Ohio River city from which to launch a truly powerful offensive into East Tennessee. The state capitol was closer to the region and afforded rail service from Louisville, the supply base for the Army of the Ohio. Still, the positive use of the railroad would only be as effective as Buell's ability to repair it as he went.[8]

Farther west, Halleck reasoned that the Confederate positions at Columbus, Kentucky, were the major impediments to seizing and occupying the Mississippi Valley. Still, Halleck had given considerable thought to the military situation. The western rivers offered the only feasible all-season routes for penetrating the Confederacy at least as far south as northern Alabama. In many ways Halleck and Buell were alike, which surprisingly made cooperating with one another quite difficult. They were both self-absorbed, professionally oriented, and viewed the war through a series of diagrams and maps. Perhaps the largest hurdle for these generals to overcome was the volunteer soldiers' lack of discipline, which they feared would result in recklessness in combat. In addition to these concerns, Buell and Halleck shared a like perspective when it came to civil-military relations: military considerations always subordinated political considerations.[9]

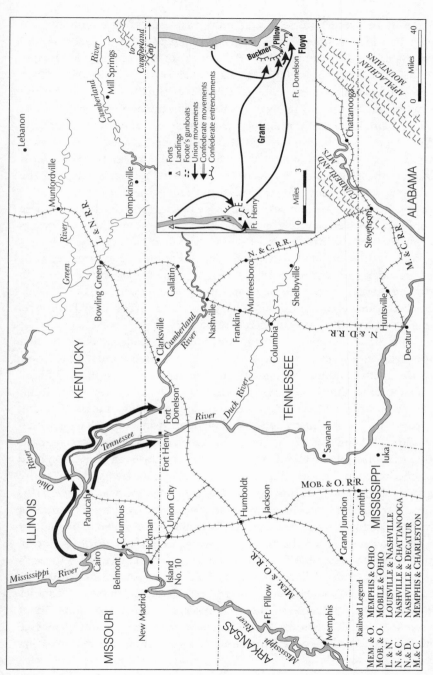

Kentucky and Tennessee, winter–spring 1862

To make matters worse, Washington was demanding attention to an area in which neither Buell nor Halleck knew exactly where his departmental authority ended or the nature of the physical landscape. Halleck's command stretched to the banks of the Cumberland River but applied only to the state of Kentucky. Buell's orders made him responsible for Ohio, Michigan, Indiana, that portion of Kentucky east of the Cumberland River, and the entire state of Tennessee; the chaotic War Department had not yet divided Tennessee because it was unclear which command would enter the state first. The problem was not only that the best choice for breaking the Confederate's entire line in the West was at the point where Buell's and Halleck's departments joined each other near the Kentucky-Tennessee border, but also because these commanders were entirely independent of each other and took orders from McClellan, who favored Buell over Halleck. Moreover, Lincoln's administration demanded the generals' attention at the opposite ends of their departments for political reasons. Halleck was concerned with driving Sterling Price's Confederates from southwestern Missouri, while Buell continued to be distracted by pressure to invade East Tennessee, though he had shown little interest to do so.[10]

Whatever the problems, the fact was Buell and Halleck both knew that the rivers could prove useful in the winter and had contemplated how to use them. Though contemporaries and scholars alike have differed on the authorship of the Forts Henry and Donelson (or twin rivers) campaign, they all generally agree that, as Benjamin Franklin Cooling argues, "the whole thing was patently obvious to anyone looking at a map in 1861."[11] Politicians, civilians, commanders, even journalists recognized the usefulness of the Cumberland and the Tennessee in penetrating the Confederacy in the West. The editor of the *New York Herald* did an entire article on those responsible for planning the invasion via the rivers. Indeed, farmers and merchants who had utilized the waterways for trading had known this for decades. Buell had written to McClellan of his idea for a water-borne invasion shortly after arriving in Louisville. From Paducah, the headquarters of the District of Western Kentucky (under Halleck's command), Capt. William D. "Dirty Bill" Porter, son of famed War of 1812 hero Commodore David Porter, had pressured Brig. Gen. Charles F. Smith and Capt. Andrew Foote, a reserved hard-nosed Connecticut seaman, throughout November and December to steam up the Tennessee and seize vulnerable Fort Henry. Smith and Foote, however, reasoned that the gunboats were not ready and that the Confederacy was threatening to go on the offensive elsewhere.[12]

While Buell had posed the invasion idea to McClellan, Halleck had pinpointed the location of the center of operations to two of his subordinates, George W. Cullum, his chief of staff, and William T. Sherman. One late December evening while sharing cigars with them at his St. Louis headquarters, Halleck turned to a map, glared at it, and asked the officers the location of the Confederate line. When Cullum finished penciling an arc from Bowling Green to Columbus, Halleck circled the Confederate forts of Henry and Donelson and announced, "That's the true line of operations." Still, knowing the location of the Confederate center on a map and doing something about it were two different things.[13]

Yet Halleck was not about to redirect his army's attention to Tennessee until Missouri was completely rid of Price; besides, he needed Buell's cooperation. Buell, though, was not ready to move and was just as stubborn about not wanting to aid Halleck in the western part of Kentucky as he had been about not moving into East Tennessee. What Halleck needed most before implementing his plan of operations was for McClellan or Lincoln to persuade Buell to cooperate. Lincoln, however, left military strategy to professionals, which was odd given his willingness to lay out for Buell the road to East Tennessee. When McClellan fell ill in December, he left the president without any indications of how the western operations might be coordinated. Though he had written to Buell that his proposed idea of taking Nashville was right, it was subordinate to the administration's wishes to relieve loyalists in East Tennessee. Buell, however, remained unpersuaded.[14]

Lincoln was certainly aware of the rivalry between Halleck and Buell, which helped explain the commanders' lack of cooperation. Still, he came to see this as nothing more than procrastination. As McClellan remained immobilized, the disheartened president sought to get Buell and Halleck moving. Hoping for good news in the new year, Lincoln wired both asking if they were in concert for operations. He queried Halleck that if Buell moved on Bowling Green, "what hinders it from being re-enforced from Columbus?" Lincoln answered his own question for Halleck, saying, "a simultaneous movement by you on Columbus might prevent" the enemy from reinforcing in Buell's front. In other words, the coordination between the two commanders would help accomplish the overall objective in the West.[15]

On the first day of 1862, Lincoln reemphasized the need for collabo-
ration between the western commanders. His message reflected his frustration over military affairs, particularly because Congress was itching to
make abolition a war measure; the longer the armies stood still, the more
Radical Republicans pressured the president to adopt their position. With
the Union high command also remaining immobile, an air of desperation
began to descend on Lincoln. It was time, he thought, to take the upper
hand in military affairs. The president borrowed several military books
from the Library of Congress, including Halleck's *Elements of Military
Art and Science,* and immersed himself in military theory. Though not a
military man, Lincoln soon convinced himself that he could do the job the
Constitution had given the president as commander in chief. He understood fully the Congressional designs for expanding the war, so he began
to play a more decisive role in articulating the administration's desires to
keep the war from turning revolutionary. When Halleck responded that
he was not ready to cooperate with Buell in undertaking a simultaneous
advance but would be ready in a few weeks to undertake a campaign
of his own, arguing that "Too much haste will ruin everything," a vexed
president simply could not understand how haste or cooperating with
Buell would ruin anything. Attorney General Edward Bates mirrored
Lincoln's frustration, lamenting in his diary: "we may [stand] to win
advantages decisive of the war. But I fear the arrangements are not perfect
as they ought to be."[16]

As Lincoln tried in vain to inspire Halleck and Buell to action, it was
painfully obvious to him and McClellan that the two generals shared
the same view regarding the whereabouts of the choice for breaking the
Confederate's entire line in the West. Moreover, both commanders agreed
that the attack upon the center should be by two gunboat expeditions on
the twin rivers. Oddly enough, Buell, whom Lincoln still could not get to
advance into East Tennessee, informed Halleck that whatever was done
"should be done speedily, within a few days" as the "work will become
more difficult every day."[17]

When Lincoln wrote urging them to accomplish what they both had
said needed to be done, Halleck lashed back that the "authorities at
Washington do not appreciate the difficulties with which we have to
contend here." Like "a carpenter who is required to build a bridge with
a dull axe, a broken saw, and rotten timber," to whom Halleck compared
himself, "it would be madness" to attempt to assist Buell. In addition,
he argued, to "operate on exterior lines against an enemy occupying a

central position will fail, as it has always failed, in ninety-nine cases out of a hundred. It is condemned by every military authority I have ever read."[18] Besides, the general had Missouri to think about, and the top-ranking officer in Kentucky was Grant, whom Halleck thought careless.[19]

Lincoln first posed the idea of a simultaneous advance on Bowling Green and Columbus to Halleck, but Buell had also thought of it and in more detail. Buell liked the idea because it positioned him on the path to Nashville with a railway for a supply line. The idea also had merit because it diverted attention away from the advance into East Tennessee, an operation to which, he indiscreetly informed Lincoln and McClellan, he had *"from the beginning attached little or no importance."*[20]

But East Tennessee was too important to be neglected altogether. "[M]y distress," wrote Lincoln, "is that our friends in East Tennessee are being hanged and driven to despair, and even now I fear are thinking of taking rebel arms for the sake of personal protection." He concluded, "In this we lose the most valuable stake we have in the South."[21] McClellan echoed the importance of liberating thousands of loyal Tennesseans, emphasizing to Buell that the "political consequences of the delay of this movement will be much more serious than you seem to anticipate."[22]

Regardless of his motives for not moving into East Tennessee, Buell caused trouble for himself by acknowledging his disinterest with the campaign. What the general failed to anticipate was that Tennessee senators Andrew Johnson and Horace Maynard would see his letter, which helped fuel the pressure on Lincoln to get commanders to fight rather than manage the war. More than that, it placed Buell in a bad position with regard to his political views of the war and his understanding of civil-military relationships.[23]

Two telegrams on January 7, 1862, reflected Buell's dilemma. On that day Secretary of War Simon Cameron wrote to Buell, "We are exceedingly anxious to have some result in Kentucky; especially towards East Tennessee." Later Lincoln wrote: "Please name as early a day as you can safely . . . move southward in concert with Major-General Halleck. Delay is ruining us; and it is indispensable for me to have something definite."[24] When Buell and Halleck wired back that neither could name the day when they could be ready to move, Lincoln scribbled his woes on the back of Halleck's response before passing it on to the War Department. "It is exceedingly discouraging," read his comment. "As everywhere else, nothing can be done."[25]

While the Union high command sparred over strategy and cooperation, on January 6 Halleck permitted Grant to make a demonstration into western Kentucky. Because he had little confidence in the Illinoisan, Halleck gave his subordinate a limited objective, little independence, and specific instructions. He ordered Grant to march on Mayfield, Kentucky, and then head to Murray. Brig. Gen. John McClernand at Fort Holt and C. F. Smith at Paducah were to move simultaneously from their bases spreading misinformation to the press and local populace that they were headed to Dover, Tennessee. Though this operation was a demonstration, Halleck hoped to deceive Johnston into thinking that Grant would be followed by a larger force of twenty to thirty thousand soldiers in an attempt to keep the Confederates riveted to Columbus. In the meantime, Halleck would attempt to assemble and dispatch reinforcements from St. Louis. Without hesitation, Grant's land and naval force departed on a cold and foggy January 10 and moved up the Tennessee River.[26]

The weather conditions were difficult for marching. Muddy roads, frozen ponds, and biting cold winds combined to make Halleck's intended demonstration worth remembering, though the conditions severely diminished the soldiers' enthusiasm. Still, the troops were on the move. For many it was their first trip through what was generally known as the "Sunny South," and they came across some civilians who were so frustrated by the devastating effects of the war already that they would have gladly joined the Union cause if only to have their own lives and families whole again. Northern reporters observed that residents wanted uninterrupted freedom. Others, however, chafed at the very thought of Federal soldiers camping on their property.[27]

Of course to the men, there was little gained by the operation, which merely amounted to advancing and returning. On the morning of January 17, however, three Federal vessels shelled Fort Henry while three transports landed a reconnaissance party on the west bank of the Tennessee. Two days later, at the request of Brig. Gen. Lloyd Tilghman (in command of Fort Henry), Maj. Gen. Leonidas Polk at Columbus sent a cavalry force to harass the rear of the Union column, which had already begun its withdrawal. A temporary calm descended on the inland rivers afterward. Though he considered the move a false alarm, Johnston could not figure out whether the demonstration was intended to trap Polk at Columbus or to threaten Nashville. He did, however, shift eight thousand men to Russellville to protect Bowling Green. Polk, nonetheless, remained committed to keeping Columbus, the "citadel of the Mississippi," protected rather than reinforce Bowling Green or the river forts.[28]

Whatever Grant's mission did or did not accomplish, one thing was clear—the Union's experience of coordinating land and naval force had proven agreeable. Though short lived, the operation benefited sailors and soldiers alike as they worked together, discovering much about the bridges, roads, and streams of the area. Perhaps the most important thing they observed was that the roads were too impassable to haul a large supply train. Thus, campaigning would have to be done on the water. Perhaps what was most revealing for the residents along the rivers, however, was that the Union's move south produced a constant fear of being subjugated.[29]

About the same time that Halleck's amphibious operation got underway, the president held what amounted to a council of war. Though the civilians and military personnel primarily discussed what McClellan should do with the Army of the Potomac, McClellan defended his inactivity, arguing that it was necessary to act first in Kentucky and that he was pressing Buell to advance. When the meeting ended on January 13, Lincoln, unsatisfied that McClellan could light a fire under Buell, wired the austere western commander describing his view of the military situation, concluding that "Halleck shall menace Columbus and 'down river' generally; while you menace Bowling-Green, and East Tennessee." The president was clearly seeing the larger picture of the Union's efforts in the West: the core of the problem lay not in the inhospitable weather or countryside but with the commanders themselves.[30]

McClellan returned to his office and dashed off a desperate letter to Buell concerning the political situation. "You have no idea of the pressure brought to bear here upon the Government for a forward movement," he warned Buell. "It is so strong that it seems absolutely necessary to make the advance on Eastern Tennessee at once."[31]

Buell seemed to use the East Tennessee excuse as a way of not helping Halleck. But McClellan continued to reiterate what had been obvious to his friend since he came to the West in November: the possession of the railroad in East Tennessee would prevent the main army from reinforcing in McClellan's front, and it was politically desirable to aid the Tennessee Unionists. To illustrate just how important an advance into East Tennessee had become, McClellan was even willing to depart from his initial orders protecting the rights of citizens. In hiring wagons and teams to facilitate the expedition, McClellan advised Buell to take on private teams, and if the people "will not freely give them, why, then, seize them." "It is no time to stand on trifles," fumed the general in chief.[32] In McClellan's mind everything was tied together in such a way that his operations were always more important than those of anyone else.

By mid-January, newspaper correspondents, convinced that the Union's best chances for success in the West flowed on the waters of the twin rivers, became concerned that Halleck and Buell were the impediments in bringing about such success. Ironically, just a few weeks before, the *New York Times* prophesied that Halleck and Buell, given their credentials, "would have driven the last spoiler out of Kentucky and Missouri by January 1."[33] Indeed, delay appeared to be the order of the day. The western commanders continued to delay while McClellan did virtually nothing to bring about what the president desired—cooperation. Meanwhile, C. F. Smith had steamed upriver aboard the *Lexington* to get a look at Fort Henry; seeing no gunboats, he concluded to Grant that two ironclads would make short work of Confederate post. The problem was convincing Halleck and McClellan to order the operation before Johnston could move to counter the mission.[34]

Fortunately, Buell's and Halleck's subordinates had more of the "go" and "fight" in them than their superiors. For weeks Buell had promised McClellan that the "roving bugbears," as he characterized the Confederate cavalry attempting to harass and upset his plans, were not going to deter him from organizing his army; Buell always emphasized preparation over movement. But just when all eyes seemed to be on the twin rivers for a major engagement, nearly five thousand Confederates led by Brig. Gen. Felix Zollicoffer and Maj. Gen. George B. Crittenden attempted to surprise Brig. Gen. George H. Thomas's command of roughly the same size in eastern Kentucky at a place called Logan's Crossroads, or Mill Springs, eight miles west of Somerset. Thomas was on his way to East Tennessee when, on January 20, the Confederates attacked his force; the day ended with the Union victorious. The completeness of the triumph provided proof that Buell, who desperately needed it politically, was finally doing something. It also gave Lincoln reason to believe that the general would now commence a major campaign into East Tennessee, since the only remaining Confederate force was at Cumberland Gap. Though not a great victory, Mill Springs not only weakened Johnston's defensive line, but it also revealed that his Confederates could be whipped, thoroughly diminishing Confederate prestige in the area. As one Ohio captain wrote to his wife, "We are beginning to feel that there is yet some life in our army."[35]

The Mills Springs victory also breathed new life into a deflated administration, particularly since Buell, despite supply difficulties but encouraged by Thomas, consented to send Brig. Gen. Samuel Carter's Twelfth Brigade to Cumberland Gap, though bad weather would ultimately stall this movement indefinitely. Thomas, meanwhile, headed toward Burkesville on the Cumberland above Nashville to thus cooperate with Buell in threatening Johnston's Bowling Green position. After months of prodding, Buell had finally moved toward East Tennessee, though only by inches and with Thomas doing the fighting. The new secretary of war, Edwin M. Stanton (Cameron having been dismissed by Lincoln), acknowledged on the president's behalf the brilliant victory and took the opportunity to declare his views of the purpose of the war as "attack, pursue and destroy."[36]

Stanton's entrance on the scene at this stage proved critical in teaching military commanders that they were subject to civil authority and in helping Lincoln prod them into action. Stanton found useful the Joint Committee on the Conduct of the War. Up to January 1861, he told Charles Dana, editor of the *New York Tribune,* "We have had no war, we have not even been playing war."[37]

After Mill Springs, Buell continued to try and convince McClellan that Nashville should be the main objective. He reasoned that Halleck's gunboats could easily move upriver, steam past Fort Donelson, destroy the railroad bridge at Clarksville, Tennessee, and then join Thomas above Nashville. Halleck, however, continued to maintain that a combined army could utilize the Tennessee River, take Fort Henry, turn Columbus and force it to surrender, and compel the abandonment of Bowling Green. He hoped that this idea would convince McClellan to send him reinforcements to undertake the operation. At the same time, Halleck would send a portion of his Missouri command into northeastern Arkansas, cut the Confederate supply line in Missouri, and have Brig. Gen. Samuel R. Curtis pursue the Confederates into Arkansas. Brig. Gen. John Pope, meanwhile, would take the Mississippi River town of New Madrid. The administrative struggle, however, was over whose advance east of the Mississippi River would take priority and who would assist whom. Buell wanted to keep Bowling Green and Nashville as his sole prizes while Halleck aided him by threatening other points of the Confederate line.[38]

Both Halleck and Buell explained to McClellan their ideas regarding how penetration along the twin rivers should develop. The responsibility for a move up the rivers, however, would have to come from Halleck, since they emptied into the Ohio River in his department. Halleck had complained throughout December and January that he would not be ready to cooperate with Buell until sometime in February. He hoped to double the size of the force at Cairo and Paducah and also secure enough additional troops to make up a combined naval and army column to head south along the rivers. Too, he was concerned about New Madrid, which Federal forces in Missouri could seize but would be of little value unless Confederates were driven from Columbus upriver. Though "the 'On to Richmond' policy here," he added, "will produce another Bull Run disaster," Halleck promised McClellan that he would be ready to move in Tennessee by early February.[39] He also implied to McClellan that Buell's moves be demonstrations and not the main offensive in the West. While he waited for approval of his plans, Halleck sent Grant and Foote out to investigate the obvious weaknesses of the western end of Johnston's line.[40]

To the thoroughly professional Halleck, Grant was perhaps the most unlikely commander he could trust. He had refused Grant's earlier requests to come to St. Louis to discuss seizing the forts. However, when Grant asked to come to St. Louis after his recent demonstration, Halleck, perhaps jealous over the Union victory in Buell's department, finally agreed. Based on a curt telegram that read, "You have permission to visit headquarters," Grant was not exactly expecting a warm reception.

The general arrived in St. Louis on January 23, but apparently overwhelmed by Halleck's bluntness, he displayed uncharacteristic nervousness and became inarticulate. Halleck had a poor command relationship with Grant, partly because he lacked confidence in and respect for his subordinate and partly because of Grant's alleged alcohol abuse. Grant did make an impression on Halleck, however, so much so that Halleck became even more concerned about his fitness for the river expedition. Whatever the case, Halleck was neither moved by anything Grant managed to get out about Fort Henry nor was he about to abandon his mid-February deadline for commencing a major campaign upriver. Moreover, the departmental chief had not yet completed his concentration at Paducah and Cairo. Still, he had ordered C. F. Smith, in whom he had more confidence than Grant, to survey the condition of the roads from Smithland to Dover and Fort Henry and the crossing points above Paducah.[41]

As excited as he had been to tell Halleck of the favorable news of the expedition, Grant returned from his unproductive visit downcast. Halleck's treatment was typical of the unproductive command relationship that existed between the two men. The incident left such an impression on Grant that years later he recalled in his memoirs how Halleck received him with so little cordiality that Grant was soon made to feel as though his plan was "preposterous."[42]

Compounding the general's rebuked feeling was that it was increasingly difficult to keep the troops busy while in Cairo. Impatient soldiers continued to think of their families and the idleness led to mischief and fighting. The navy's inability to acquire the necessary crews and equipment for the expedition against Fort Henry also gave him concern. Foote pained over reports by subordinates that given the swift river currents, gunboats would have to tow mortar boats up the Tennessee and Cumberland to get at the forts. About the only encouraging news from camp was that Smith's surveying mission had given Grant reason to hope the time was right to move and that Foote was primed to undertake a joint venture in seizing the forts. An inspired Grant and Foote wired Halleck that they were prepared to move and only needed permission to launch the joint operation. "With permission," a persistent Grant wrote back to Halleck, "I will take Fort McHenry on the Tennessee and hold & establish a large camp there." He argued in a follow-up letter that such a move would have "a moral effect upon our troops to advance them towards the rebel states. The advantages of this move are as perceptable to the Gen. Comd.g Dept. as to myself, therefore further statements are unnecessary."[43] Still, Halleck remained skeptical about Grant's idea, thinking it was premature.

Fear, more than the urging of Buell, Grant, or even Foote, was the great motivation that finally caused Halleck to give the go ahead against Fort Henry. Far off to the east, McClellan had learned that Confederate general Pierre Gustave Toutant Beauregard was heading to Kentucky with fifteen regiments, and he wired Halleck the news on January 29. Naturally, this struck a chord of anxiety in Halleck, who decided instantly to rush to the offensive and get Grant moving. No longer did Halleck consider Buell's suggested dual advance up the Cumberland and the Tennessee "madness." Furthermore, he also may have considered that sending Grant on an advance might keep him from drinking and keep the soldiers occupied.[44]

Though "Old Brains" had thought about such an offensive for some time, he had not received additional troops for his department and had not effected coordination with other commands for such an offensive. The impassibility of the roads would require that the expedition be conducted on water, something Halleck really had little experience in organizing.

He had recently complained to the secretary of war that he was unable to cooperate with Buell in a campaign to Nashville because his own units were so scattered that to do so would weaken Federal forces in Missouri. The general had informed McClellan earlier that the distribution and arrangement of forces—what Halleck termed a "pepper-box strategy"— had been done to satisfy political expediency and that the "want of success on our part [was] attributable to the politicians rather than to the generals."[45]

Halleck felt confident that he could draw on the new secretary of war in supporting his ideas for operations in the West, so he appealed to Stanton to rectify the command situation. Although the twin rivers were the "great center line in the Western theater of war," the problem was that once Grant crossed into Tennessee, he left Halleck's department and entered Buell's command. This seemed unimportant at the time the War Department created the western departments, but now Halleck was concerned that Buell would claim a victory by capturing Bowling Green and Nashville precisely because Johnston would reinforce Columbus. He also thought that Buell might gain command of the entire West not only because of his friendship with McClellan but also because of Thomas's Mill Springs victory. That success had opened the path to East Tennessee and gave Lincoln some much-needed political relief, reflecting favorably on Buell. Halleck knew he had to counterbalance Buell's success and establish his own force in Tennessee before Beauregard arrived. He suggested to McClellan that Tennessee be added to his department. This would not only enlarge the area of Halleck's command and allow him to oversee the entire operation as it progressed further into Tennessee but also subordinate Buell's operations. McClellan ignored this request and instead sent Buell a map of Tennessee to make sure he knew the terrain when Grant came into his jurisdiction.[46]

Though Buell had urged Halleck to move into Tennessee for two months to aid his advance on Nashville (and had in fact said that Fort Henry could be taken in a matter of two hours based on the reports of his Paducah spy, John Lellyett, when the operation commenced), he was shocked by its haste. He wired Halleck on January 30, "Please let me know your plans and force and the time, &c." Halleck responded briefly that he had already ordered movements against Fort Henry and the railroad between Columbus and Dover. Buell fumed in his reply: "Do you consider active co-operation essential to your success, because in that case it would be necessary for each to know what the other has to do."

He ended his message with a threatening bit of advice for Halleck that his operation "ought not fail."[47]

Halleck's decision to unleash Grant incensed Buell, since he was not ready to move, certainly not with haste. Though he was convinced that an advance into East Tennessee would prove futile, he had, nonetheless, arranged his army to make it appear as though he might strike at anytime. Part of this had to do with the mounting political pressure against him. Thus, to shift his army to aid Halleck quickly was impossible. On the same day Buell learned of Grant's operation, he halted the advance toward East Tennessee, which he knew he would have to explain to Washington.[48]

It was imperative that Buell and Halleck cooperate to bring about success in the West, particularly since they agreed on where the Confederates were weakest. The fact that they refused to get along reflected the inherent defects of the Union departmental command system. What made matters worse was that the two men were pugnacious and too much alike, governing in similar situations. Administering vast and diverse regions, both were forced to position parts of their armies to satisfy politicians both locally and nationally, which greatly inhibited their ability to concentrate the whole. Halleck and Buell were perfectionists who sought to minimize risk and maximize security in war. Moreover, it was mentally and emotionally exhausting for them to rely on subordinates in whom they lacked confidence. As a result, caution and thorough preparation had become for them the means to increase the safeness of war. McClellan, apparently too absorbed by the pressure in his front on the Virginia Peninsula and the mounting political pressure against him in Washington, refused to interfere in any tangible way to bring about better cooperation. Thus, Buell and Halleck's similarities made cooperation difficult, and action would only be forthcoming whenever either was willing to relinquish the importance of his personal desires. While the generals stalled for time, the men of their armies spent the tedious winter weeks dominated by bad weather, repetitious drilling, and military inertia while waiting for something to happen. Grant, however, was preparing to advance.[49]

Congressional Republicans, already fed up with the annoyingly slow prosecution of the war, came to view the uncooperative spirit of the two commanders as a general lack of appreciation for the political nature of the war. This led some political leaders to conclude that Buell and Halleck lacked not only fighting spirit but also moral vitality. In order to be successful in the West, the Union would have to designate one of the generals as overall commander to get efficiency from both. Had

McClellan acted on this assumption earlier, Buell might have been given the greater authority, but when McClellan fell out of favor with Stanton and Lincoln, so too did Buell. The president, however, could no longer afford to wait and decided in late January to issue a strange comprehensive paper entitled "President's General War Order No. One." This called for a general land and naval movement against the Confederates beginning February 22. Though it had little impact on the surface, it did goad McClellan into responding about his overall intensions, including goals, timetables, and forces involved. Lincoln's order also had significance for Halleck and Buell, since McClellan's plan called for joint efforts between those in the East and West. Moreover, the Joint Committee on the Conduct of the War was now primed to expect results.[50]

Though the Union high command spent the early winter frozen in inaction and dissension, the Confederates at least had one overall commander for the West and an excellent advantage of interior lines afforded by the rail communications linking commands in Kentucky and Tennessee. Still, the Southern army in the West was cursed with an embarrassing lack of resources and manpower, incompetent subordinate officers, limited railroad facilities, and an unsupportive administration. Though he had three separate armies under his authority, Gen. Albert Sidney Johnston was greatly outnumbered. He had positioned his forces to take advantage of the railroads in the region, but not the rivers. Polk's eleven thousand soldiers faced Grant's twenty to twenty-five thousand men; Johnston had twenty-five thousand troops under William J. Hardee at Bowling Green in the path of Buell's seventy-thousand men heading south; and Crittenden had about four thousand soldiers facing a Union force of about the same size in eastern Kentucky.[51]

Despite his problems, Johnston firmly believed that Buell's obvious path of advance was over rail to Nashville. The Ohioan's reported seventy-five thousand men kept Sidney Johnston focused on the Tennessee capital, and if he had not completely forgotten about his flanks, he had neglected the river defenses. Nevertheless, he was concerned about the natural river gateways that paralleled each other south behind his Bowling Green position into the Confederate heartland. Johnston kept a close eye on Polk, whom he alerted to the importance of the land between Columbus and Bowling Green, a region not unlike that of northern Virginia and the Shenandoah Valley in its strategic importance. But the commander's warnings throughout the fall and winter produced little change in the situation. He failed to persuade President Davis that the painfully obvious situation in the West, especially Tennessee, was crucial enough to the overall war effort to commit the resources necessary for its security. Though Davis was convinced that Johnston was capable of doing much with what few resources he had, the Confederate president had not really appreciated the situation's gravity. As William Preston Johnston later wrote, "It was the error of the Administration not to have perceived that the defense of Tennessee was vital, and that it was in more immediate peril even than Virginia—that a stab in the back is as fatal as one in the breast."[52]

Once the Confederates moved into Kentucky in the fall of 1861, the twin rivers attracted considerable attention, as did the dual forts that lay about ten miles south of the Kentucky line and roughly the same distance apart. While Kentucky remained neutral, the state of Tennessee commenced construction of Henry and Donelson. Unfortunately for the Confederacy, political exigencies more than strategic location or terrain governed the selection of the sites, which resulted in the injudicious decision to construct them dangerously close to the riverbanks. Confederate authorities respected Kentucky's neutrality and went ahead, though lethargically, with strengthening the forts. When Johnston assumed command of the department, he thought Polk was responsible for evaluating the strategic significance of the positions, either fortifying them where they were or possibly relocating them. Convinced that Henry and Donelson were fine as established, Polk initially called on Col. Adolphus Heiman, a German émigré, to oversee their completion. Because he apparently did not consider them to be in his district, though, Polk turned his sights to strengthening Bowling Green. Heiman repeatedly warned of the forts' weaknesses in defensive works, but throughout December and January, Polk did little to change the situation.[53]

The neglect of the river defenses on the Cumberland and Tennessee stemmed from confusion in district alignments and Polk's failure to devote the necessary attention. He knew the forts' weak conditions, but he had become as obsessed with the defense of Columbus as Johnston had been with Bowling Green. Polk lived in daily fear that Columbus was in peril, so much so that it immobilized him. When in mid-November Brig. Gen. Lloyd Tilghman, a Kentuckian and the department's chief engineer, replaced Heiman in command of Forts Henry and Donelson, Johnston ordered him to complete his predecessor's preparations with haste. Though concerned about their obvious weaknesses, the general's directives failed to impress Polk, who continued to allow the forts' con-

struction to continue arbitrarily. For two months Tilghman proved ineffective as Polk repeatedly denied his requests for troops, reasoning that the
forts were not in his district. In late December, anxious to get something
going, Tilghman warned that no other point in the entire Confederacy
needed more assistance than Henry and Donelson.[54]

Polk's neglect was not the only reason the forts remained incomplete and undermanned. Johnston was partially to blame because he
allowed his subordinates too much independence of judgment and held
too much confidence in Polk. Though Tilghman was in command of the
troops at Henry and Donelson, Johnston had assigned his chief engineer,
Col. Jeremy Gilmer, to prepare defenses at Bowling Green, Nashville,
Clarksville, and the river forts. Unlike Tilghman, Gilmer was convinced
that given the chaotic mess of their new departments and the brutal winter
weather, neither Halleck nor Buell would venture a campaign until spring,
so he exercised little haste in fortifying any of the assigned locations,
least of all ones that represented the least path of resistance. Joseph
Dixon, Johnston's chief of the department's engineer corps, contributed
to Gilmer's decision, since he shared ideas on spreading out the river
defenses, despite Johnston's orders to concentrate on those at Donelson.[55]

The cumulative impact of these failings was that by January the most
important projects such as the river forts and the defenses at Clarksville
and Nashville had been neglected. Tilghman's entire command now
numbered only 4,600 troops, of whom almost 2,000 were unarmed. The
total effective force at Donelson numbered 600, and of those there were
still no trained soldiers to man the river batteries. Finally, in mid-January
Johnston concluded that the Union commanders had found the weakest
point in the Confederate line, and he finally realized something was wrong
with Confederate defensive preparations, which he should have known
four months earlier. He wired a desperate note to Tilghman: "Occupy
and intrench the heights opposite Fort Henry. Do not lose a moment.
Work all night."[56] The order came too late. As Grant's force steamed
upriver, the Federals found just what they had expected, a weakly held
Confederate line. Although Tilghman warned that the enemy column was
in a position to advance again on Fort Henry, a temporary calm descended
on the inland rivers. With the exception of Tilghman, the Confederate
high command considered the move a false alarm rather than a precursor
of events to come.[57]

Meanwhile, Johnston, burdened with cares elsewhere, organized his
entire command east of the Mississippi River to meet the anticipated Fed-

eral advance of Buell against Bowling Green and Nashville or of Halleck along the line of the Mississippi River, perhaps using the Tennessee River to support his movement. The Confederate commander also continued his efforts to raise an adequate army, but he failed to keep pace with those of Buell and Halleck. As Johnston sought to strengthen his forces through volunteers, he also tried to impress upon Davis the strategic importance of the Mississippi Valley. Preoccupied with the defense of Richmond, Davis seems to have been insufficiently aware of the danger through the broad western approach. Johnston saw it with clarity, but the region remained neglected. A powerful Federal army was about to march south from Louisville, he warned Secretary of War Judah P. Benjamin, "They [the Federals] have justly comprehended that the seat of vitality of the Confederacy if to be reached at all is by this route." Johnston concluded, "It is now palpable that all the resources of that government will, if necessary, be employed to assure success on this line."[58]

Disappointed by the lack of public support in volunteering for service, contributing labor for digging defensive works, and providing war material, along with the administration's preoccupation with Richmond, a dejected General Johnston attempted to concentrate his scattered forces to hold the line in Kentucky. However, in this defensive mentality, state governors and other political leaders sought to guard every corner of Confederate territory, and neither Davis nor Johnston were able to achieve an effective concentration of forces. The general was realistic about the impossibility of a complete concentration, so he made modest requests to Davis for reinforcements that helped focus the attention of political leaders on points of weakness. He displayed a passive attitude toward pressing the government for things needed in his command, and consequently his army suffered. Still, Johnston suggested to the president that units in departments not similarly threatened by the enemy might be transferred to his command. In mid-January, however, he bypassed the chain of command and dispatched Col. St. John R. Liddell to Richmond to ask the president in person for troops from Virginia, Charleston, Savannah, Pensacola, and New Orleans. A frustrated Davis lashed out that he had neither troops nor arms to spare. "Tell my friend, General Johnston," he told Liddell, "that I can do nothing for him; that he must rely on his own resources."[59] Davis could not be shaken from his apathy regarding the situation in the West.

Johnston knew that Buell and Halleck were aware of his lack of strength, which gave the Federals a tremendous advantage in choosing the time and place to strike south. Grant's January demonstration had frozen the Confederates. Thomas's victory at Mill Springs was Johnston's first defeat in the field and resulted partly because Zollicoffer displayed more spirit than wisdom. It came also because Johnston, faithful to his command theory, turned over the area of eastern Kentucky, like he had done in western Tennessee, to an untried subordinate and relied on that officer's judgment as to how the mission could best be accomplished. Allowing commanders such as Polk and Zollicoffer considerable independence was partially the result of Johnston's inexperience in directing a large army on a vast and exposed front. The defeat intensified the general's desire for reinforcement, and he increased his pleas for more troops. Still, Richmond authorities were unable or unwilling to send sorely needed resources west. Thus, Grant's January demonstration at the center of the Confederate line simply confirmed what Johnston already knew to be true about his situation. He was desperate.[60]

For weeks the Confederate command structure functioned in a confused and anxious state, reflecting the frailty of Johnston's tempering influence and Polk's fear. Richmond's lack of appreciation for the Tennessee situation was evidenced by the administration's lack of support for things such as men and arms needed in Johnston's command. Polk's fear of an attack from Cairo convinced him to amass twenty-one thousand men and about one hundred fifty fixed and field guns at Columbus, producing the strongest single force in Johnston's department. Fear controlled Polk's attitude so much that in January he announced his intentions of retiring into a state of siege at Columbus unless more troops were forthcoming. He even declared to Johnston that a Federal strike aimed at any point elsewhere in his district would have to be the responsibility of the War Department and other Confederate forces in the region. Johnston, however, made no effort to force Polk to be responsible for defending the eastern part of his district.[61]

Throughout the fall and early winter, Johnston had concealed his army's weaknesses by staging a series of raids along his entire front, especially to the east, while he strove to create a real army behind this screen. He had better luck masking his weaknesses than overcoming them largely because Union commanders such as Buell spent considerable time anticipating moves and reacting rather than acting; Confederate raids placed Buell on the defensive for fear of an attack on Louisville. But as much as Johnston pained over the lack of soldiers and equipment, Fort Henry's position mirrored that of the Confederacy in this region—

vulnerable to robust rivers. Located on the east bank of the Tennessee on low land, the position was commanded by hills within rifle range on both sides of the river. More alarming was the fact that the Tennessee River flooded Henry annually in an ordinary February rise, which put the highest point of the fort under two feet of water.[62]

Twelve miles away on the west bank of the Cumberland, Fort Donelson, however, was a far more formidable post. It was constructed on a bank nearly a hundred feet above the water and was protected on the north by Hickman's Creek, deep and wide in the high water of winter, and on the south by Indian Creek. In a crescent around the fort ran a line of rifle pits, largely following a ridge and protected by felled trees forming an abatis. Two water batteries positioned in the northern face of the bluff thirty feet above the river held twelve guns and one 10-inch Columbiad. Attacking infantry would find Hickman's Creek almost impassable, and to reach the rifle pits they would have to struggle at most points up hillsides some seventy feet high. Still, even with its imposing physical and geographical strengths, Donelson was rendered weak because it lacked the garrison to exploit its advantage. Not only did the eighteen thousand ill-trained, ill-armed, ill-provisioned recruits lack spirit but they also lacked competent leaders. The ranking officer was Brig. Gen. John B. Floyd, the same political incompetent who had been President James Buchanan's secretary of war. Under him was Simon Buckner, the only West Point graduate whose authority matched his ability and who had served with the Kentucky State Guard. Tennessean Gideon Pillow had resigned from the army shortly after Christmas 1861 because he refused to serve under Polk, whom he considered wholly unqualified to command.[63]

Though the cold winter days were indistinguishable from one another, January passed into February. Colonel Gilmer and engineer Joseph Dixon had done as much as they could to strengthen Fort Henry, though it still lacked heavy ordnance. Lt. Col. Milton A. Haynes, Polk's heavy artillery specialist, took over gunnery instruction at the river forts, organized the available men and guns into a provisional battalion, and drilled the men in an attempt to prepare them for action. The frenzy of activity by the Confederates was necessary since winter floodwaters had already begun to envelop Henry.[64]

Although these forts had undergone a marked transformation in a relatively short time, one month had passed since Lincoln demanded that Halleck and Buell cooperate in the West. The two commanders, however, were still sparring over how to comply. When Buell had offered to assist after learning that Halleck had ordered Grant south, his counterpart replied on February 1 that cooperation was not essential. This incensed Buell, who wrote McClellan the same day arguing that when he had first proposed cooperation, Halleck had answered, "I can do nothing." Now, Buell fumed, his counterpart had ordered an advance without consultation. "I protest against such proceedings," exclaimed Buell, "as though I had nothing to do but 'Commence firing' when he starts off."[65]

Buell obviously wanted to head out first, which would have subordinated Halleck's campaign to his own move against Nashville, but he needed more time to repair the railroad to Bowling Green. That would help justify the explanation to Halleck why Buell felt pushed into action when he wanted to start for Bowling Green anyway. Nevertheless, Buell's slow advance transfixed Johnston's forces in their positions.

Halleck's abruptness had momentarily distracted the War Department and saved Buell from the trouble of advancing into East Tennessee. In the same note in which he complained about Halleck, Buell wrote McClellan that although the conditions in East Tennessee were serious, its citizens were loyal and would remain so, "though submitting to the power that has subjugated them." He concluded: "They will rise whenever they can see themselves properly supported and we can put arms in their hands, but not before in any efficient manner. It would be cruel to induce them to do so on any other conditions."[66]

Secretary Stanton acknowledged Buell's letter, approving, as had McClellan, the campaign on Nashville. He added, however, that they urged cooperation, arguing "that your two heads [Halleck's and Buell's] together will succeed."[67]

But Halleck desired to keep the upper hand in the campaign on the twin rivers and elaborated to Buell on February 2 what he intended Grant to do. The confident commander envisioned taking Fort Henry and then Fort Donelson as well as cutting the railroad from Columbus to Bowling Green. Despite his anger over not being consulted by Halleck, Buell thought it useful to perhaps send a larger force into East Tennessee to keep the Confederates debating over which end of their line to reinforce. Whatever the case, Buell and Halleck were showing signs of urgency.[68]

The next few days witnessed the exchange of a barrage of telegrams indicating a troubled Union high command, particularly because Halleck was concerned about Grant. Beauregard's reported fifteen thousand Confederates might arrive at Fort Henry and crush Grant's small force. He wired Buell asking for either some troops or for a diversion at Bowling

Green. Buell responded that his progress had been slowed by the need to repair the railroad. Besides, he argued: "My position does not admit of diversion. My moves must be real ones."[69]

Halleck took his plea to a higher level and pressured the general in chief. McClellan, however, avoided making any decisions, though he did inform Buell of Halleck's needs. This prompted Buell to dispatch a brigade west, but wrote to Halleck—almost as if he were demanding proof—that he would send it only if the latter "absolutely" required it. With the acknowledgment that he would send the brigade, Buell concluded his telegram with the words he had voiced the week before: "You must not fail."[70]

Though nervous about the operation on the Tennessee, Halleck was still hopeful. Buell's help would have gone a long way toward relieving his fear about Grant's potential vulnerability. It might also have been a much-needed cooperative gesture that would have added to Buell's recent victory at Mill Springs and may have benefited him in the eyes of Washington. Still, the general continued to reason to McClellan why he could not assist Halleck. He had not only positioned his forces to make it look like he might advance on East Tennessee but also did not want to be diverted from Nashville, his main objective. Buell lectured McClellan that Halleck should have "weighed his work well" before starting out, so that his expedition would be prepared to meet all contingencies in striking at Fort Henry in haste. If Halleck failed, Buell thought, it would surely teach him a lesson about moving without complete preparation and concert.[71]

Buell was not the only one who would have benefited by Halleck's failure. Given the friendship between Buell and McClellan, and the latter's ambition to continue to manage the Union armies, the general in chief shared Buell's sentiments in not wanting Halleck to bring about the great victory in the West. Buell was not ambitious for a larger or more significant command, certainly not McClellan's position. Consequently, he was not a threat to McClellan. In fact, Buell might be useful in helping McClellan maintain his position as general in chief. A defeat caused by premature movement might convince political leaders that despite military inertia in his own department, McClellan was at least successful in getting Buell to move, something he had promised Lincoln during the council of war meeting three weeks in January.[72]

While McClellan, Halleck, and Buell squabbled over strategy in the West, Stanton dispatched his assistant secretary of war, a former railroad executive named Thomas A. Scott, to the Midwest to examine the possibility of a transfer of troops from the East to the West as proposed by McClellan some weeks earlier. By early February, Scott had made his way to Louisville, where Buell convinced him that Halleck's river advance would be accomplished easily and that the troops from the East should be transferred to his own department for the move on Nashville. When Scott sent his opinions to Stanton, the secretary of war replied brusquely that the assistant had been sent on an inspection mission and not on a tour to make policy. At that point, according to Scott, it was clear that whether the secretary of war liked Halleck or not, he preferred him to Buell.[73]

Buell concluded that the key to winning the war was not only in the West but also in his department. The austere Ohioan was contemplating changing the main line of his operations from the Bowling Green–Nashville line to help Halleck; McClellan had obviously persuaded Buell to at least consider the idea. While he decided what to do, Buell fumed to his friend that Halleck's whole move, "right in its strategical bearing," was commenced "without appreciation—preparative or concert—has now become of vast magnitude." He could not have been more right. On January 22, Albert Sidney Johnston wrote to Samuel Cooper: "Our people do not comprehend the magnitude of the danger that threatens. Let it be impressed upon them."[74]

CHAPTER THREE

Henry and Donelson

As obvious as the weakness of the Confederate line was to Federal authorities, so too was the unmistakable sign to the Confederates that the Tennessee and Cumberland Rivers flooded every winter. In past years this was a time of great advantage for farmers seeking to use water transports to carry their supplies upriver. Now, Union commanders shared that benefit as routes of supply became strategic military arteries. Northern snows swelled the Ohio and Mississippi Rivers, and Northern soldiers at Paducah watched as the confluence of the Tennessee and the Ohio gave them great advantages to move south by water. Fort Henry was the sole Confederate obstacle in the path of invasion into northern Mississippi and Alabama, and the high water of the Tennessee had flooded the position, giving the Union a tremendous advantage. Grant knew that his future in the military resided in his ability to pull off a successful river campaign, even more so to impress Halleck and compensate for his mishandling of their recent meeting. The department commander had ordered that Fort Henry be taken before reinforcements could arrive, and this meant moving quickly, secretly, and with a combat-ready force.[1]

If Grant felt eclipsed by Halleck's intimidating presence, Brig. Gen. C. F. Smith made him feel at ease, despite the latter's formal manner stemming from a thirty-five-year service career. Smith was a seasoned veteran and towered over his commander, both physically and intellectually. After all, he had been a commandant of cadets when Grant was at West Point and had made the army his life's profession. Now Grant, a stubby, impulsive, unprofessional-looking political appointee in whom Halleck had little confidence, was his superior. Still, Grant was a West Pointer and Smith came to respect him. Flag Officer Andrew Foote did little to relieve

Grant's discomfort by complaining that, to carry out the combined army-navy expedition, he lacked sufficient transports to haul the seventeen thousand soldiers of the Army of the Tennessee in one lift. Not only did he lack ships but also sufficient crews to man both the transports and the gunboats detailed for escort and bombardment duties. The energies of Foote and Grant, however, managed to compensate for these impediments by borrowing replacements from other vessels and converting army recruits into seamen. Still, the shortage of steamboats forced the Union expedition to move forward sequentially, protected by gunboats.[2]

When Brig. Gen. John McClernand arrived with his division of troops at Paducah late in the night on February 3, he joined two eager commanders in Foote and Grant. McClernand had participated in the Black Hawk War and had served in the Illinois legislature. It was rumored that he was trying to obtain an independent command through President Lincoln, his friend and former colleague in the Illinois legislature. When Grant visited Halleck in St. Louis, McClernand assumed command of Grant's district and took the liberty of recommending to Halleck that an advance of Union forces to either attack Columbus or occupy the region between that river city and the Tennessee River was in order. The recommendation offended both generals because it assumed that neither Grant nor Halleck had thought of such an idea. Still, McClernand was eager to push forward and fight. The three brigades of his First Division were comprised of Illinoisans who were elated when they learned that they were the vanguard of an amphibious offensive to move up the swollen river. Two of Foote's five ironclads, the *Essex* and the *St. Louis,* shielded the transports as they headed sixty-five miles upstream to Pine Bluff, Tennessee. Grant was forced to move the infantry in two trips and invest Fort Henry from land while Foote shelled it from the river. McClernand's force was to land quickly and as near Henry as possible but beyond the range of the artillery, so the steamers could return for Smith's Second Division and Col. William H. L. Wallace's Third Division. Grant remained at Paducah until the last of the troops embarked for the campaign. Before leaving, he wired Halleck that his entire force would be on the river by six o'clock in the morning. Some soldiers were so confident they would be returning shortly that they left their overcoats and blankets behind.[3]

Grant intended for McClernand's division to land south of Panther Creek, a few miles north of the Confederate position, to avoid crossing the swollen tributary. Before issuing the order, though, he boarded the *Essex* and requested Capt. William D. "Dirty Bill" Porter to approach

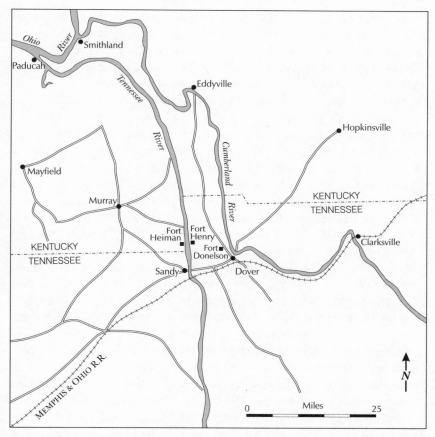

Twin rivers area

Fort Henry to draw Confederate fire, which ultimately forced Grant to conclude that his troops would have to debark below (north of) the mouth of the creek at Bailey's Ferry. In the darkness of a cheerless winter morning, McClernand's division marched off the steamers and onto the muddy and impassable road, which severely restricted and delayed the march for several hours. Still, Grant expected McClernand to secure the road between Henry and Donelson to prevent the Confederate garrison from escaping. Meanwhile, Grant returned downriver to Paducah to hasten the remaining troops under Smith forward. Smith's column would land on the river's west bank and march southward to seize the unfinished Fort Heiman before crossing to Fort Henry.[4]

For the Confederates, the winter gloom was darker than expected as the Federal invasion proceeded virtually undetected. In fact, McClernand's troops had sloshed ashore into the woods before Confederate scouts discovered them. Brig. Gen. Lloyd Tilghman and Col. Jeremy Gilmer had been overseeing the construction work at both river forts, and on the night that Grant's force started upstream both commanders were at Dover, Tennessee (near Fort Donelson). When they heard Fort Henry's batteries begin firing early on the morning of February 4, Tilghman and Gilmer concluded that the situation required their attention, but they did nothing until midday, when Col. Adolphus Heiman informed them that Union soldiers were at the landing. Still, riding throughout the day and evening, they managed to arrive at the fort shortly before midnight.[5]

Heiman commanded less than three thousand men, all of whom were pathetically armed with shotguns and old "Tower of London" flintlock muskets that the Tennessee militia had used during the War of 1812. He immediately sent steamboats upriver for reinforcements. Under the circumstances, he positioned his men at both Fort Henry and Fort Heiman, dispatching what little cavalry he had to block the ford across Panther Creek and monitor the road heading north. Meanwhile, he sent Maj. Gen. Leonidas Polk an urgent note just before sundown on February 4 stating that his position was serious and he needed reinforcements. Polk, however, concluded that to send soldiers to support Tilghman would prove disastrous, because the seventy-five miles of railway were in no condition to transport troops quickly. When Tilghman arrived at the post around midnight, he immediately decided to abandon the unfinished Fort Heiman and concentrate his forces at Henry, which was quickly taking on water. Polk wired him that he had sent some cavalry, much to Tilghman's surprise; the Kentuckian thought it an odd offering given his real need for infantry. Tilghman also sent a note to General Johnston that if he would send reinforcements, "we have a glorious chance to overwhelm the enemy."[6]

Being overwhelmed was precisely what Halleck was anticipating when he commandeered Assistant Secretary of War Thomas A. Scott for a confidential mission. Halleck thought it essential to impress upon him the necessity of getting Buell to cooperate with the now underway twin rivers campaign and urge Midwestern governors to hasten the mustering of troops for his department. Having heard nothing from Grant since his landing in Tennessee, Halleck grew concerned about his subordinate, who potentially faced a concentrated and larger Confederate force to defend the forts.[7]

Union forces did not need reinforcements in taking Fort Henry, which was in fact, already besieged by the Tennessee River. Though Johnston had now come to appreciate the tremendous significance of the potential loss of the position, he simply refused to commit troops to a venture by now doomed. He wired Beauregard the same day Tilghman asked for support that he would not reinforce Henry; Bowling Green and Nashville were more important. With no real assistance expected, Tilghman decided not to venture out and strike the Federals but rather to fortify as best he could and await the inevitable assault.[8]

On the evening of February 5, even before the last of the Federals trudged off the transports, Grant composed readiness and attack orders for the next day. He anticipated that his army would be at full strength by morning and was anxious to commence the operation against Fort Henry. As ordered, McClernand would head out along the swampy road leading to Fort Donelson to prevent a Confederate escape. Smith's division would make its way to Fort Heiman on the opposite side of the Tennessee, leave a force to hold that position, and then march back to the landing, where he would recross the river and reinforce McClernand. Although the roads were dreadful and the troops would be delayed in carrying out these orders, Grant provided Foote with permission to attack even if the infantry was not yet in position. "It will be the special duty of this command," he ordered, "to prevent all re-enforcements to Fort Henry or escape from it."[9] As if a signal from the divine that all was right for the Federals to give battle the next day, the rain poured during the night. Meanwhile, Grant observed to his wife: "To-morrow will come the tug of war. One side or the other must to-morrow night rest in quiet possession of Fort Henry."[10]

As the sun crested the surrounding hills of Fort Henry on the morning of February 6, it belied the doom that was about to break open upon the Confederates. The garrison awoke after a night of hard rain to find that what they had been defending had finally succumbed to the floodwaters of the Tennessee. Artillery specialist and gunnery instructor for Forts Henry and Donelson Lt. Col. Milton A. Haynes concluded after rowing his way into the fort that it was untenable and should be abandoned before the troops inside were captured. Tilghman agreed, and he detailed a small force to remain behind and delay the impending attack, allowing time for the rest of his force to head to Fort Donelson twelve miles to the east. Donelson was in a more reasonable defensive position, and the delay would allow time for Johnston to send reinforcements from either Polk or Hardee.[11]

True to Grant's orders, Foote's black-bottomed gunboats steamed upriver toward Fort Henry during the morning and anchored in battle formation behind Panther Island. At half past noon, the gunboats' combined sixty-five Dahlgrens opened fire on the partially submerged fort. Though the initial shots fell short, the accuracy of the Federal gunners improved as the gunboats steamed to within a few hundred yards. Tilghman's artillerymen responded by unleashing the twelve heavy guns they had managed to move into position. Each man directed his gun at one of the enemy ships; soon the shells raining into the water turned the once calm river into a stormy sea. The Confederates managed to score an early blow to the Union flotilla by taking out the *Essex*. The garrison, however, was hindered from the inability to utilize a plunging fire on the gunboats because the fort was built on low ground. Moreover, the Confederates suffered a decisive self-inflicted blow when a 24-pounder rifle exploded, killing and wounding the entire crew. Similar catastrophes disabled some of the 32-pounders. Tilghman himself refused to surrender and manned one of the few remaining guns shortly after the engagement commenced. Less than a half-hour later, he, Gilmer, and Heiman, considered it pointless to continue the fight with only four effective guns.[12]

Shortly before two o'clock, a thoroughly disheartened Tilghman ordered that the Confederate flag be lowered. Soon a white flag of surrender, mounted on a stick, appeared to Union spotters through the smoke. Foote ordered the gunboats to cease fire. Minutes later, a small white boat appeared rowing out of the fort containing two officers, who requested a conference when they got closer to the *Cincinnati*. Foote's sailors erupted in cheers as they concluded that the Confederates wanted to surrender Henry. When the *Cincinnati* steamed up to the fort, Foote debarked into a boat and rowed into the fort, where he found Tilghman. "I am glad to surrender to so gallant an officer," remarked a combat-weary Tilghman. Foote replied cockily, "You do perfectly right, sir, in surrendering, but you should have blown my boat out of the water before I would have surrendered to you."[13]

In victory, the Federals had been as anxious to get inside Fort Henry as the Confederates had been to flee it in defeat. The majority of Tilghman's men were now at Fort Donelson, and what had constituted the delaying defensive force evaporated across the countryside. As the Federal soldiers surveyed the interior of the fort, they found large quantities of food and supplies, leading some to conclude that the enemy had simply been surprised and confused. When McClernand arrived with his troops, he bestowed the name "Fort Foote" on the new Union prize, though without authority, in honor of the naval commander. Interestingly enough, he had named his previous camp along the river "Camp Halleck." Thus, in trying to flatter Halleck, perhaps into giving him a larger command, and Foote, whom he considered the person most responsible for the capture, he apparently wanted to insult Grant. Still, when Grant arrived at three o'clock, he congratulated Foote on the naval victory and ignored McClernand's tribute; he had more pressing concerns. To Halleck, Grant wired that he would take Fort Donelson within the next two days and then return to Fort Henry. Meanwhile, Union steamers carried the Confederate captives to Paducah, where they would be dispersed among Northern prisons. To his wife that evening, Grant confided: "Fort Henry is taken and I am not hurt. This is news enough for to-night."[14]

So it was. If the Northern press had been preoccupied with George McClellan's army and the lack of events on the eastern front, about which reporters sarcastically wrote "all quiet on the Potomac," the Union victory at Fort Henry highlighted that all was not quiet on the Tennessee. It was unexpected news from a region that few Northerners east of the Appalachian Mountains had even heard of. For months, the war stood still as Halleck and Buell sparred over strategy. The gray skies and the dreary winter weather mirrored the lack of warmth between the Union departmental commanders. Now Halleck boasted to Buell: "Fort Henry is ours. The flag of the Union is re-established on the soil of Tennessee." To flaunt his victory, and perhaps stake his claim on command ability, he also boldly asserted to McClellan, "It will never be removed."[15]

The news sped through the Union army and Northern newspapers carried the headlines of victory. Grant's alarming prediction about taking Donelson, however, eclipsed Halleck's enthusiasm, since he had yet to authorize such a move. Halleck knew that Grant's force had its back against the swollen Tennessee River, and he also learned that some of Foote's gunboats had continued upriver. To make matters worse, Buell was moving toward Bowling Green, albeit slowly, and refused to provide any aid. Thus, Halleck ordered Grant to hold on to Fort Henry "at all hazards" while he anticipated Johnston's reaction.[16]

Kentuckians and Tennesseans were dumbfounded over Tilghman's surrender, particularly because it came at the hands of a few gunboats, which Southerners would quickly come to respect. When news finally reached Richmond, it alarmed though hardly surprised Confederate authorities. After all, Johnston had bemoaned his lack of resources to hold all the vital points in the West for months. Nevertheless, it was an embarrassing defeat stemming from a number of factors that plagued the Confederate war effort in the region, not the least of which was lack of troops, poor generalship, and navigable rivers that flooded. Tennessee governor Isham Harris echoed the embarrassment as he wired the news of the disaster to Secretary of War Judah P. Benjamin. The governor warned that if Johnston was not significantly reinforced, the injury to the Confederacy would be "irreparable."[17] In relaying the unfortunate news to his wife, Kentucky's provisional Confederate governor, George W. Johnson, remarked that "The South has now waked up."[18] Indeed it had, and residents of the twin river countryside were now contemplating either thoughts of deliverance or fears of subjugation.

Johnston had little confirmation of the news about the Fort Henry damage, but he knew an attack on Fort Donelson was eminent. He was in a precarious situation. Johnston reasoned to Confederate authorities that given the Union penetration on the rivers, he was contemplating concentrating his entire force somewhere below Nashville. This meant either diminishing or eliminating the positions in central Kentucky and East Tennessee. Furthermore, he had to think about Columbus and Bowling Green on the southern bank of the Green River. To weaken either of these points meant leaving open either the Mississippi River or the road to Nashville. He recognized that Polk had failed to defend his own district, which included Henry and Donelson, but continued to think that Grant would follow up his expedition with a move on Columbus.[19]

Not fully aware of the situation in Tennessee, President Davis had no choice but to allow Johnston independence in judging what was necessary to prevent a Union occupation in the state. A disciple of concentration of forces, Johnston had repeatedly called on Richmond for reinforcements to achieve the necessary resources to hold Columbus, Fort Donelson, and Nashville. Confederate authorities, however, never shared Johnston's sense of urgency, forcing the western commander to make judicious decisions regarding where and when he should concentrate with the forces he had and not weaken other points. It was apparent that the leadership among the Confederate high command was collapsing at a time when it could not afford disarray.[20]

The fall of Fort Henry signaled a departure from the Union inertia in the West. Even Horace Greeley, the New York journalist generally at a loss for anything positive to say about the military conduct of the war, editorialized, "A few more events such as the capture of Fort Henry, and the war will be substantially at an end."[21]

Halleck telegraphed to have the gunboats pushed up the river, so Foote's flotilla steamed ahead on the Tennessee, a natural thoroughfare winding south to Florence, Alabama, destroying railroads and bridges spanning the river as they went. Only the Muscle Shoals kept Foote from steaming another forty miles to Decatur. Johnston appealed to local authorities to protect the bridges because the army may need them. The residents of the Tennessee countryside quickly recognized that the war was at their door. To acquiesce would mean they had committed themselves to the Confederate war effort, if they had not already; to refuse would mean living in fear of retribution from neighbors sympathetic to the Southern cause. As the Union gunboats steamed south, Lt. Seth Ledyard Phelps aboard the *Conestoga* met hundreds of loyal people expressing gratitude toward the Union. Southern families, rich and poor, gathered at the wharfs of Savannah, Eastport, and Florence to greet Union forces, reported a correspondent to *Harper's Weekly*, and "old men cried like children at the sight of the stars and stripes." At least twenty-five men "enlisted in the gunboat service," Grant wrote to his wife.[22] "Tears flowed freely down the checks of men as well as women," observed Phelps. "These people braved everything to go to the river bank, [and] this display of feeling and sense of gladness at our success and the hopes it created in the breasts of so many people in the Heart of the Confederacy astonished me not a little."[23]

This was not a universal feeling to be sure, and frightened residents sent delegates to call upon Phelps to plead for the safety of their women from the dreaded Yankees. The seaman responded amicably and in tune with the administration's lenient attitude toward Southern civilians, saying that the Union had arrived to "protect them from violence and to enforce the law." Still, the same correspondent observed, as much as the Union soldiers were there to protect citizens, it would soon become clear that disaffected residents would have to be handled with a heavy hand. Editorialized *Harper's Weekly:* "The rule of statecraft is the same as in agriculture. You must not knock off the leaves of the weeds; you must dig up their roots." Certainly, Union control of the rivers would go a long way in digging up secessionist roots.[24]

Despite Halleck's restraining order, Grant continued to think offensively. His success led him to believe that he would be in Fort Donelson shortly, particularly because Henry had been a walkover and Gideon Pillow was in command at Donelson. After the Civil War, Grant remembered remarking to his staff at the time that he had known Pillow in Mexico, and from what he witnessed in his ability concluded, "with my force, no matter how small, I could march up to within gunshot of any entrenchments he was given to hold."[25]

Grant was so confident that he decided to march without transportation and only a few cannon. The fact was, however, that he, like many of his soldiers, had greatly underestimated the difficulty in marching across a waterlogged countryside in an unpredictable winter. The rapidly rising river waters alone were problematic, and Foote had returned the gunboats to Cairo for repair. Because he was convinced he could move quickly, Grant brought neither the equipment nor the wagons to march overland to Donelson. Though Halleck ordered Grant to hold Fort Henry, the Federal commander considered the partially submerged fort of no use to anyone. The arrival of Halleck's reinforcements was evidence that Donelson too would be reinforced if the Federals delayed much longer. Besides, Halleck had dispatched Sherman to hold Fort Henry. While he waited for the roads along the Tennessee to dry out, Grant held a council of war on the afternoon of the February 10 aboard the *New Uncle Sam* to determine whether he should move against Fort Donelson or wait for more soldiers. By this time the rains had ceased, the rivers were dropping, and the terrain was passable. Smith, McClernand, and recently promoted Brig. Gen. Lew Wallace agreed that movement was essential. "[L]et's go, by all means; the sooner the better," Wallace declared.[26] That same evening Grant wrote his sister: "I intend to keep the ball moving as lively as possible. . . . G. J. Pillow commands at Fort Donaldson, I hope to give him a tug before you receive this."[27]

Grant's enthusiasm and movement suited the administration and the Federal army by increasing the momentum of war and keeping the soldiers out of camp. Still, it had not suited Halleck and especially not Buell. Indeed, the Federal commander's optimism caused Halleck and Buell great distress. Each day it took Grant to get to Donelson, the tighter the spot he found himself in and the more Halleck became emotionally unhinged. Halleck did the worrying about the rear (and Buell) that Grant apparently refused to do, calling on McClellan to send everything he could spare from other commands.

Interestingly enough, Buell, who had thought the rivers were the way to go in the winter, argued that he was confused by Grant's move. The truth was he simply did not want to commit troops to assist the operation, given the circumstances—Grant had initiated something Buell had hoped would not cause him to change his course of action. The Ohioan exasperatingly wrote to McClellan that he could not "on reflection, think a change of my line would be advisable."[28] Buell never doubted the potential success of the twin rivers campaign. He simply thought the overland approach to Bowling Green and Nashville was more strategically vital to the Union war effort in that region because he was covering Louisville and in the process the vital Louisville and Nashville Railroad. Besides, Buell argued, he had arranged his army to make it look like he was preparing to head into East and Middle Tennessee despite refusing to commit any real force to the east and complaining that the railroads precluded swift movement on Bowling Green.[29]

As Grant's men prepared to trudge across twelve miles of marshy roads toward Fort Donelson in unpredictable weather, Halleck fretted that his reckless subordinate had promised more than he could deliver. His fear was compounded because Grant was no longer in the Department of the Missouri and there seemed to be some confusion about who had operational command over the Henry-Donelson area. Naturally, Halleck sought to clarify the discrepancy by urging McClellan to "create a geographical division to be called [the] Western Division, or any other suitable name." Though he claimed he had no desire for a larger command, Halleck reasoned that placing everything "under one head, [would] avoid any clashing of interests or difference of plans and policy," as had already occurred.[30]

Although this made sense, McClellan refused to consider the idea and instead remained committed to Buell's idea that Nashville was important enough not to commit too many troops to the twin rivers campaign. The general in chief refused to exercise any leadership in effecting a more harmonious command relationship between Buell and Halleck. He simply wired Buell to watch Fort Donelson closely, for McClellan was "not certain as to the result there."[31]

Even if the Union high command had enjoyed productive command relationships, Halleck should have expected that McClellan would not desert Buell, given their friendship. Though "Old Brains" shared little affinity for his counterpart, he nonetheless preferred him to Grant as a commander. At one point Buell even confessed that although he was against Halleck's idea, he was willing to move on the twin rivers line, though it would take him time to do so; besides, as general in chief, McClellan would have to direct the execution of such a move. Still, Halleck was in a frenzy to support Grant. "Give us the means," he argued to McClellan, "and we are certain to give the enemy a telling blow."[32]

Halleck, meanwhile, was concerned that the troops were not moving through Cairo fast enough, and he ordered George Cullum, his own chief of staff, there to hurry things along. A frustrated and panicky Halleck wrote on February 11 to spur Foote: "You have gained great distinction by your capture of Fort Henry. . . . Make your name famous in history by the capture of Fort Donelson and Clarksville."[33] Inspired, Foote responded the same evening that he would be casting off in two hours. Grant at this time had given marching orders to McClernand, who by dusk that same day had made it several miles beyond Fort Henry on the road to Dover. Lew Wallace and twenty-five hundred men would stay behind to hold Henry, at least until Sherman arrived, an upsetting assignment for the former Indiana politician who hoped to use his military service to boost his political career after the war—being away from the action would not gain him distinction. The weather had become unseasonably warm, dry roads prevailed, and many soldiers, thinking they would make short work of Fort Donelson, left their blankets, coats, and knapsacks alongside the road as they marched.[34]

The departure of Grant's army from Fort Henry was a significant turn in the western war. It forced the Confederate high command to make grave strategic defensive decisions and make them fast. It was obvious what the Federals had in mind, but General Johnston continued to delay deciding just how much of his limited manpower to commit to saving Donelson. He was not convinced that it was the right place to concentrate at that moment and considered gathering his forces at another point where he stood a better chance of defeating the Federal army. In a council of war at the Covington House in Bowling Green on February 7, Johnston, Hardee, Beauregard, and William Mackall failed to agree on what should be done. It was the first time Johnston and Beauregard had met—the Creole general was passing through on his way to Columbus to supersede Polk as commander. Interestingly enough, Beauregard arrived without the rumored fifteen thousand reinforcements that had inspired Halleck's urgency to get Grant moving in the first place.[35]

Buell's arrangement of forces in January had required Johnston to counter the Federal commander's moves with what meager means he had, with little ability for concentrating quickly due to the disabled railroads. Consequently, the Confederates were lamentably scattered and pathetically inferior in size at any one point. Although Union naval superiority on the rivers revealed that Halleck's army could be the main advance and very likely to continue to succeed, the Confederate commander had come to believe that Buell's column was the principal one, no doubt because Nashville seemed a more important prize to Johnston than the land between the rivers. Johnston thought Clarksville might be Buell's point of attack, and he consequently positioned a significant portion of his forces in that area. He sent Gideon Pillow, who had recently rejoined the army and was at Bowling Green, to Clarksville to collect all the available forces to move wherever Federal forces struck next. Johnston, however, was conducting operations in the darkness of indecision.[36]

Though new to the West, Beauregard could clearly see the advantages of holding on to the forts as long as possible. Thus, he favored abandoning Bowling Green and concentrating on the rivers. (Why neither Beauregard nor Johnston personally went to the most endangered point of the Confederate line and conduct operations from there remains a mystery.) Still, Johnston feared for Nashville's safety. Recognizing the vulnerability of Fort Donelson and the Kentucky-Tennessee line, the western theater high command decided not to concentrate there but instead fall back to Nashville, which meant evacuating Bowling Green. Because the winter waters allowed navigation of the Cumberland River beyond Clarksville, however, agreeing where to concentrate behind Nashville was difficult. If the Union navy steamed past Donelson unscathed, they were surely able to make it to Nashville, since the defenses at Clarksville were incomplete.[37]

Johnston determined that Polk at Columbus and Hardee at Bowling Green would act as independent armies and ultimately fall back below the Tennessee border to reunite. He sent Beauregard to Columbus to supercede Leonidas Polk and, leaving only enough men to hold the Mississippi River forts, take the rest of the force south in anticipation of a concentration somewhere south of the Tennessee border. While Beauregard's assumption of command infuriated Polk to the verge of resignation, Johnston's strategy more importantly meant giving up a major portion of the Southern heartland. This would naturally devastate morale among Confederates there. George Johnson, the provisional governor of Confederate Kentucky and a member of Johnston's staff, remarked that the consequences would "spread dismay over the whole Confederacy."[38]

The council of war at Bowling Green underscored the fate of Johnston's command and reflected its deteriorating leadership. The Confederate commander knew Donelson was untenable, yet he committed a strategic error in deciding to send more men to the fort than he could afford to lose. He also assumed that if he retired to Nashville, his subordinates could at least maintain delaying actions to hold off the bulk of the Union army until Confederate forces could assemble elsewhere. For a major part of his plan, however, the general had to rely on Pillow and John Bell Floyd, another political general in over his head. Floyd had requested that Johnston make a trip to Fort Donelson so that the department commander could determine what should be done. Johnston, however, apparently thought the visit unnecessary and mysteriously turned over command in the area to Floyd, thereafter deferring to his judgment. "When [Johnston] shunned the Donelson responsibility," conceded historian Thomas Connelly, "he gave indication that he was losing command of himself and of the Army."[39] The Texan continued to think that the forts were Polk's responsibility and that Buell was his immediate threat. For some reason, according to historian T. Harry Williams, who was more charitable, Johnston "seemed obsessed with the idea that he personally had to conduct the column at Bowling Green to safety."[40]

When Pillow arrived at Donelson with his troops from Clarksville, he took direct command and inspected the fort for Floyd. Johnston told the Tennessean to hold the position as long as possible and then retire to Nashville via Charlotte. Pillow took special care in gauging the mood of the men, whose demeanor was gloomy. The fragments of the Henry garrison had trickled in to Donelson, filling the soldiers there with stories of the power of the Union gunboats. Though reinforcements had arrived, Pillow's force was still too small. The general, however, concluded to fight to save the Cumberland River stronghold and sent for Maj. Gen. Simon Buckner at Russellville to help command. Vowing not to surrender, the vain and conceited Pillow sought to restore the soldiers' confidence that they could reverse the Fort Henry loss by saving Donelson. "Drive back the ruthless invader," declared Pillow, "and again raise the Confederate flag over Fort Henry. . . . With God's help we will accomplish our purpose." Armed with "our battle cry, 'Liberty or Death,'" Pillow attempted to motivate the men. He and Brig. Gen. Bushrod Johnson set out immediately to form the units into two divisions to be commanded by Johnson and Buckner (when he arrived). Pillow requested that Floyd himself come to Donelson with some heavy guns from Clarksville to strengthen the defenses, declaring, "I will never surrender the position, and with God's help I mean to maintain it."[41]

The Tennessee general was busy overseeing the garrison of the fort when Buckner arrived on the evening of February 11. As if the problems the Confederate command was experiencing were not bad enough, Buckner's arrival renewed a prewar animosity stemming from political disagreements. Buckner carried orders from Floyd that conflicted with Pillow's position about Donelson. Floyd and Buckner had previously discussed a plan that called for a concentration of forces at Cumberland City, a place more feasible for maintaining communication with Nashville and for operating against Grant's land forces. Buckner's orders deflated Pillow's hopes of holding on to Donelson, since it meant his force would be significantly reduced. To rectify the situation, Pillow, who refused to believe the orders, decided to visit Floyd, ascertain exactly what he intended, and argue in favor of standing at Donelson.[42]

As Pillow steamed upriver to Clarksville, news arrived at Donelson that Union gunboats had been spotted on the Cumberland some miles below the fort and a column of infantry was advancing overland. When Pillow received the news, he suspended Floyd's orders for Buckner to fall back and hurried himself to Donelson. There he wired Johnston that he needed to retain Buckner's division; apparently Pillow thought it better to ask forgiveness than permission with regard to superseding his superior's orders. Floyd then decided to take his men from Clarksville to Donelson. Johnston had "determined to fight for Nashville at Donelson," as he later informed President Davis, and "gave the best part of my army to do it."[43]

Though the Confederate commander had finally consented to fight at Donelson, the situation in the West was so confusing that it was too late to arrange his army to win. Still, the soldiers considered fighting more pleasing than enduring the indistinguishable winter days in camp. Inside the fort, troops busied themselves strengthening the batteries as Milton Haynes continued to drill the cannoneers who would engage the Federal gunboats. Outside the walls, Colonel Gilmer supervised the soldiers working on a series of rifle pits running three miles along a series of ridges to the west and the rear of the fort. South of the camp, the tiny bluff-top hamlet of Dover was transformed into a drilling ground for the new arrivals who passed through on their way to reinforce the Donelson garrison. In the flurry of activity to bolster the defenses, however, Grant's column marched practically uncontested to within yards of the Confederate lines. Pillow could sense the closure, remarking, "The enemy are all around my position and within distance to close in with me in ten minutes' march."[44]

By sunset on February 12, McClernand's division, the vanguard of Grant's force, had come within sight of Donelson and deployed behind a ridge and tributary of Hickman's Creek. As they moved into position, the right flank came under fire briefly from a Confederate battery. George Washington Cullum continued to direct supplies such as tents, food, and ammunition upstream to meet the men. As the night wore on, the weather turned cold; both Confederates and Federals suffered. Those who had cast aside their coats at the beginning of the march east now wished they had brought them along. What started out as an inspiring march to Donelson soon dissipated as the huddled masses of soldiers sought warmth. To prevent drawing Confederate fire, campfires were forbidden. It was a long night of howling and biting cold wind, so cold that Grant remembered the night twenty-three years later as one of "absolute suffering."[45] To make matters worse for the Federals, the Confederates had decided to make a stand at Donelson and reinforcements were arriving.

The Southerners awoke on the thirteenth to General Floyd's arrival, accompanied by the remnants of his brigade, which brought the total strength of the garrison to roughly seventeen thousand men. Floyd assumed command of all the troops gathered in the fort, though he was even less willing to advance beyond the ramparts than Pillow, who became second in command. Johnston had given him direct instructions to defend Donelson (or withdraw without sacrificing the army) until Johnston had evacuated Bowling Green and had made it to Nashville with the Central Army of Kentucky. That morning, Floyd and Pillow inspected the outlying fortifications, though it was too late to make any improvements. Pillow had continued to assure Johnston that with Buckner's men he could hold Fort Donelson. Floyd, however, continued to waiver until finally concluding that the fort was a trap. It was an uneasy situation for Floyd. He feared his capture and sure imprisonment for his unsavory handling of the War Department's funds prior to the war. Moreover, he knew Grant was a trained soldier, and Grant knew Floyd was not.[46]

As the sun rose above the Cumberland River, Grant's fifteen thousand mud-weary troops, traveling without supplies and on crude roads, were closing in around the fort. Meanwhile, Grant awaited the return of the gunboats, which unbeknownst to him had been progressing slowly upriver

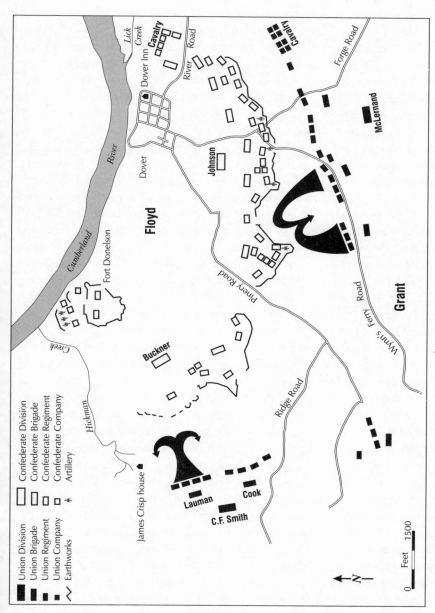

Legend:

- ■ Union Division
- ■■ Union Brigade
- ■ ■ ■ Union Regiment
- ■ □ ■ Union Company
- ∧ Earthworks

- ☐ Confederate Division
- ☐ Confederate Brigade
- ☐ Confederate Regiment
- ☐ Confederate Company
- ✦ Artillery

The Battle of Fort Donelson, first day, February 13, 1862

due to the swift current of floodwaters. McClernand and Smith had orders to close in on the Confederates while Henry Walke's *Carondelet* would create a diversion on the river. As Grant waited, he sent for Lew Wallace's force to hurry from Fort Henry and telegraphed Halleck to send replacements.[47]

Despite both sides being ordered not to bring on a full engagement yet, it was hardly possible not to do so. Smith's approach toward Buckner's works along the Eddyville Road brought on the day's opening shots. As the brigades of Jacob Lauman and John Cook inched forward, it soon became apparent that what was intended to be a reconnaissance had developed into an assault. For nearly two hours, Smith's Midwesterners fought a fierce battle only to be forced back into their original positions. McClernand's division attempted to encircle the fort and Dover and in doing so touched off another major engagement. Richard Oglesby, W. H. L. Wallace, and William Morrison deployed along Wynn's Ferry Road until they reached Forge Road, where they anchored the left flank of the Union cavalry. Throughout the early morning, Confederate batteries shelled this portion of the Union line, and by midday McClernand decided to respond by ordering Colonel Morrison's Third Brigade to charge the Confederate guns. Within an hour, however, Confederate fire completely diffused the assault. The *Carondelet,* meanwhile, steamed around a bend to within yards of Donelson and engaged the Confederate river batteries, only to be turned away after a two-hour duel.[48]

During the day the weather deteriorated as the winds picked up and the temperature dropped. Grant continued to worry over the whereabouts of Foote and his reinforcements. Until these appeared, the Federals could not bring on a major fight. Besides, Grant was not sure exactly what he could expect from the enemy army, which he estimated at thirty thousand. Grant needed Foote's gunboats to support his land forces. By dusk it began to drizzle and the thermometer dipped well below freezing. The icy ground stalled land operations, and soldiers simply huddled together to stay warm as best they could. Lew Wallace and his twenty-five-hundred-man brigade arrived at daybreak. Foote's fleet had already arrived during the night and debarked reinforcements, which Grant assigned to Wallace, who now became commander of the newly christened Third Division. More confident than the day before, Grant was sure he now had enough men to take the fort. When the ironclads commenced shelling, he would throw his right wing at the fleeing defenders of Donelson.[49]

Although Grant was confident that the combined land and naval assault would surely bring victory and with it several thousand Confederate prisoners, Foote recalled the heavy casualties his flotilla had endured at Fort Henry. He remained apprehensive about the attack but acquiesced. At almost two o'clock in the afternoon of February 14, Foote's six iron-clads chugged away from the dock and proceeded upriver, followed by four timberclads a quarter-mile behind.[50]

When the Union flotilla came into full view of Fort Donelson, Foote concluded he could silence the water batteries and then continue upriver. Covered with chains, lumber, and coal bags for protection, the four ironclads *Carondelet, St. Louis, Cincinnati,* and *Pittsburg* would have an advantage at a distance. A thousand yards behind steamed the wooden gunboats *Tyler* and *Conestoga.* Still, Foote had overrun Fort Henry by closing in and pounding it at close range. Moving closer to Donelson, the Union gunboats opened fire. The Confederate batteries replied with a severe barrage, which initially did little damage to the floating column. Soon the firing became intense, and the accuracy increased as both sides were fighting furiously. Confederate cavalryman Nathan Bedford Forrest witnessed the Union barrage and shouted to his aide Maj. D. C. Kelly, a former minister, "Parson! for God's sake, pray; nothing but God Almighty can save that fort."[51]

Watching the battle against the ironclads, Floyd wired Johnston at Nashville that the fort was doomed. In actuality, the Union gunboats found Fort Donelson a more formidable opponent as they drew closer. Their position above the river allowed Confederate batteries to take advantage of plunging fire, which was more effective than pecking away at the ironclads straight on. Despite the ineffectiveness of the smaller guns, the Columbiad and rifled cannon hammered away at the gunboats, disabling almost every one and forcing the flotilla to retire downriver. Foote had not the good fortune at Donelson as he had at Fort Henry, the result of several factors, not the least of which had to do with the swift current and the narrowness of the Cumberland. Steaming at less than three miles per hour, the gunboats were essentially sitting ducks. "Their fire was more destructive to our works at 2 miles than at 200 yards," reported Confederate captain Bell G. Bidwell. Two hours of fighting on the river ended with the badly bruised flotilla retreating downriver much quicker than it had come upstream. Floyd and Pillow arrived just before dark to congratulate the gunners. There Floyd dashed off a note of renewed confidence to Johnston, stating that the gunboats had been driven back and the day's fight had concluded in victory. Johnston forwarded the premature but good news to Richmond. Inside the fort the celebration began. The artillerists had redeemed their Fort Henry loss without losing a single gun or man.[52]

Grant was disappointed by the naval disaster, since the battle that the Union had brought on would now have to be fought solely on land. After all, he had been the one to complain that Foote had not come up when Grant was ready, and now the general had done nothing to help Foote on the river. He had not counted on the navy losing, or at least not so quickly, and the defeat heightened his fear that there would be no repeat of Fort Henry unless Halleck could help him. Among other things, Grant worried that Polk might get between Henry and Cairo, cutting his communications. Still, on the evening of the fourteenth, Grant wrote his wife, "when this is to end is hard to surmise but I feel confidant of ultimate success."[53]

Halleck, meanwhile, continued to fret. He had been impressed enough with Grant's operation that he gave him command of the newly formed District of West Tennessee, placing Sherman in command of the Cairo district. Still, the fact that it took Grant longer to get to Fort Donelson gave Johnston time, in Halleck's mind, to reinforce the garrison. Thus, he called on Assistant Secretary of War Scott to urge McClellan to send men, arguing that he would be successful, *"if they will give me the forces which are now useless elsewhere."*[54]

The general in chief of the armies shared Halleck's apprehension about Grant's operation, though he did even less to relieve anyone's fears. With every passing hour Halleck's anxiety increased. Still, McClellan was not about to commit any more of Buell's troops to the twin rivers until he had more information. Buell also needed word about Grant's operations and never missed an opportunity to strike at Halleck's decision to go ahead with the movement in haste. It was as if Buell wanted Halleck to fail, if only to teach him a lesson.[55]

The Union commanders in the West never really cooperated, and the consequences of not getting along became more apparent in the midst of Halleck's river campaign. Halleck had been so desperate to have someone else commanding the columns on the twin rivers that he previously considered pulling Ethan Allen Hitchcock out of retirement for the assignment. Hitchcock refused, and Halleck was forced to continue to badger Buell to take the command personally. Buell too refused. Acting the part of the general in chief, McClellan finally stepped in and informed Halleck that if anyone was going to take overall command in the West, it would not be Halleck. On February 14 he responded that if Halleck did not personally go to the river command, he would more than likely send Buell to Tennessee in order to further the Nashville campaign. Besides, with Bowling Green evacuated, McClellan declared to Buell, the "movement on Nashville is exactly right."[56]

Halleck and Buell, however, continued to quarrel over strategy. Old Brains was convinced that if McClellan would force Buell to aid him, he could ensure "complete success." Halleck apparently cared little about offending the general in chief, since he was informing McClellan that moving on Nashville was wrong. Grant, meanwhile, contemplated the next day's operations. He scribbled a late-night note to Halleck that "Appearances now indicate that we will have a protracted siege here." Still, he concluded, "I feel great confidance, however, of ultimately reducing the place."[57]

Even had Johnston concentrated his army against the Union forces on the river, it would still mean that the Confederate defense line had fallen back from Kentucky into Tennessee in a few short months. Though losing Fort Donelson might be considered a minor setback compared to Clarksville or Nashville, it would be nonetheless a significant strategic loss for the Confederacy. In light of the situation, Johnston should have gone to Fort Donelson, but now the Texan was between a rock and a hard place: he had to choose between losing strategic points and saving vital ones. From Nashville, Beauregard, who was quite ill, wrote to Roger A. Pryor, a former aide and now a Confederate congressman, a biting letter. "I am taking the helm when the ship is already on the breakers," he lamented, "and with but few sailors to man it. . . . We must give up some minor points, and concentrate our forces to save the most important ones, or we will lose all of them in succession. . . . The loss of Fort Donelson (God grant it may not fall) would be followed by consequences too lamentable to be now alluded to."[58] The problem for the Confederacy in the West was that it could not afford to give up any strategic points, but it had no choice. Thus, when Johnston read the dispatches from his Donelson commanders, he determined to send Hardee there, which exposed Bowling Green to Buell.[59]

By darkness on the night of the fourteenth, the rain that had drizzled and then poured during the late afternoon finally turned to snow. It was during the downpours that Floyd drastically revised his view of the situation. After two days of hard fighting, he now realized that the threat to Donelson came no longer from the gunboats but instead from Grant's infantry. He had come to this realization earlier in the morning of the same day, when he met with his division commanders and decided to attempt an escape south from Dover along a road that ran south and then east toward Nashville. The generals had already prepared the troops for the breakout when the Union flotilla came upriver and opened fire on the fort. The Confederates were forced to redirect their attention to the gunboats, and by the time they had defeated them, there was not enough time to effect the plan.[60]

Consequently, Floyd canceled the attack and, seeking the advice of his commanders, summoned them for another council of war late that evening at the Dover Inn. He was convinced that despite the naval victory, Grant was still heavily reinforced. Floyd's cynical view led him to conclude that Grant's total force was around forty thousand and that the Confederates needed more men. After considerable debate, the officers agreed to attack the well-fortified Union right flank across the road south of Dover before daylight and "pass our people into the open country lying southward towards Nashville." Pillow would command the first stage of the attack and bring on a full engagement, then Buckner would attack with his division and hopefully catch the Federals in the flank and rear, pinning Grant to the river. The generals were determined to achieve success; Bushrod Johnson wrote orders that considered "every contingency," but nothing was said about blankets, rations, and knapsacks. Floyd consented to the plan, and the council broke up to realign for the morning's attack.[61]

In the twilight before the morning on Saturday, February 15, Pillow's Confederates had worked tirelessly to move their guns (and themselves) from the advanced trenches to the Confederate left flank. Pillow massed the rest of Johnson's column, with Nathan Bedford Forrest in the lead. Surprisingly, the positioning of the men went undetected by the Federals. By now it was 6 A.M., and the entire force of eight to ten thousand Rebels began their advance in the biting wind and cold. Within a short time, they came under fire from Union pickets, even before Buckner's units were in position. The battle of Fort Donelson was again renewed, and though neither side was equipped to make the most of the fight, the Confederates were certainly better prepared.[62]

Meanwhile, at the Crisp farmhouse behind C. F. Smith's division on the Ridge Road, an aide woke Grant at 4 A.M. with a message that Foote's flotilla was in a desperate situation, Foote himself was incapacitated, and the boats were unable to come to Donelson. Grant bundled up, mounted his horse, and galloped off to the landing to visit the naval comman-

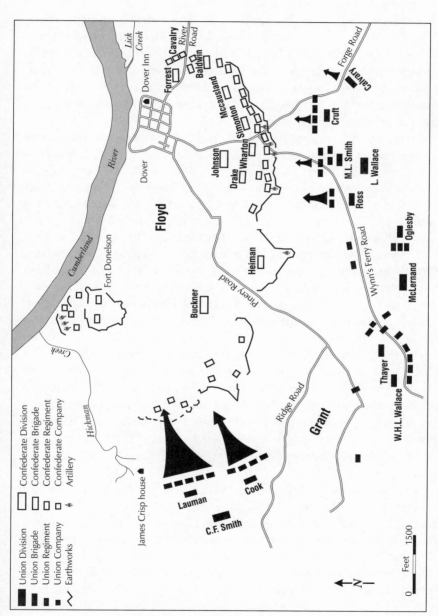

The Battle of Fort Donelson, third day, February 15, 1862

Legend:

Union Division
Union Brigade
Union Regiment
Union Company
Earthworks

Confederate Division
Confederate Brigade
Confederate Regiment
Confederate Company
Artillery

Labels on map:

Lick Creek
Cavalry River Road
Forrest
Baldwin
Dover Inn
McCausland
Simonton
Wharton
Johnson
Drake
Floyd
Dover
Cumberland River
Fort Donelson
Creek
Hickman
James Crisp house
Heiman
Piney Road
Buckner
Lauman
Cook
C.F. Smith
Ridge Road
Grant
W.H.L. Wallace
Thayer
McClernand
Oglesby
Wynn's Ferry Road
L. Wallace
M.L. Smith
Ross
Cruft
Cavalry
Forge Road

0   1500
Feet

N

der. Before departing, he gave his aides instructions to visit division
commanders and caution them not to bring on a general engagement
during his absence. Many years later, Grant recalled that he had "no idea
that there would be any engagement on land unless I brought [it] on
myself." The army's second in command was McClernand, who made
no secret that he wanted command of the army, and Grant wanted to
prevent a potential glory-seeking McClernand from attacking during his
absence. Still, contemporaries and later historians have speculated as to
what prompted him to leave the front, and their conclusions have ranged
from simple fatigue to drunkenness.[63]

In the frosty morning rain while Grant was away, the Confederate
attempt to break out took the Federals by surprise. By 8 A.M., six thousand gray-clad soldiers had managed to force McClernand's division
back, despite a stiff resistance, and compress it against the Union center
as planned. After trying to stem the Rebel tide, McClernand sent a
courier to inform Grant of the situation. When the rider came upon
Lew Wallace on McClernand's left, he urged him to help, but Wallace
had direct orders to prevent the enemy from escaping. Consequently,
Grant's instructions preventing division commanders to move without
his consent prompted Wallace to send his own courier to headquarters
pleading for permission to help McClernand. Grant, however, was still in
consultations aboard Foote's gunboat. Wallace's courier approached the
landing and met Grant, who was about to return. Informing the general
of the news from the front, the messenger galloped back to Wallace. In
Grant's absence, the new division commander, a combat amateur and
not a professional soldier trained to obey orders, decided to reinforce
McClernand on his own authority and moved the recently arrived green
brigade from Buell's army in that direction. Before Wallace could get into
position, the Union army found itself fully engaged. Before returning
to his command, Grant ordered Foote back to Cairo with the disabled
ironclads.[64]

The Confederates of Buckner's division joined Pillow's offensive and
together pressed the attack, managing to exhaust Union resistance on the
right wing, which was wearing down from fatigue and supply shortages.
Pillow concluded from this that the Federals were on the verge of defeat.
Still, he later reported that the enemy "contested the field most stubbornly," stalling the Confederate advance nearly two hours. By noon, the
attack had broken the Federal lines and opened a seam between the river
and the left flank through which the Confederates could escape south to

Nashville. The overwhelmed Federals retreated from Wynn's Ferry Road. The Confederates then formed a line that curved a mile from the river to Bufford Hollow, within an hour securing a way out of Fort Donelson. If they could hold Wynn's Ferry Road, the fort's defenders could escape to Nashville and safety. Pillow and Buckner personally remained at the front, and at one point Pillow sent a note to Johnston boasting that the Confederates had won the day.[65]

As the sun began to descend, the daylong struggle was ending and the Confederates prepared to take advantage of the opening. However, Pillow, without consulting Floyd or Buckner, ordered Buckner's men back to their original positions in the fort. When the Kentuckian learned of this, he erupted in anger, vehemently protesting against such a move. He blamed Pillow for a disaster at the front because he had denied Brown's brigade reinforcements when it was apparent it was being forced back. Consequently, the Confederate leadership remained divided on their next move. About this time Floyd rode up, whereupon Buckner explained that he thought they should continue with the original plan to break out. Pillow, however, argued that the men were tired, hungry, and needed their blankets and coats. Under the circumstances, he recommended that the Confederates should regroup at their defensive perimeter and attempt to escape later, particularly since he thought they had beaten and disorganized the Federals sufficiently. Not wanting to reverse his second in command, Floyd agreed, and the troops shuffled back to their original lines. As the evening gave way to night, the fort's garrison, except for the nearly thirteen hundred wounded soldiers who lay in the snow on the battlefield, had returned to their morning positions on the ridge. "It was a move," as historian Steven Woodworth aptly observed, "of sublime stupidity that probably could have been achieved only through the combined efforts of a Floyd and a Pillow."[66] The failed Confederate breakout was more than a defeat; it signaled disaster for the entire Confederate army at Fort Donelson.

The day's fight had nearly ended before Grant even made it to the front around 1:30 P.M. After listening to McClernand describe the battle and receiving reports from the front, he sent a message to Foote that despite the condition of the gunboats, he needed them on the river simply to make a diversion and redirect Confederate attention away from his divisions. At the front, Grant found bodies strewn across the field and his men badly demoralized, though not defeated. Indeed, he considered they might be on the verge of victory if Foote came through with his flotilla. Grant realized that by concentrating on their left flank, the Confederates had weakened their right, and he ordered Smith to prepare to attack. Besides, the Federals had already forced the Confederates back to their original lines. He was confident that if he counterattacked now, his men could bag the entire Rebel force.[67]

The winter landscape had darkened by midafternoon, but Grant was determined to seize the opportunity given him by Pillow with the remaining daylight. When he rode to Smith, whose division remained unengaged, and informed him that all had failed on his right and that it was up to his men to take Fort Donelson, Smith boldly remarked, "I will do it."[68] The soldiers fixed bayonets and prepared to launch their assault. In their path were the Tennessee battalions of Maj. James Turner. Smith's blue wave advanced toward the Confederate works as the Tennesseans let loose a tremendous fire, but the Federals overwhelmed the thin line and forced it back to a ridge five hundred yards away. Buckner's men were returning to their original positions when they caught sight of their fleeing comrades. Quickly counterattacking, Buckner's troops stalled the Federal advance. As the afternoon wore on, it became clear that neither side had gained any advantage. Still, Smith's brigades had captured Buckner's outer defensive line. That night, the old-army veteran determined to complete the task the next day.[69]

With Smith assaulting on the left, McClernand and Wallace successfully reclaimed the ground they had previously occupied at dawn. Grant sent word that they were to wait until morning to complete the Confederate repulse. As the sun set on the combatants, all that had been accomplished during the day's fight was that both sides had retained roughly the same positions they had when the sun rose. The breakout attempt had cost the Confederates more than just casualties, but the opportunity to save the garrison from capture as well. The fate of the Southern soldiers, though, had been sealed during the night. As the wind howled and the snow fell, the dead and dying bore witness that although some minor gains had been made, these had come at a heavy price. Indeed, it was a wretched night. Grant's exhausted force, deprived of food and shelter, would simply open the engagement the next morning, though success was a far cry from what the soldiers were thinking they could achieve.[70]

As Sidney Johnston slept at his Edgefield headquarters on the night of February 15, one of the most significant discussions in Civil War history was taking place at Fort Donelson. There was something prophetic about the dramatic events with the Confederate commanders that miserable evening. Pillow and Floyd somehow had ended up in a place where their ineptitude could severely hurt the entire Confederate war effort. As historian Charles Roland later wrote, the night's events were "a tactical comedy of errors turned into high tragedy for Johnston and for the South."[71] Whatever the case, the strategic results of losing Donelson subordinated all else.

After midnight, Floyd called a council of war of all regimental, brigade, and division commanders at Pillow's headquarters in the tiny Dover Inn. It was a tense atmosphere given the day's happenings. With reports that the size of Grant's army was significantly larger than estimated and that the woods were alive with Union troops, Floyd decided that the army should attempt to break out once again. Reports indicated, however, that the Federals had cut off the escape route. Any attempt to ford freezing Lick Creek would cost the men dearly. Besides, the soldiers were exhausted, demoralized, and in no position to effect anything resembling a formal retreat. Pillow was unmoved by the army's condition and advocated fighting out of the fort before sunrise. Buckner, however, already furious with Pillow for ordering the troops back that afternoon, had resolved to surrender, arguing that his four thousand men would only be able to put up a brief struggle before succumbing to the enemy's superior forces. Moreover, he cited the return of Foote's gunboats among other reasons for desiring capitulation. Around midnight, Floyd summoned Col. Nathan Bedford Forrest to the inn to solicit his opinion. Surprised and angered, the daring cavalryman protested acrimoniously against surrender. He vowed to escape. Still, it was evident to Pillow and Floyd that the Kentuckian was hopelessly defeated in mind and in spirit, and in the end they agreed to capitulate.[72]

Surrendering was not something easily done. It was naturally an unpleasant task for the Confederates and involved serious problems for both Union and Confederate commanders. Floyd was concerned that if he gave up the army to Grant, he might be hanged by the Federals for prewar crimes, namely treason. "We will have to capitulate," the former U.S. secretary of war remarked, "but, gentlemen, I cannot surrender; you know my position with the Federals; it wouldn't do; it wouldn't do!"[73] He asked Buckner if he would give him time to get his brigade out and Buckner agreed. Thus, he turned the command over to Pillow, who refused it himself and passed it on to Buckner, who said, "I will accept and share the fate of my command." The Kentuckian, a general with more ability

but less seniority than either Floyd or Pillow, sent for a bugler and a pen
with which to formally open surrender negotiations. As Pillow prepared
to depart the room, Forrest asked him what he should do, to which Pillow
replied, "Cut your way out, sir." Forrest boldly answered, "I will do it,"
and left the room. He and his column reached Nashville two days later.[74]

Before dawn, Pillow and his staff crossed the river on an empty scow
in disgrace, a rather fitting departure for the failed commander. Floyd
meanwhile shamelessly boarded his Virginia regiments on the *General
Anderson,* which ironically had debarked reinforcements that would only
be surrendered shortly, and escaped to safety. Soon, news of the capitulation tore through the camps, and a mad scramble ensued to get aboard
a steamer and leave. The thought of going to a Northern prison inspired
thousands with the determination to flee or die trying. Some two to three
thousand soldiers actually managed to escape by steamers, on foot, or on
horseback.[75]

Under the circumstances, Buckner thought it wise to officially inform
the soldiers of the surrender and his hope that it would be conducted
with dignity and honor. These orders had little effect on the men. The
Kentuckian ordered white flags to be posted on the fort's outer works,
and he dispatched a conference party to search for Grant and request
an armistice; Maj. Nathaniel F. Cheairs led the party with Buckner's
surrender note in his pocket. Surely, Buckner thought, his old friend Sam
Grant would be charitable in his terms. After all, Grant had been polite in
his business with Leonidas Polk regarding the exchange of prisoners and
had been honorable at Belmont when the wounded required evacuation.
More personally, Buckner had loaned him money before the war to settle
a credit in a New York hotel and helped out with his finances until Grant
could return to Missouri.[76]

When the party came upon Brig. Gen. C. F. Smith at about 3 A.M.,
the crusty old commander refused to accept any terms of surrender
and went along with the soldiers to the Crisp house, where they found
Grant. There Smith handed the dispatch to Grant and conversed about
the surrender. The Federal commander also refused to consider terms.
The surrender would be unconditional, as Grant proposed to attack
Donelson immediately. He fully understood the implications. The entire
nation was waiting to hear what had become of Halleck's river campaign;
Grant was not about to disappoint Washington. When Buckner received
Grant's reply, the terms stunned him to the point of outrage. This seemed

so ungentlemanly of Grant, Buckner thought. Still, Grant signed the message, "I am, sir, very respectfully, your obedient servant."[77]

Later that morning, when Buckner and Grant finally met at the Dover Inn to discuss the details of the unconditional surrender, it reflected the uniqueness of a nation at war with itself. For example, the Confederates were naturally concerned with what would happen to them since they were supporting a treasonous cause. Grant, however, was charitable in allowing the captured Rebels to retain their clothing and blankets and by providing them Union rations. They would later be paroled. Though soldiers were stripped of equipment, Grant allowed officers to retain their side arms. After their initial meeting at the hotel, Buckner and Grant met again aboard the *New Uncle Sam* to complete the arrangements. At one point, Buckner mentioned that Pillow had escaped, to which Grant remarked that the Tennessee commander might have saved himself the trouble. "If I had captured him," Grant joked, "I would have turned him loose. I would rather have him in command of you fellows than a prisoner." Joking aside, in four days of fighting, Grant had achieved the greatest victory of the war thus far. Ironically, the brigade of Brig. Gen. Stephen Hurlbut arrived in time only to police the battlefield.[78]

As the Confederate prisoners of war, including Buckner, all huddling to keep warm, were shipped from the Dover landing on their way to Cairo during the subsequent days, the Federals wasted no time in lauding their victory to those at home. "It was the hardest Battle ever fought on the American continent," boasted James F. Drish of the Thirty-second Illinois to his wife, "the endurance of the men is wonderfull they fought for three days without scarsly any thing to eat and they had to lay down on their arms in the snow for three nights in sucsision without blankets."[79]

Grant also sped the news of his victory to Halleck. He was so confident that he had dealt the great blow to the Confederacy in the West that he wrote his wife the end of the war was in sight: Donelson was "the largest capture . . . ever made on this continent."[80] Grant's news elated Secretary Stanton, especially since he was used to getting bad news from Halleck and Buell about how they could not cooperate. Grant was rewarded for his efforts, as John Nicolay recalled in his diary: "Tonight the Secretary of War brought over the nomination of General Grant to be Major General of Volunteers, which the President signed at once." Still, many administrators and newspaper editors attributed the success to Halleck, because they could not believe that an unknown could have achieved such a victory. As the light began to shine on the Union war effort in that region, though, it illuminated someone whom few expected to win a victory, much less the capture of twelve thousand enemy soldiers. No longer would Grant be an unknown in the war: his given name would forever be changed to "Unconditional Surrender" Grant. "Was it not a funny sight," wrote Stanton to Charles Dana of the *New York Tribune*, "to see a certain military hero [McClellan] in the telegraph office at Washington . . . organizing victory and by sublime military combinations capturing Fort Donelson *six hours after* Grant and Smith had taken it sword in hand and had victorious possession."[81]

Ironically, Grant had achieved the victory that the Confederates had expected from Johnston. The South had lost the line of the Cumberland and Tennessee. With it, the whole western defensive line collapsed, and no one, except Buckner, escaped criticism. The strategic consequences were vital, for half of the remaining Confederate army was at Columbus and the other half was at Nashville two hundred miles away. As historians Herman Hattaway and Archer Jones have argued, Confederate leaders failed to see the defensive line in the West as a whole, and "allowed themselves to lapse into a cordon defense with each of the separate detachments in the department committed to the defense of a particular point or locality. Instead of using the Cumberland River and the railroads to concentrate at a threatened point, each of the Confederate commanders thought only of his individual responsibilities."[82] As Leroy P. Walker, former Confederate secretary of war, observed to Judah P. Benjamin: "better to lose the seaboard than this line. The Memphis and Charleston, is the vertebrae of the Confederacy, and there are no troops for its defense. The people will abandon the country to the occupation of the enemy."[83]

Victory in this instance proved as worrisome to Halleck as Grant's impulsive nature, for Union occupation presented problems. His fears turned to defeat, concerned that Grant had penetrated so far into the Confederacy that the army was in jeopardy of annihilation from Polk at Columbus and Johnston at Nashville. Both Union generals worried about guerrillas forming in the rear of the army's advance along the rivers. If, as it had been reported by the navy heading upstream, Unionism existed in the occupied region, Grant would have to protect the loyal citizens while warring against resident secessionists. Moreover, now that Johnston's troops were abandoning Middle Tennessee, Southerners found themselves unprotected, which encouraged them to find ways to compensate for the lack of organized military protection and defend themselves.[84]

Though guerrillas were worrisome, Halleck still wanted to resolve the command problem in the West. Although on a map it was obvious that a divided command had its advantages, given the poor experience of the last few months, it had not worked in practice. Halleck counseled Washington that the Union army should concentrate its efforts on moving up the Tennessee River and splitting the Confederacy. Given his successes on the twin rivers, he thought the time was right to again urge McClellan to give him sole command of the West. With this and fifty thousand reinforcements, Halleck believed he could increase the scope of the river campaign and provide Buell the necessary force to overrun Nashville. "Give me command in the West," he demanded of McClellan, "I ask this in return for Forts Henry and Donelson."[85] This was an odd statement for a commander who the same day had written McClellan that what was happening at the fort was "the crisis of the war in the West" and that he was "certainly in peril."[86]

Halleck's ideas were strategically sound, though neither the administration nor McClellan were insightful enough to adopt them. Still, the general in chief wired Halleck the day Fort Donelson fell that he should move against Nashville as soon as possible either by water or land. With Clarksville abandoned, it appeared that the Cumberland was the quickest route. But the city was still in Buell's jurisdiction, and Halleck withheld his forces. He continued to emphasize the move on the Tennessee and harassed Foote to get his flotilla in shape, since Buell could easily capture the Tennessee capital. Middle Tennessee belonged to Buell, and Halleck had his sights on larger claims, with which he thought McClellan agreed.[87]

The problem with the command situation in the West, however, was that the administration and the high command were torn between the conquest of the Confederacy for political reasons and the occupation of the heartland for military reasons. Nonetheless, the army had just won for the Union a fairly large region to police, which would prove a complicated and difficult task over the years. Because the Lincoln administration never let up on East Tennessee, McClellan could not dismiss the political concerns, no matter how much he agreed with Halleck and Buell regarding the operations of each in the overall strategic picture. Part of this had to do with the fact that "Little Mac" enjoyed his status and position as general in chief, and to keep it he frequently had to succumb to the desires of the politicians. Fortunately for McClellan, the desire to seize East Tennessee helped his own strategy in the East. But he continued to lack a sense of purpose in issuing directives to Halleck and Buell. When he did offer his strategic ideas to them, McClellan contradicted Halleck by reminding him to cooperate with Buell until Nashville was in Union hands. Still, Washington had a victory to celebrate. "I have just heard the glorious news from Fort Donelson," wrote Salmon P. Chase to M. D. Potter, manager of the *Cincinnati Commercial.* "The underpinning of the rebellion seems to be knocked out from under it." In some respects, Halleck was right: Donelson "was the turning point in the war."[88] As church bells rang throughout the North, the *New York Herald* concluded that thanks to Grant's victory, "the backbone of the rebellion is broken."[89] The capture of Donelson and its defenders was just as significant as jubilant Northerners believed.

CHAPTER FOUR

Missed Opportunities

If anyone was regretful during the bleak winter days following the fall of Fort Donelson, it was Albert Sidney Johnston. Most of the nearly seventeen thousand inhabitants of Nashville had initially welcomed his army euphorically to the city having read in the local paper of Brig. Gen. John B. Floyd's earlier telegrams indicating victory. The editorials of defeat on Sunday morning, however, cast a dark cloud over the Tennessee capital and Johnston's exhausted army. Rumors that Buell's troops would arrive any day motivated Governor Harris to order the women and children out of the city. As a sense of urgency fell upon on the residents, pastors dismissed their congregations so that parishioners could gather their belongings and leave town. Nashvillians feared they had but little time to escape from the approaching Federals. Some citizens, however, became enraged by Johnston's failure to protect them. Angry mobs rioted, and at one point a group forced its way into the home where Johnston made his headquarters, demanding an explanation for the defeat and his plans for the future. Kentuckians shared this fear as the Union's penetration deeper into the heartland alarmed Confederate sympathizers. Provisional governor George W. Johnson wrote his wife, "the time of our severest afflictions has now come—our state is about to be abandoned by our armies."[1]

General Johnston became the target of unprecedented criticism for the fall of Fort Donelson. Newspapermen forgot that just a few weeks earlier they had lionized the commander as the savior of the West. Then, they argued, Johnston was a hero in whom the Confederacy could expect great things. Now, they concluded, Grant and Buell had outgeneraled Johnston, and his blunders had transferred the war from Kentucky to Tennessee. Editors throughout the South led the way, conjuring up outlandish accusations charging him with incompetence and treason. The *Richmond Enquirer,* for example, lamented that the losses of the forts "were for our own good," because defeat taught the Confederacy a lesson in appointing someone whose authority exceeded his ability. The government, the editor argued, had put too much stock in one commander.[2]

Political animosity followed closely behind public opinion. Tennessee congressmen sent a delegation to President Davis in the second week of March calling for Johnston's removal, claiming that "confidence is no longer felt in the military skill of Gen. A. S. Johnston." Some representatives declared that Johnston had inexcusably lost the Mississippi Valley and demanded that Congress vote to investigate his conduct in the recent losses. At first, the president thought of going to the West, not to replace Johnston but rather to reassure the people there that all was not lost. Indeed, he was concerned about these disasters, citing them on February 22 as he officially accepted the presidency of the Confederate States of America. Though an unpopular move at the time, Davis stood by his trusted friend and kept him in command. "If [Johnston] is not a general," Davis remarked, "we had better give up the war, for we have no general." Critics then turned on Davis for his refusal to dismiss Johnston, arguing that the president himself should come to the West and take command, which was, they believed, the only way to revitalize what many came to believe was a thoroughly demoralized army. In the heat of criticism, Davis remained silent on the subject in his correspondence to Johnston.[3]

The consequences of losing the Forts Henry and Donelson went beyond military defeat. Middle Tennesseans now contemplated Yankee occupation of their rivers and communities, and military authorities worried about the vulnerability of the Memphis and Charleston Railroad to Union raids. Also, important cotton ports such as Florence, Tuscumbia, and Eastport might now come under Union control, and residents questioned whether or not the Confederate army would return and when. A correspondent to the *New York Times* wrote that the women and old men in and around Dover, Tennessee, complained bitterly of the war in their vicinity. They had not wanted to take any position with regard to secession but simply wanted to be left alone. The reporter had no reason to doubt them, arguing, "as they are women, and privileged to say what they choose, it may be supposed there is some sincerity in their sentiments." In the meantime, families whose sons had joined the Southern army would be forced to condition their lives around an uncertainty that threatened the stable society they had cultivated in the years before the war. It had been Confederate policy to establish camps in the midst of loyal pockets in the region such as at Corinth, and when the Federals arrived in such communities, the citizens risked their very lives if they made their sentiments public by aiding Union troops. The defeats not only cut into the fabric of Upper South society but also into the Confederacy's ability to elicit foreign recognition, which Davis so desperately desired. Virginian James Mason wrote from London that the losses of Henry and Donelson "had an unfortunate effect upon the minds of our friends here." He tried to minimize the consequences of the loss by insisting that only six to seven thousand prisoners were captured.[4] The *Memphis Daily Appeal,* which had been generally critical of Confederate operations, supported Johnston in the face of tremendous criticism, arguing that "a general of less ability would have lost his whole army under the circumstances."[5]

As the seemingly endless line of Maj. Gen. William J. Hardee's seventeen thousand Confederates, plagued by sickness and disease during the icy retreat from Bowling Green, plodded through the Tennessee capital, their physical appearance proved disturbing and quite revealing to civilians. Hardee himself had disclosed privately that "nothing can save us except the presence of the President, who ought to come here, assume command, and call on the people to rally to his standard." To make matters worse, the soldiers frightened residents with stories of Buell's savage troops closing fast upon their heels and powerful gunboats that would destroy the city. The people responded to their first experience of military defeat unkindly, since the consequences were much more devastating then they had imagined. The frigid conditions mirrored the cold reception the soldiers received as they came into the city, accompanied by more precise news of the surrender. Ironically, by remaining with his troops and surrendering with dignity, Buckner was spared the criticism and eventually "achieved Confederate sainthood."[6]

Though he refused to respond to the unforgiving criticism, the complaints of the people were not lost on Johnston. He kept his composure and exhibited a quiet dignity of character that had earlier won him supporters. He privately remarked to Davis: "[The] test of merit, in my profession, with the people, is success. It is a hard rule, but I think it right. If I join this corps to the forces of Beauregard . . . , those who are now declaiming against me will be without an argument."[7] Indeed, it was a hard rule he learned, so much so that he vowed never to repeat his mistake.

Though Davis's support for Johnston was unchanged by the loss of

Donelson, Johnston's dilemma, however, remained the same. The vast-
ness of the area he had been charged to defend still dwarfed the few
resources allowed him by an administration blinded by the war nearer
Richmond. As overall commander in the West, whatever irresponsibility or
failures had occurred ultimately came back to the general. He alone bore
the responsibility for not personally inspecting the vital anchors to the
Confederate heartland along the rivers and for allowing his incompetent
subordinates too much independence of judgment. The consequences
of his actions highlighted the fact that his scattered and disconnected
forces in Tennessee were in a critically dangerous situation. About the
only saving grace for Johnston was that his retreat from Bowling Green
had been effected with some strategic insight. Still, three hundred miles
separated his forces in Middle Tennessee from those at Columbus.[8]

The Union was moving south in Middle Tennessee and the Mississippi
Valley and Johnston had to decide quickly which area to give his full
attention and forces. Because of the distance between the two armies,
Johnston thought it wise to allow Beauregard a free hand in making
decisions. Columbus could be relinquished, he told the Louisianan, but
only if Richmond approved. After their meeting, Beauregard departed
for Kentucky, but an illness delayed him at Jackson, Tennessee. When
Fort Donelson fell, Johnston retreated from Nashville south to effect the
concentration of his forces safely behind the upper Tennessee River at
Murfreesboro, thirty miles southeast of Nashville. He also made preparations to fall back to northern Alabama if necessary.[9]

Johnston's retreat from Bowling Green and the evacuation of Nashville
were made in good order, mainly because the Army of the Ohio was moving slowly overland, contrary to Johnston's belief that Buell was marching swiftly, while Grant's command ascended the river. During these
monotonous weeks of indistinguishable days of boredom and gloom,
weather and disease forced the Union forces into a quasi-paralysis of
repetitious drilling while waiting for something to happen. Grant's river
victories shocked the residents of Clarksville, an attractive river city, and
the nearby Tennessee capital, and panic gripped both cities. Residents of
Memphis shared this fear. One alarmed woman wrote to the *Memphis
Daily Appeal* demanding to know what was holding the men of the city
back from doing something about the impending doom. "Are you really
willing," she goaded the city's male population, "to be slapped in the face,
snubbed, pricked with bayonets . . . and insulted by every epitaph that a
gloating jubilant Yankee can manufacture?"[10]

The flood of demoralized Confederates from the forts threw Clarksville and Nashville into a weeklong hysteria. The ragged appearance of Johnston's army and the sight of Governor Harris rushing to get aboard a special train with the state archives added to their anxiety. The Southern press had portrayed Yankees as ruthless and brutal, infamous for murdering civilians, shamefully undisciplined, and longing for "booty and beauty." Nashville mayor Richard B. Cheatham, alarmed that Buell's army would soon overrun the city, promised the residents all the Confederate provisions that Johnston's army did not take to Murfreesboro. On the Sunday morning that Johnston learned of the surrender of Donelson, the general assured residents with whom he and his staff had taken their meals that although he could not make a fight at Nashville, he knew Don Carlos Buell well—indeed, had served with him before the war—and that he was a gentleman who would not "suffer any violence to peaceable citizens or disturb private property." When Brig. Gen. Gideon Pillow arrived the following day, he attempted to calm the scrambling citizens. In a speech on Public Square, he declared: "The Federals will be with you only for a time, and I pledge to you my honor that this war will not end until they are driven across the Ohio River. The officers who will come among you are gentlemen, and of course, will behave as such towards you." Still, the sullen displays of the governor packing for Memphis and the soldiers crossing the wire bridge over the Cumberland en route to Murfreesboro made Pillow's and Johnston's reassurances seem hollow. After all, these were the same commanders who had given up Henry and Donelson. Residents convinced themselves that the worst was yet to come, setting off a scramble for safety.[11]

Johnston left to John Floyd the chore of burning the bridges across the Cumberland River and of salvaging the government stores. When Nathan Bedford Forrest arrived on March 19, a Wednesday, Floyd put the cavalry commander in charge of securing Confederate stockpiles before leaving Nashville himself. The politician-general had mismanaged the evacuation so badly that it was all Forrest could do to get his own men out of the city safely, since residents were furious over what the Confederates had done. Dr. William Cheatham, brother to the mayor, recalled the unpleasantness of the day the Confederates departed, complaining that they "had swept by or loitered in the neighborhood [and] took whatever they needed or found untaken."[12]

The fall of Bowling Green, combined with the imminent capture of Nashville, influenced Halleck to continue pressing McClellan for

supreme command in the West and Buell to join him in campaigning
on the rivers. With Grant's force moving on Clarksville, Halleck pleaded
with his counterpart to assist him. "The battle of the West is to be fought in
that vicinity," he argued. "Don't hesitate. Come to Clarksville as rapidly
as possible. Help me and I will help you. We came within an ace of
being defeated." Had it not been for the help of David Hunter, who had
sent troops from Missouri to support Grant during the Fort Donelson
crisis, Halleck concluded that the army would surely have been defeated.
His words of desperation continued: "It is evident to me that you and
McClellan did not at least accounts appreciate the strait I have been in.
Help me, I beg of you. . . . You will not regret it. There will be no battle
at Nashville."[13]

As it turned out, Halleck was right in perceptively recognizing that
there would be no battle at Nashville. Buell, however, clung to the belief
that the Confederates were falling back from Clarksville to defend the
Tennessee capital. Unable to convince Buell to cooperate, Halleck pressed
McClellan for a solution once again. "I must have command of the armies
in the West," he demanded on the evening of February 20. "Hesitation and
delay are losing us the golden opportunity. Lay this before the President
and Secretary of War. May I assume the command?" Complaining that
Buell "acted like a dog in the manger," he badgered Assistant Secretary
of War Thomas Scott, who was in Louisville at the time, to assume the
responsibility of ordering Buell to accommodate Halleck's desires. Scott
refused. Halleck's bypassing the chain of command once again infuriated
McClellan. To say the least, the general in chief's mind was made up:
Nashville was the key. In the meantime, he would wait to hear from Buell
before laying Halleck's request for overall command before Lincoln and
Stanton.[14] McClellan's program was a "slow and sure" strategy, wrote
the editor of *Harper's Weekly*, though it was not swift enough to satisfy the
"idle gossips [in Washington] who indulge in tea-party strategy."[15]

As predicted, Clarksville fell on February 20. The residents of the
bustling river city, known for its tobacco and iron industry, bore witness to the aftermath of the Fort Donelson battle as the wounded and
disheartened soldiers filtered through town on their way to Nashville.
Some residents stayed long enough to plead with the soldiers to protect
the city, but it was no use. By the time Foote's gunboats showed up,
all the soldiers had fled south, along with a majority of the city's five
thousand inhabitants. As white flags flew throughout the town, slaves
who knew of the retreating Southerners, and who had been restless

for days, gathered at the waterfront to see the arriving Union warships and accompanying soldiers. The correspondent to the *New York Herald* wrote that the residents who were not able to flee had been deceived into thinking that they were being "invaded by a band of Germans and Negroes." To highlight the significance of the Union capture, the *Herald* did an entire front-page spread on Clarksville, characterizing it as a city that "gave great promise of being a rising place" before the war. Now, wrote the correspondent, "the whole country looks as if the inhabitants thereof had been frightened from their homes by a terror worse than that of Lisbon when the earth quaked, or of Marseilles when the plague ravaged every household. Terror and desolation are on every hand."[16]

Mayor George Smith, Judge Thomas Wisdom, and Cave Johnson, a friend of Andrew Foote's father, greeted the arriving gunboats. The commodore met the delegation and promised to protect those residents professing loyalty to the Union. Still, Clarksvillians had overwhelmingly supported the Confederacy in 1860, and Foote was careful not to tolerate any displays of disloyalty or dissension. All things having to do with the military would be surrendered, and "no secession flag or manifestation of secession feeling shall be exhibited," Foote ordered. Two days later Grant visited the city, surveyed the situation, and ordered Brig. Gen. Charles F. Smith's division to occupy Clarksville. He gave Smith no specific directives but did cite orders preventing soldiers from invading the private homes of the residents and "annoying the citizens generally." This meant avoiding disturbing the "peculiar institution" or being bothered by slaves themselves.[17]

With Clarksville in Union hands, Halleck decided not to participate in the capture of Nashville, particularly not by water. Commodore Foote was furious that his gunboats were prevented from ascending the river and taking the city. Capt. Seth Ledyard Phelps recalled that Halleck's decision meant that "Genl. Buell must have his chance to glorify." Still, according to Phelps, it was apparent that the gunboats had made an enduring impression on Southerners, as one Nashville paper reported, "while we have nothing to fear from the Yankee army those gunboats are the devil."[18] Phelps and his seamen came to believe that the river victories at Henry and Donelson were responsible for the evacuation of Bowling Green and Nashville, perceptively concluding, "we shook the bush while Genl. Buell was sent to 'gather' the fruit in the capture of Nashville."[19]

An occupied Clarksville made Halleck's panic unnecessary and his demands all the more irritating to McClellan. The general in chief was anxious for Buell to move on Nashville quickly and wired the commander an inducement: "Have your commission as Major General on the field of battle in taking Nashville." Now Halleck was in no hurry to help Buell, instead he boasted that because of his recent successes on the twin rivers, as well as crushing the rebellion in Missouri, he was now able to concentrate entirely on Tennessee. Columbus and Nashville, he complained, should already be in Union hands had Buell cooperated and moved swiftly. Fed up with McClellan's favoritism, Halleck wired Stanton in order to get control of Buell's army. "Give me authority," he demanded, "and I will be responsible."[20]

Stanton was apparently growing somewhat fond of Halleck; at least the Union commander's confidence impressed the war secretary as much as Buell's lethargy disturbed him. Though he had heard the rumors swirling around Congress, particularly from East Tennessee politicians, that Buell lacked the aggressive spirit necessary for a commander, Stanton was just now beginning to see confirmation of those accusations. He confided to Assistant Secretary of War Scott that as soon as Buell "fights a battle or makes any decisive movement with the large force under his command, I will be glad to recommend him for major general."[21]

Stanton was also irritated by Buell's allegiance to McClellan. The self-absorbed Ohioan continued to trust only his close friend and immediate superior. Buell's loyalty to McClellan rubbed an already irritated Stanton the wrong way. The secretary of war wanted McClellan to change his mind about Nashville and acquiesce to Halleck's demands. "Little Mac," however, continued to defend his friend's strategy, even when it meant losing political allies. Still, neither Lincoln nor Stanton desired a change in the departmental arrangement and instead thought whatever strategic problems existed could be overcome by full and zealous cooperation.[22] In the meantime, it was Grant who claimed the entire front page of *Harper's Weekly* and with it instant fame; the caption under his portrait read: "The Hero of Donelson."[23]

Though the Confederates did not have the problems of a divided high command, they had lost more than just a golden opportunity when they had not fallen back from Bowling Green and concentrated at Clarksville, where they could have driven Grant out of Fort Donelson as Halleck contemplated. Allowing the Union army to penetrate farther into the Southern heartland proved crucial to the Confederacy's ability to remain a slaveholding society. The Lincoln administration's willingness to continue its attitude of conciliation in a region where it seemed doomed was the first real test of the policy's viability. Had the Union army seized eastern Tennessee, where few slaves existed and where considerable Union support could be found, the administration would most likely have been immediately successful in luring citizens back to the Union. But to test conciliation where it was least likely to succeed, because of the absence of loyalty and the presence of slavery, was in effect more significant for the Union and the future nature of its war aims. Thus, the "accident of war" in beginning reconstruction where it was least likely to succeed, caused by the capture of the river forts, proved to be the kind of collision that helped bring about a change in Union policy that ultimately found wide reception.[24]

In its infancy, the Lincoln administration had initially insisted that abolition would not be a war aim and that conciliation toward the Southern populace would reduce civilian resistance to the soldiers campaigning and occupying portions of the South. These conceptions formed the basis for the way in which Federal armies were to shape military strategy, conduct the war, and deal with civilians in the Confederacy. These attitudes had particular significance for the Border States because those areas provided the testing ground to gauge the validity and durability of the administration's assumptions; not only could conciliation be applied to reopening river and rail commerce but also, more importantly, to slavery.

As the Union army occupied territory on the periphery of the Confederacy such as Kentucky and Tennessee, slaves by the thousands headed for Federal lines. Initially, commanders simply returned fugitive slaves, some with more enthusiasm than others, until it became policy not to do so. Handing over slaves to their masters was seen as a way to enforce the administration's pledge to protect the rights of Southern civilians, thereby mollifying their hostility. By February, however, the Union's occupation of Middle Tennessee provided the impetus for policymakers to depart from this attitude. Despite the intentions of political leaders, the Union penetration south loosened the bonds between master and slave. The arrival of Federal soldiers disrupted the world of the slaveowner and destroyed the plantation community and its daily routines. Though initially slaves were confused and reacted cautiously to this situation, they soon began sneaking away from the plantations and gravitating toward Union camps. Slaves and masters alike quickly perceived the significance of the nearby presence of Federal troops. Conversely, Northern soldiers, typically ambivalent about fugitives, increasingly came to believe they possessed some value. Writing from Fort Donelson, Illinoisan James F.

Drish observed to his wife that most regiments had "contraband," a euphemism for slaves. "I have a very fine mulatto fellow and we find them very useful[,] they are very good cooks. I am bound to have a half dozen if the war lasts much longer, and when I come home I am going to get a girl to cook for you if I can find one."[25]

The occupation of Southern soil by Union soldiers also highlighted the inevitable friction between civilians and military personnel, reflecting the fundamental dilemma of the civil nature of the war. It soon became apparent that no matter how well conceived the Union policy was, the daily experience of dealing with these issues proved more useful in providing alternatives for resolving the inherent conflicts. Federal policy directed commanders to exclude runaway slaves from camp, confiscate only identifiable Confederate property, suppress only active resistance, and conciliate noncombatants to Federal authority. Although some soldiers were astonished to experience what one called a "Union revival . . . going on in this state [Tennessee], especially around here," other soldiers found themselves in a countryside that proved increasingly hostile even in what was believed to be the most loyal regions.

Clearly these campaigns were beginning to leave their imprint on soldiers and civilians alike. Civilian hostility forced soldiers and commanders to question, if not challenge, the Union's rationale for carrying out a limited war. The consequences incurred by the Federal army while maintaining strict adherence to the administration's desires ultimately forced commanders to deviate from the limited-war policy in the occupied South. Some officers simply abandoned trying to decide who was and was not loyal to the Union. In dealing with fugitive slaves, civilian property, and active resistance, they assumed more practical responses for individual cases. This conflict indicated that, in a larger context, the administration's handling of the occupied South conflicted with what a significant portion of an impatient Northern populace had come to believe was a tiring way to fight and win. More so, this departure from policy would create problems within the armies as soldiers came to resent commanders who refused to deviate from the administration's initial conceptions.[26]

Northern abolitionists and Radical Republicans, particularly some governors of the Midwest, had never wavered in their desire to see the war eradicate slavery. On the opening day of Congress on December 2, 1861, Rep. Thaddeus Stevens introduced a joint resolution favoring emancipation, arguing that because "Slavery [had] caused the present rebellion in the United States, . . . there can be no solid and permanent peace and union in the Republic as long as the institution exist[ed] within it." To highlight the relationship between the political responsibility of the government and its armies, pro-abolitionists kept what they believed was the war's ultimate purpose at the vanguard of military policy. War offered the North the opportunity to carry out with the army what politicians failed to achieve in Congress—the extinction of slavery. Because initial policies had been unable to produce victory, or at least the kind of victory political leaders sought, Grant's successes encouraged their thinking that the addition of emancipation as a war measure could now be implemented. Abolitionists and Radicals presented a plausible way of weakening the rebellion at a time when Union armies seemed uninterested in the revolution they could achieve. Whatever the experience of war had taught policymakers about their initial conceptions, abolitionists and Radicals had thought long about abandoning conciliation and implementing emancipation, pressuring the administration to accept these goals. Thus, as Federal troops came to occupy more of the South, which accelerated the collapse of slavery, the role of the Union armies changed.[27]

In his success, Grant had unknowingly given abolitionists and Radicals ammunition to increase their pressure on the administration to expand its war aims. Lincoln, however, understood that whatever support he gained by adopting confiscation and abolition to please abolitionists and Radical Republicans was minimal compared to what he stood to lose in the support of Northern conservatives and Southern Unionists. He had hoped for either a massive victory or the occupation of a suitable region that would allow him to institute his brand of reconstruction before congressional Radicals gained the upper hand in directing the war. While he would have preferred Union success in East Tennessee rather than in the western or central sections of the state, Lincoln saw in the Union's occupation of Middle Tennessee the opportunity to make a broader political statement regarding his view of reconstruction.[28]

As expected, Federal success in Tennessee created problems for the army and its commanders. Like all Union leaders, Halleck, Grant, and Buell were greatly concerned about how to treat Southern civilians in an occupied region, particularly since they were aware of the rumors that partisan guerrillas were surfacing. Fortunately for the Union, Gen. A. S. Johnston was too preoccupied with his retreat to organize any of these irregular forces to prove effective in harassing the Federals. Grant too was preoccupied during the weeks immediately following the fall of

Clarksville, particularly in handling the problems presented to his army by runaway slaves. Dealing with slavery was difficult for Grant, as it was for Halleck and Buell. Halleck had emphasized to his subordinate the need to keep civilians out of war but authorized him, citing the First Confiscation Act, to impress slaves under the pretense that they helped construct Confederate fortifications. Soon, slaveowners appeared in Union camps demanding the return of their human property. The consequences of such a policy soon taught Grant that such a practice "leads to constant mistakes and embarrassment to have our men run[n]ing through the country interpreting confiscation acts and only strengthens the enthusiasm against us whilst it has a demoralizing influance upon our own troops."[29]

Officers learned immediately the extent to which slavery and emancipation were volatile and complex affairs closely intertwined with reconciliation. As one perceptive correspondent to *Harper's Weekly* who had been traveling for weeks with Grant's army observed, the Union penetration, "though militar[ily] successful," was sure to change the opinion of some Southerners "who felt they may join the Confederacy" as a result.[30]

While Grant's thirty-five-thousand-man Army of the Tennessee accumulated around Fort Henry, regrouping and awaiting orders for another move south, Buell's Army of the Ohio was experiencing many of the same hardships during its march toward Nashville. While he occupied northern and eastern Kentucky and now Bowling Green, Buell carried out the administration's policy in dealing with slaves and civilians. For him, however, his experience in Kentucky, where the majority of slaveowners were loyal to the Union, confirmed for him that protection of the institution proved an effective device in maintaining that allegiance. Since coming to the West, Buell insisted that slavery had nothing to with the war and that violating the rights of owners would simply disfranchise the countryside. Still, Buell knew that conciliation had its objectors and that civil disobedience would surface regardless, which would require him to deal practically with sentiment.[31]

On Sunday, February 23, the vanguard of Buell's army reached Edgefield, on the north bank of the Cumberland River opposite Nashville, just as Johnston's army pulled into Murfreesboro thirty-five miles south. His command had come to gather the fallen fruit of the tree shaken by Foote and Grant. It was a beautiful spring-like day, and the disheartened residents who remained in the city gathered along the river to watch the anticipated arrival of those whom they believed were merciless Yankees. Watching the citizens depart the city caused Tennessee soldier W. H. Mott to lament that it was indeed a "death blow to the valor of Tennesseans. . . . Of all the gloomy pictures that I have witnessed, the one presented that morning wore the palm, the streets and the walk were a complete jam of citizens and soldiers with cast down looks and muddy clothes."[32] What compounded the situation was the conduct of the Confederates not only in Nashville, who pillaged, looted, and conducted themselves disgracefully, but also those in other areas. Addison Croft, acting assistant adjutant general, complained from Iuka, Mississippi, that in falling back, Southern soldiers had been guilty of the most "disgraceful plundering of private property; that chickens had been stolen, hogs had been killed, a horse wantonly stabbed, [and] private gardens robbed." The military losses, the discontented civilian attitudes toward the soldiers in the occupied region, and the substantive display of loyalty were so great, that writing to his wife, Grant concluded, "'Sesesh' is about on its last legs in Tennessee."[33]

The anxious residents feared the Yankees would no doubt commence shelling the city, and they pressed the mayor to cross the river to surrender Nashville in order to save it. Cheatham persuaded the Ohio captain in charge not to fire on the capital. Had Buell moved swifter in getting to Nashville, he might have saved the Cumberland River bridges, which had recently been built, and bagged Johnston's entire army. A missed opportunity indeed, lamented some Northern newspapers.[34]

The morning of Tuesday, February 25, brought a temperate and "bright, glorious day," according to a soldier in the Sixth Ohio aboard the *Diana*, headquarters for Brig. Gen. William "Bull" Nelson's division.[35] As the steamer approached the wharf just before nine o'clock, a crowd of those fearful but courageous citizens who had long awaited liberation from the Confederates had assembled to see the Yankees. A *New York Times* correspondent said he knew of one such merchant who in the summer of 1860 bought sulfuric acid in Louisville and got a permit for it on a pledge that he would not sell it to the secessionists. He kept his pledge and in late February still held eight thousand pounds of it, despite being offered four dollars per pound by Rebel authorities when it cost him only eight cents to purchase. The reporter was impressed because the merchant and his family had been threatened repeatedly until the Nashville Vigilance Committee visited him and offered the option of hiding out until Union troops arrived. The first chance he got, the shopkeeper flew the Stars and Stripes above his store. The arrival of the Yankees also impressed Capt. Thomas J. Wright of the Eighth Kentucky, who remembered that the slaves who had gathered along the river to witness the day of jubilee "made many demonstrations of joy, clapping their hands, swinging their hands and patting and dancing." Some slaves "hung on the fences along the road in Sunday attire," recalled Lyman S. Widney, "and gazed for the first time upon the Yankees with open-eyed wonder."[36] What seemed like a painfully long journey in the eyes of Congress had finally ended. Buell's army at last occupied a significant target in the heart of the western Confederacy.

As Old Glory was hoisted above the Tennessee capital, Union soldiers broke into celebration. Later that same day, Buell and a delegation of residents led by the mayor negotiated the terms of capitulation. The general convinced Mayor Cheatham that he had no intention of harming the people, just as Johnston had said. He demonstrated his guarantee by pledging safety and protection to the citizens "both in their persons and in their property" as well as aiding the local police force in restoring and maintaining order. After the conference, Buell and his staff crossed the river and established headquarters. To Stanton, Buell wired the news: "Nashville was taken possession of to-day."[37]

Hearing of Nashville's capture, soldiers at Paducah concluded that "the war will be closed in less than six months from this time."[38] In some respects, as historian Stephen Ash asserts, the war had already ended for some Middle Tennesseans, particularly farmers. Southerners came to realize that Lincoln's armies would remain in their midst until they produced the desired change, at least with regard to loyalties. As the winter months brought a close to the year's agricultural activities for the most part, so too did it reflect the bleak and barren Middle Tennessee landscape. Livestock was scarce, winter harvests were diminishing, and the devastation they had feared revealed that war had not discriminated in its destructive effects.[39]

When Buell tried to get Smith's division to Nashville, the move encouraged Grant to travel to the Tennessee capital early on the twenty-seventh, without Halleck's permission, to survey the situation. Like Foote, Grant had wanted to move upstream and take Nashville before Buell, but Halleck remained steadfast in his refusal. After spending some time in the city, Grant returned to the wharf, where he finally met Buell; it is doubtful if the two men had seen each other since the Mexican War. Grant tried to convince Buell that Johnston was heading south to Murfreesboro and posed no threat to Nashville. An alarmed Buell responded that Johnston's return was a real possibility, particularly since there was fighting just ten miles southeast of the city. "Quite probably,"

Grant curtly responded. "Nashville contained valuable stores of arms, ammunition, and provisions, and the enemy is probably trying to carry away all they can. The fighting," he added, "is doubtless with the rear guard who are trying to protect the trains they are getting away with." Buell disagreed, arguing that Nashville was indeed in danger and that he "knew" his information was accurate.[40]

Though they met only briefly, Buell and Grant had managed to offend one another. Grant's unauthorized trip to Nashville also upset Halleck, who after a week of getting no correspondence from his subordinate and needing to support Pope's advance on New Madrid, Missouri, complained to McClellan that Grant's behavior required censure. In the weeks to come, Halleck would act on his anger, partly because he was jealous over Grant's victories and the notoriety they had brought him.[41]

Though Buell was given Nashville without even crossing the river, his army's presence nonetheless represented a new order for its citizens. Buell had captured the city and now had to hold it while allowing its residents to return to their normal activities. Thus, he remained cautious and uncertain about how to proceed. The Tennessee capital was indeed one of the great prizes of the war. Its strategic location alone was an important point of departure from which to launch campaigns south and east. The city's tremendous economic benefits was an added bonus as its factories produced military ordnance, munitions, and supplies ranging from saddles and sabers to belts and uniform cloth. Nashville, observed a *New York Herald* correspondent, was an "imposing city" with a new capitol building, a new courthouse, new railroad bridges across the Cumberland River, a university, Shelby Medical College, historical society, state library, a paid fire department, and a tremendous book publishing company. New York journalist Henry Villard thought of it "more as a Northern than of a Southern city." With Federals now in Middle Tennessee, Johnston had lost his logistical and industrial base. Moreover, Kentucky seemed safe in Union hands, the Mississippi River was open as far as Island No. 10 on the Confederate's left flank, and Buell's sizeable army now was anchored in Middle Tennessee, holding the junction of key railroad and river connections. Moreover, they gained the benefit of tremendous quantities of supplies left behind by the fleeing Confederates.[42]

Despite the military inertia and frustration of the past months, the Union had made significant gains in February. Still, success and occupation created problems not only for Tennesseans bewildered by a profound apprehension regarding what would become of them but also for the high command that struggled to capitalize on this success. Lincoln viewed the capture of Nashville as an opportunity to subject civilians to his policy of reconstruction. The president decided to extend civil guarantees to the citizens of Nashville and Middle Tennessee by allowing them to participate in civil processes. Even in a region where slavery and Confederate sentiment were deeply entrenched, Lincoln was convinced that the latent Unionism of the citizens would surface if only nurtured by the army's protection. Efforts to politically reconstruct Tennessee were sure to burden an already turbulent relationship between civil and military authorities. The sheer demand of having to deal with the civilian populace, slavery, the local economy, and Confederate property would have troubled even the most productive and favorable civil-military relationships. Attempting to deal effectively with these issues forced politicians and commanders to refashion the political objectives of the war, which had to this time remained subordinate to military concerns.[43]

Buell's determination to deal effectively with these issues was articulated in what became the most controversial orders of his command, General Orders 13a. In sum, Buell reminded his troops of the policy they were to pursue in Tennessee. "We are in arms," he declared, "not for the purpose of invading the rights of our fellow-countrymen anywhere, but to maintain the integrity of the Union and protect the Constitution under which its people have been prosperous and happy." No longer would aid to the enemy be viewed with indifference, but only authorized persons could take action against it. Peaceable citizens were not to be molested "in their persons or property," and "any wrongs to either" would be "promptly corrected and the offenders brought to punishment." Soldiers were to pay for the use of private property, and no seizures of private property were to be made without the authority of the highest commander present. Soldiers were forbidden to enter private residences or make arrests without Buell's authority. Anything less than what he prescribed in occupying the city would bring shame on the army.[44]

The Ohioan had every expectation that erring Southerners would be convinced that his army was not representative of an allegedly wicked and corrupt Northern society. Instead, he set out to prove that his soldiers represented the best of a democratic society, which meant not infringing upon the constitutional rights of noncombatants. General Orders 13a was his attempt to ensure that the army would act responsibly and to maintain an atmosphere in Nashville that was favorable to regaining the daily functions of life both in business and among the private residents.

George B. McClellan. Massachusetts Commandery, Military Order of the
Loyal Legion, and the United States Army Military History Institute (USAMHI).

(*Above left*) Henry W. Halleck.
Massachusetts Commandery, Military
Order of the Loyal Legion, and the
USAMHI.

(*Above right*) Don Carlos Beull.
USAMHI.

(*Opposite*) Ulysses S. Grant. USAMHI.

(*Above left*) Andrew S. Foote. From
*Frank Leslie's Illustrations: The
American Soldier in the Civil War.*
(New York: Bryan, Taylor, 1895), 264.

(*Above right*) Albert Sidney Johnston.
Massachusetts Commandery, Military
Order of the Loyal Legion, and the
USAMHI.

(*Left*) Simon Bolivar Buckner. From
Frank Leslie's Illustrations, 264.

(*Opposite*) P. G. T. Beauregard.
Massachusetts Commandery, Military
Order of the Loyal Legion, and the
USAMHI.

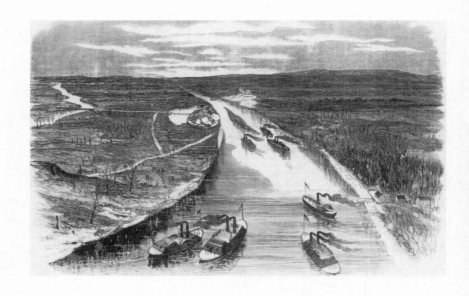

(*Above*) Union Gunboats on the Tennessee. *Harper's Weekly.*

(*Opposite top*) Surrender of Fort Donelson. *Harper's Weekly.*

(*Opposite bottom*) Group of Confederate prisoners captured at Fort Donelson. From *Frank Leslie's Illustrations*, 108.

Southern Unionists welcoming Federal gunboats in Alabama. *Harper's Weekly*, March 1, 1862.

Nashville. *Harper's Weekly*.

Pittsburg Landing. *Harper's Weekly*.

Shiloh Church. *Harper's Weekly*.

Battle of Pittsburg Landing. *Harper's Weekly*.

Corduroying roads to Corinth. *Harper's Weekly.*

Deserted Confederate fortifications, Corinth. From *Frank Leslie's Illustrations,* 161.

Before leaving the city, Governor Harris had characterized the Federals as ruthless cutthroats, and so Buell's words of conciliation came as both a shock and a comfort to the townspeople. Whitelaw Reid, correspondent to the *Cincinnati Gazette*, however, perceptively warned his readers from Nashville that before the Union could again claim popular support in the Tennessee capital, citizens "must be assured that the power of the nation is re-established throughout the State beyond peradventure."[45]

Given the hectic state of affairs, Buell remained confident that his policy would prove effective because he saw little evidence in Nashville that the citizens were actively resisting occupation. Still, he ordered his subordinates to remain cautious of civil disobedience. What made him anxious was what actions the president would take in Tennessee. "As a matter of great importance and delicacy," he warned McClellan, "I would advise you to use all the means you have to induce the President to pursue a lenient course, and as far as possible to reconstruct the machinery of the general Government out of material here." With his army acting properly, Buell had "reason to hope that a great change will take place speedily in the attitude of the Tennesseans, in both the manner of the military and political policy to be observed."[46]

When Buell was confident that Johnston's army was no longer a threat to Nashville, the general breathed a sigh of relief about retaining the city. Assistant Secretary of War Scott confided to Stanton that Buell's course was "very prudent and conciliatory which I think the present temper of these people absolutely requires."[47] In light of the undisciplined mobs of Confederate troops fleeing the capital, Buell's orderly and mannerly soldiers earned the respect of Nashvillians. Indeed, it was as Johnston predicted before he left, wrote resident Margaret (Maggie) L. Lindsley of Nashville to her grandmother in Louisville, the "Federals have interfered with no one whatever, and have behaved much better than the rebel army."[48] Another pleased observer was so impressed that he complimented Buell's efforts to the War Department, saying that the soldiers were "truly gentlemen—gentlemen of a high order in all their bearing." With the Federals present, this resident "never felt more secure in my life, both in property and person."[49]

A week after crossing the Cumberland River into the city, Buell wired McClellan that all was calm. The general in chief no doubt wished for the same pleasing atmosphere in Washington. Though Buell's capture of Nashville delighted Union authorities, some dissatisfied politicians continued to press for an advance into East Tennessee. Lincoln, in the meantime, mused on the appointment of a military governor for the occupied capital. The very thought of this bothered Buell. He was convinced that most of the region's citizens, if not coerced into submission, would cooperate with military commanders in restoring local government and maintaining law and order. He called on his friend McClellan to discourage the idea in the Washington. "Use all your persuasion against the appointment of a military governor for Tennessee," he wrote. "It will do incalculable harm. Beg the President to wait."[50]

Buell's opposition was based on the belief that such an appointment would mean military government in his department. The imposition of martial law, he reasoned, represented a hasty decision and fragile attempt by the administration to restore loyal Tennesseans to the Union politically without considering what might happen if the army was forced to withdraw. Some citizens, such as Maggie Lindsley, feared the possibility of a reverse: "that the Confederates should get back here. Then *our* doom is spoken—either flight—beggary or, remaining death."[51]

Perhaps even more significant with regard to Buell's authority was the fact that such an appointment would create a conflict of power between himself and a military governor. He thought even loyal Tennesseans might resent power imposed on them by the Union, and large numbers of otherwise passive citizens might become motivated to retaliate against the army. One of Buell's primary doctrines argued that "Wars of invasion, always difficult, become tenfold so when the people of the invaded territory take an active part against the army." He added to this, "These considerations are of such importance to success that there is no exception to the rule of securing the neutrality if not the friendship of the population [in rebellion]."[52]

Buell vowed not to trample on the citizens' sensibilities, but he feared a military governor would. Assistant Secretary Scott agreed with Buell's attitude and policy, worried that any change might create more trouble. He was not alone in his presumptions about a change in attitude. Although the Union army had been in the city only a few days, William Nelson concluded that the "tide has already turned," as the citizens "seem to be awakening from some unpleasant dream."[53] Still, the longer his army remained in the region, the more problems it would have in dealing with the population. In time the optimistic assumptions about the loyalties of the citizens and conciliation would be challenged.

Lincoln was anxious to introduce his brand of political reconstruction. On March 4 he appointed Sen. Andrew Johnson of Tennessee as military governor of the South's first occupied region; he gave Johnson the military rank of brigadier general for added authority. Without precisely defining the office Johnson would hold, the president nonetheless gave the new governor the power to exercise and perform the duties and functions pertaining to the office of military governor. Without working out the details, Lincoln had sent Johnson to get loyal state government functioning again as soon as possible.[54]

The appointment alarmed Buell. Not only had Lincoln created the position but also named to the post the very person who resented Buell for not moving into East Tennessee the previous year. It was Johnson who himself had visited the army's commanders and the president desiring to get Buell to move. The general, however, had not budged, arguing at the time that such an advance was impractical due to the lack of roads and inhospitable terrain. Consequently, the Tennessean arrived in Nashville with not only political reconstruction on his mind but also to assert himself above Buell in handling affairs in the state. Though Johnson came "with the olive branch in one hand and the Constitution in the other," he also came with a vengeance to punish secessionists and to purge them from high-ranking positions. Nelson warned Treasury Secretary Salmon Chase that Johnson was "too much embittered to entrust with a mission as delicate as the direction of a people under the present circumstances."[55] Pro-Confederate Governor Harris remarked, "If Johnson were a snake, he would lie in the grass to bite the heels of rich men's children."[56] After all it seemed, as Assistant War Secretary Scott had determined, that Buell was "managing matters with great prudence." The developing animosity between the politician and the general was so widely known in the ranks that a perceptive Maj. Joseph Warren Keifer of the Third Ohio concluded to his wife, "there will be no harmony between Johnson and Buell."[57] Indeed, this may have been Lincoln's intention in appointing Johnson.

The cumulative effects of Buell's first two weeks of occupation proved that the Union's policy of conciliation was not only cultivating loyal support but also benefiting Buell's army. He was further encouraged by the news from the foot of the Cumberland Mountains in eastern Tennessee and Kentucky, where a portion of his army had advanced, that judicious treatment of civilians had resulted in the rise of loyal sentiment. He continued to return fugitive slaves to their masters, which won him wide support among the wealthy elite. Soldiers who violated his General Orders 13a were quickly punished. Thus, by the time Johnson arrived on March 11, Nashvillians had responded receptively to the general's lenient policy, and Buell feared any other course would undo what he had accomplished.[58]

Naturally, Buell's occupation policy had its detractors, principally because it could not completely stop civilians from assisting the Confederates or the depredations committed against Federal troops in and around Nashville. Some soldiers harbored a feeling of complacency, and although Nashville was in Union hands, it might just as well not be an occupied city. Buell's occupation policy was becoming more difficult to enforce. Not only was it becoming increasingly controversial, but also the tremendous influx of slaves into camp complicated his task of returning them. Of course, not everyone, including some of his division commanders, shared Buell's enthusiasm about a lenient occupation. Brig. Gen. Ormsby Mitchel, for example, quickly came to resent Buell's policy and wrote Chase that this "extreme leniency" would ultimately "work evil not good. The poison of rebellion has penetrated deeply into the systems of our Southern people . . . , [and] [i]t needs some powerful antidote."[59] Whether or not conciliation would bear fruit for the Union, the fact was it forced Southern citizens, as well as some Union soldiers, into a crisis of faith.

Maj. Joseph Keifer agreed that Buell's policy needed modification and hoped Johnson would bring about significant change. "Nashville is second only to Charleston in her rebel proclivity," he complained to his wife. "I predict the policy of Genl. Buell will be promptly changed for the better. . . . We must punish the secesh of this place and state in a more *severe* and *summary* manner."[60]

As the initial weeks of the occupation passed, it was clear that Andrew Johnson would have pleased Major Keifer, as the governor carried out a decidedly different policy than Buell. Johnson purged the city government of political dissidents, editors, and preachers who printed or preached sedition. With the help of the army, Nashville began to deal with the new problems of crime, disease, and poverty posed by war. Buell, meanwhile, continued to regroup his Army of the Ohio as units came into city. As Halleck had predicted, the war in the West was moving in the direction of Memphis, not Chattanooga or even back to Nashville, where Buell had anticipated. Buell, however, remained cautious, and the tug-of-war continued between the department commanders over the true strategic design for the West. As often as he could, Halleck complained that others simply could not see what he saw. To Assistant Secretary Scott he complained that he could not "make Buell understand the importance of strategic points till it is too late."[61] To his wife he was less charitable, connecting Buell to McClellan and Stanton as culprits in denying him due credit for the success of Henry, Donelson, Nashville, and New Madrid. "The newspapers give the credit of these things to Stanton, McClellan & Buell," he fumed, "but fortunately I have recorded evidence that they even failed to approve them after I had planned them."[62] Halleck believed that if he had supreme command in the West, he could take advantage of the Confederates' mistake in not holding on to Fort Donelson or Clarksville.[63]

After the euphoria of Grant's river victory, Halleck outlined his next strategy. The Union penetration into Tennessee forced the Confederates to abandon Columbus, Kentucky, their northernmost stronghold on the Mississippi River. Now Brig. Gen. John Pope applied pressure farther south on the great river. When Leonidas Polk evacuated Columbus, the Confederates attempted to defend the Mississippi where the boundaries of Kentucky, Tennessee, and Missouri come together. The principal positions were Island No. 10, a strong fortification in the Mississippi at the southern end of a loop in the river, and New Madrid at the northern end of another big loop. Because Island No. 10 prevented Pope from attacking New Madrid by water, he decided to approach the tiny river hamlet by land from the north and west. On February 21 Pope went on the offensive against New Madrid and Island No. 10 with the promise that Halleck would send reinforcements.[64]

By the time word reached Grant on February 26 that he should send reinforcements to Pope, he was in Nashville seeking to visit Buell. Halleck wired Grant with requests for troop strengths but received no answer. He began to complain to McClellan: "It is hard to censure a successful general, but I think Grant richly deserves it. . . . I am worn-out with this neglect and inefficiency." This admission, coming on the heels of McClellan's telegram chiding Halleck for wanting a larger command when he could not keep track of the forces he had, angered Halleck. McClellan agreed with the department commander's handling of the situation, though, arguing, "Do not hesitate to arrest [Grant] at once if the good of the service requires it."[65]

Stanton apparently approved of Halleck's action too, and on March 4 "Old Brains" replaced Grant as commander of the Army of the Tennessee with recently promoted Maj. Gen. Charles F. Smith, obviously the only dependable officer in the department. It was clear that as much as Halleck disliked Buell, he preferred that general to Grant, who had outshone Halleck at a moment when he had come under attack for wasting too much time sparring with Buell. Grant's victory increased the demand for more aggressive action, something that suited his temperament. Still, Halleck was Grant's superior, and jealousy motivated him to make an example by punishing Grant for his independence in going to Nashville and for failing to communicate regularly. Thus, just two weeks after giving the Union its first significant victory of the war and making national headlines, Grant found himself shelved.[66]

About the same time that Andrew Johnson arrived in Nashville, Pope, commanding the new Army of the Mississippi, had forced the evacuation of New Madrid, a significant Union victory because of the town's great importance to the Confederates' ability to hold the Mississippi River. Though Island No. 10 had yet to fall, it was beginning to look as though Halleck, or at least Halleck's subordinates, was winning the war in the West. It was simply a matter of time before Island No. 10 capitulated, which then would force the Confederates farther south, possibly all the way to Fort Pillow, fifty miles north of Memphis. Still, with McClellan at the helm of the government's armies, Halleck would have to go around him to get what he wanted—overall command of the West. Fortunately for Halleck, disgust with McClellan in both Congress and the Lincoln administration was developing. On March 7 Stanton asked Halleck what areas he would desire in a new western department. The St. Louis commander wanted most of the region west of the Alleghenies. With this in mind, he exploded to McClellan three days later that the general in chief's friendship with certain individuals had influenced his judgment against a unified western command. Soon, despite McClellan's misguided loyalty, Halleck would "fight a great battle on the Tennessee unsupported."[67]

Halleck's ability to forecast the future was no accident, since he usually foretold what was obvious to an alert observer. The Confederates had lost a golden opportunity to concentrate against and defeat Union forces in the region piecemeal, and now there would have to be a great battle in the West on the Tennessee. Buell had been busy politically trying not to incite more aggression from pro-Confederates in Nashville or to alienate loyalists, while Johnson vowed to make treason odious. At the same time, Halleck won another decisive victory in the western command struggle in the form of Presidential War Order No. 3. Lincoln's disgust over McClellan's inactivity compelled him to think that Halleck might be able to do what Little Mac could not if given what he desired. This directive abolished the Department of the Ohio and placed Buell's forces along with Smith's under Halleck's command. In his first message to

Buell under the new letterhead "Hdqrs. Department of the Mississippi," Halleck attempted to assure his newest subordinate that the unified arrangement would not interfere with his command. Buell would still have to deal with Johnson and the situation in Nashville.[68]

What made Lincoln's War Orders No. 3 all the more striking was that it also relieved McClellan as general in chief of the armies, ordering him back to the field as the commander of the Army of the Potomac. To be sure, McClellan had invited the political pressures against him by failing to get the government's armies, especially his own, moving with the war. Halleck was as delighted as Buell was angered to know that McClellan was demoted in the same order that gave Halleck the combined western command. "I think Halleck is second to none of our Genls," confided Major Keifer to his wife. "I *think* I have changed my mind somewhat in reference to Genl. McClellan."[69] Obviously, attitudes were changing toward the progress of the war in the West. From the ranks to the administration, Halleck, or at least his subordinate Grant, demonstrated more vigor.

The Union high command appeared to overcome the organizational handicap of two independent departments by placing Halleck in command of the West. With McClellan out of the way, Halleck could not only deal directly with Stanton and Lincoln but also direct the war as he saw it. The role he would play in the next few months was pivotal, and as historian Stephen Ambrose put it, "one more victory in the West and he might be able to choose his position."[70] Still, Old Brains was his own worst enemy, and dealing with Stanton directly would strain their relations.

Halleck was full of confidence and boasted of many laurels. He had bright prospects for the future. "Of course I have been very, very busy," he confessed to his wife, "not only in carrying out these plans, but in forming new ones."[71] Nashville's capture and Halleck's assumption of command was a turning point in the war, concluded Major Keifer: "I predict the whole character of the war will be changed."[72]

Lincoln, however, remained cognizant of the political problems the West manifested with regard to the Republican Party. In consolidating the western command, there were compelling political ramifications that eclipsed the organizational command structure. Many of the leading generals in the Midwest were Democrats, whose party had stood for conservatism, tradition, and maintaining the status quo. This was manifested in many ways, the most significant of which for Lincoln was that

Democratic commanders in the West resisted new approaches to fighting the war, including the abolition of slavery. The limited-war attitude of generals such as Halleck and Buell harmonized with the Democratic vision of the war. These commanders led soldiers from the same region who shared the same attitudes. Moreover, Democrats were quite strong in Congress and quite influential in resisting the progression of Radical legislation. Thus, Lincoln would have to tread softly in attempting to expand the war in a region where civilians and soldiers would surely resist.[73]

When the spring rains and gloomy skies came early in Middle Tennessee, so too came the realization that the Confederates would need to react to all that had transpired in February. Confederate authorities were concerned that Kentuckians and Tennesseans sympathetic to the South would not be able to endure long in a region occupied by the Union armies. Albert Sidney Johnston needed to return his forces to the region and reassert Confederate control. As the demoralized Southern army, comprised of five brigades, was concentrating at Murfreesboro, a prosperous town of two thousand residents, Johnston thought of nothing else but redemption. The evacuations of Fort Donelson, Clarksville, Bowling Green, and Nashville disintegrated the Confederate western defense line.

At Murfreesboro, Johnston's army was reinforced by the arrival of Maj. Gen. George Bibb Crittenden's two brigades, which brought the strength of his army to seventeen thousand men. Johnston organized his command into three divisions under William J. Hardee, Crittenden, and Gideon Pillow. Brig. Gen. John C. Breckinridge commanded the reserve division, while Forrest's horsemen and John Wharton's Texas Rangers remained independent units. No doubt unenthused about the prospects of an offensive, Johnston apparently gave little care to creating an effective force, for the structure of his army showed little effort on his part and proved unmanageable. Moreover, the soldiers lacked tents, food, and adequate medical assistance to aid them in recovering from what had been a long and weary retreat south. Many of the soldiers who had been at Fort Donelson had come to resent their commander, agreeing with Col. St. John Liddell that "the conclusion is almost universal that [Johnston] is totally unfit for the position he holds in the Confederate army, and if he does nothing more to retrieve his character soon, he will be regarded as hopelessly embicile [sic]."[74]

Though the army's dissatisfaction with Johnston appeared most critical at the time, the fact was that the Confederate strategic position had rapidly deteriorated. The loss of Nashville, at a time when Southern papers had reported that Johnston would make a stand to save the city at all costs, stunned the infant nation. Many assumed that the staggering losses of the previous weeks alone would have been incentive enough to stand at Nashville. When Johnston departed the Tennessee capital, he initially planned to head to Stevenson, Alabama, while Beauregard acted independently in western Tennessee. At Murfreesboro, however, Johnston rethought his strategy given the limited options. Sensing that Halleck's next move would be in western and not Middle Tennessee, Johnston and Beauregard thought it only reasonable that they should unite their forces and concentrate on defending Memphis and the surrounding region. The commanding general had concluded that Decatur, Alabama, a hundred miles from Stevenson, would be the Federals' next destination. Thus, the Mississippi Valley became the focus for the Confederate defense in the West, though the exact location was yet to be determined.[75]

Thomas Connelly has credited Beauregard with convincing Johnston to move west instead of east and unite their forces at Corinth, Mississippi. In his defeated state, so Connelly argues, Johnston allowed Beauregard to assume conceptual superiority in designing the Confederacy's next move. In doing so, Beauregard was drawing the Southerners almost completely out of Tennessee and assuming the independence of judgment Johnston had allowed him. While Connelly paints Beauregard as formidable and conniving in this situation, historians Steven Woodworth and Larry Daniel have perceived an emaciated and weak man in the Creole. Perhaps more significant was that Jefferson Davis refused to assert his own authority in making decisions for either of them. Regardless, reinforcements were arriving to the army, as Brig. Gen. Mansfield Lovell, commander at New Orleans had wired Johnston that a brigade of reinforcements under Brig. Gen. Daniel Ruggles would travel to Corinth first, since it was the obvious rail connection, before moving on to join Johnston's gathering army, wherever it may be.[76]

Beauregard assumed command of Polk's troops on March 5, and though still suffering from throat trouble and colds stemming from recent surgery, he vowed to make the enemy "atone for the reverses we have lately experienced." Despite being only in command of the forces that had recently abandoned Columbus and fallen back slowly to Corinth, once the Creole found his place in the Confederate high command, he never relinquished his authority. Throughout the withdrawal from Kentucky, he had flooded Johnston with warnings that the Federals would pursue their advance farther up the Tennessee River. Although Buell had sent Mitchel's division toward Decatur, Alabama, to give the impression that his entire army would follow, Beauregard was not taking that bait. Also, thanks to President Davis, Maj. Gen. Braxton Bragg was sent from Pensacola with reinforcements, making it to Corinth on March 4. His arrival greatly relieved Beauregard, for he knew his responsibility would be shared by someone on whom he could rely. Though Bragg held a lower rank, Beauregard would have welcomed a role reversal—a sentiment that reflected the Creole's self-doubt regarding his new command.[77]

To stir public support for reinforcements being sent to the Mississippi, Beauregard composed a confidential circular to be sent to the governors of Louisiana, Mississippi, Tennessee, and Alabama to supply troops to strengthen the army in anticipation of striking north to Paducah. Though this violated his earlier agreement with Johnston about concentration of forces, it stirred the attention of the citizens and politicians of the region as well as Confederate authorities in Richmond. Shocked and dismayed by the domino-like collapse of vital heartland cities and river strongholds, Richmond responded with reinforcements. There was little response from the governors. Leroy Walker observed of this: "a general conviction has seized hold of the minds of the people of the valley of the Tennessee . . . that that entire section is to be abandoned to the enemy, and that apprehension is bearing its legitimate fruits in a general panic most unfavorable to the cause of enlistment. . . . I am convinced that stationing a respectable force among them would have a most salutary political effect in serving to restore public confidence and as a nucleus around which to gather volunteers."[78]

Fear of losing yet more of the heartland to the Union and not having sufficient forces to restore public confidence motivated the administration to do what Johnston had asked of it in January. Not only had Davis ordered Bragg north, but he also ordered newly commissioned Maj. Gen. Edmund Kirby Smith and his small command of East Tennesseans to cooperate with Johnston. Additionally, the president wired his western commander that he was hoping to supply some naval support.[79]

The attempt to concentrate Confederate forces at Corinth reflected the stirring of the high command, coming from the apparent loss Johnston had allowed to occur and the vigor with which Beauregard managed to operate. Discouraged by his numerous futile attempts to garner re-inforcements from the administration, Johnston simply decided not to renew the effort. He was aware of the demoralized state of his men, particularly his subordinates, who now looked to Beauregard to restore the Confederate hopes that Johnston had diminished. Although lacking the official authority to form the newly arriving troops into a large army, Beauregard and Bragg would soon take charge of them anyway and do, according to historian T. Harry Williams, "what Johnston should have done." The Texan still controlled the army, but Beauregard and Bragg were constructing it. Beauregard even characterized himself as the commander of the "Army of the Mississippi Valley."[80]

In assuming a more decided role in the Confederate high command in the West, it cannot be denied that Beauregard provided a stabilizing influence that was badly needed. He reconceptualized the western sector, creating a more precise departmental organization and coordination of effort. Johnston had allowed his subordinates too much independence, particularly in the areas of accumulation and distribution of supplies, and Beauregard established better means of facilitating the army's needs. His almost complete restructuring of Polk's command into the Army of the Mississippi Valley resulted in a more tightly organized left wing. The reconsolidation of the various independent forces would replace the formerly fragmented structure and more readily absorb the reinforcements sent by Davis. Finally, the army as a more fully unified command began to take shape at a critical time in the West. It gave evidence of being a force capable of defending the region from which it came.[81]

A reconfigured Confederate army, however, suffered from serious liabilities. Beauregard considered the defense of the heartland subordinate to that of the Mississippi Valley. Middle Tennessee already being in Union hands meant that northern Alabama and the vital Memphis and Charleston Railroad, the veritable spine of the western Confederacy's rail lines; Chattanooga; and all of East Tennessee were now vulnerable. Though the army was on the move, it did little to raise the soldiers' spirits after all that had been lost. Johnston's focus on Buell and Bowling Green had allowed Polk to exercise considerable independence, which resulted in the loss of the river forts. The inability to better coordinate his army's actions weakened the entire defensive line in the West. Still, Johnston was confident in the possibilities that a concentration of his forces might bring in the region, and he was heartened that the general condition of his troops was good and effective. "The General wears a very anxious face," wrote chief engineer Col. Jeremy Gilmer. "Still he expresses that better fortune awaits us."[82]

If Johnston had convinced himself that indeed better fortune awaited his army, the wounded pride and abused confidence of thousands of Southern soldiers, citizens, and politicians would need immediate restoration. Still, for so much loss, the army had ironically done so little fighting. If the retreat from Tennessee had blanketed the countryside with gloom, at least it had not destroyed his army's confidence in its fighting ability; in fact, it may have hardened it. The chance to reverse the losses and prove their mettle as warriors perhaps served as motivation to regroup and quickly retake the offensive. The Southerners would soon get that chance.

CHAPTER FIVE

Toward Pittsburg Landing

By mid-March, as Johnston and Beauregard debated the logistics of gathering their armies, Charles F. Smith was preparing for the upcoming Tennessee River expedition, an operation eagerly awaited by the troops who were "anxious to fight if we have a show," asserted one Illinoisan. Western commander Henry Halleck had given Smith the Army of the Tennessee, formerly led by Ulysses Grant, who had recently come under a cloud of Halleck's disapproval. When the change came, Grant was dutifully preparing to head up the Tennessee River, establish a base at some point, and wait for Halleck's next order. Now it was Smith who led the advance.[1] A snubbed Grant yielded his command and harbored no animosity toward his old teacher, since Smith was popular with the men. Still, he wrote to his wife that the change of command "may be all right but I don't see it."[2]

Grant reserved his anger for Halleck, whom Grant thought had unfairly chided him based on unfounded charges. It was obvious that Halleck was simply waiting for the opportunity to eliminate him from command. Rather than stifling unfounded rumors alleging that Grant had been relieved because of misconduct at Fort Donelson—referring to his absence on the battlefield at the moment of the Confederate attack—and of his drinking, Halleck used these as partial justification for his actions. But Grant benefited from maintaining his innocence because it simply endeared him to his soldiers all the more. Several officers, including Smith and John McClernand, came to his defense and denounced Halleck's treatment of the commander. Old "Unconditional Surrender" found he also had support in Washington. Both Lincoln and Stanton, impressed by Grant's vigor and recent victories, while generally annoyed by Halleck's dawdling in getting things done, bickering with Buell, and general pettiness in handling military affairs, came to Grant's aide. In the weeks to come, the president would press Halleck to produce facts of Grant's alleged misconduct and drinking to put an end to the harsh rebuke. In the meantime, the Army of the Tennessee set out on the offensive.[3]

Halleck compensated for the hard facts he lacked against Grant with ideas to win the war in the West, or at least to occupy strategic enemy locations. He realized that with or without Buell's assistance, the Confederates had given the Federals the "golden opportunity" Halleck had earlier predicted. The quick and decisive move south needed to attack Johnston's weakest point, however, could only be achieved, as earlier, by using the Tennessee River. Johnston's weakness was where the Memphis and Charleston Railroad and the Mobile and Ohio Railroad came together at the tiny northern Mississippi town of Corinth. Although Grant's, now Smith's, entire twenty-seven-thousand-man army would depart Fort Henry and move upriver toward Savannah, part of Halleck's plan included a cavalry raid near Corinth, perhaps to lure the Confederates to mass their forces nearby. Halleck thought that by waiting for the Confederates to concentrate, it would give him the necessary time to gather an overwhelming force of his own that could bring the enemy to its knees with one decisive battle. Thus, he warned Grant and Smith to avoid a general engagement no matter what the circumstances until Buell arrived with his Army of the Ohio.[4]

Typical of Halleck, his plan was well conceptualized, but its success weighed heavily on too many contingencies; once the campaign started, he began to get nervous. Although he had complete command of the West—and after the Union victory at Pea Ridge, Arkansas, he could concentrate on operations along the Tennessee and the Mississippi—Old Brains would have to rely on Buell to support the expeditionary force when the time was right. This implied that Buell would have to move when ordered. Furthermore, it placed Smith's army in a vulnerable position deep in Confederate territory until Buell arrived. Halleck, however, had thought far ahead and expected few difficulties. Once the campaign got underway, he wired Buell for assistance, claiming that Beauregard had fifty thousand troops along the Mississippi River. The Ohio commander, however, was preoccupied with attending to details in Nashville and pacifying Andrew Johnson. Buell was unconvinced that Halleck's estimation of troop strength was correct and that it warranted immediate support.

Though Halleck's attempt to pull his forces together continued, so too did the sparring with Buell.[5]

Instead of capitulating to Halleck, Grant had busied himself by scrounging for steamers and assembling the expeditionary force. By early March he had managed to collect twenty steamers capable of transporting fifteen thousand men for the advance. A week later, nearly thirty-one thousand infantry and nineteen hundred cavalry had assembled at Fort Henry, prepared to advance upriver on Halleck's campaign. William T. Sherman, Grant's close friend, commanded the expedition's vanguard, the newly organized Fifth Division, comprised mostly of green recruits.

By focusing his attention on strategy and preparation, Sherman had managed to avoid the Halleck-Grant and Halleck-Buell power struggles. In the process, he managed to turn his life around after some early emotional instability and enjoy some military success thanks to Grant. The spirited commander reasoned that the only way to reclaim what was once an esteemed military reputation was in combat, and now with his own unit, a volunteer division, he was anxious to prove himself on the battlefield. Sherman's eagerness worried not only his superior but also the new recruits, who saw in his fidgety temperament signs that justified his previous removal for alleged insanity. Already fast becoming one of Halleck's favorites, Sherman would embark on a campaign that would prove to be among his finest as a commander. On March 9, 1862, the Army of the Tennessee set out on perhaps the war's greatest Union campaign in the West. Aboard the steamers, anxiousness prevailed among the soldiers, since the daily rains forced the river out of its banks. Although it was an uneasy trip, the high water made for good navigation, and by March 12 most of the transports had docked at Savannah, Tennessee. Along the way, Sherman penned to his wife, "the People gathered on the Shore and manifested pleasure by the waving of handkerchiefs, clapping of hands &c., but I noticed that the young men took little part in their manifestations." He observed also that the "enthusiastic love of the Union of which you read in the newspapers is a form of expression easily written, but it is not true. The poor farmers certainly do want peace, & protection, but all the wealthier classes hate us Yankees with a pure unadultereated hate."[6]

Smith could not have picked a better place for the landing of his army. Savannah was the county seat of Hardin County and home to some eight hundred residents, mostly Unionists. It was an unassuming place in the middle of what some soldiers considered a pale countryside, hardly worth writing home about. "It is a quiet, sober looking old town," observed W. H. L. Wallace, "with a single street, a square brick house, a number of buildings scattered along the street, with some pretty and rather stylish residences in the suburbs." One of those residences belonged to staunch Unionist William H. Cherry, who besides owning much of the county also owned slaves. Cherry lived in a white brick mansion atop the bluff overlooking the river. Not surprisingly, the river itself was the barrier between Union and Confederate loyalties, for the residents east of the river, tied to small farms of corn and other agricultural staples, remained loyal to the Union. Cherry would offer his home for use as Union headquarters, while the army prepared to camp.[7]

Smith knew that Sherman's cavalry raid on the railroad would need support, and on the evening of March 12 he visited Maj. Gen. Lew Wallace and told him to take his Third Division to Crump's Landing four miles up and across the river. Wallace was a noted Indiana politician and political appointee who had performed admirably at Fort Donelson, which had earned him promotion to major general. Smith alerted him that Maj. Gen. Frank Cheatham's Confederate division was supposedly at Pittsburg Landing nine miles upstream on the west bank. Afterward, Smith made his way back to his transport, but while stepping into the skiff he slipped and severely injured his leg. Though initially forcing him to simply hobble about, in the weeks to come an ultimately fatal infection would set in, and his condition steadily deteriorated.[8]

Wallace's division made its way across the river in the driving rain in the early-morning hours of March 13. The Hoosier commander dispatched Maj. Charles S. Haynes's battalion of the Fifth Ohio Cavalry to cut the railroad between Bethel Station and Brown's Station. By midmorning the Ohio cavalry had succeeded in breaking the bridge over Beach Creek, and before midnight the horsemen had made it back to the landing. The entire division returned to the transports and steamed back to Savannah. Though Wallace's men had fulfilled part of Halleck's plan, its significance lasted but a day, for the Confederates were able to repair the bridge the following evening.[9]

While the Confederates were working on the damaged bridge, Smith ordered Sherman's division to the northern Mississippi hamlet of Eastport to break the Memphis and Charleston Railroad. By sunset on March 14, Sherman's troops, aboard nineteen transports, had steamed past Pittsburg Landing and docked at Tyler's Landing, Mississippi, at the mouth of Yellow Creek. Later that night the four hundred horsemen of

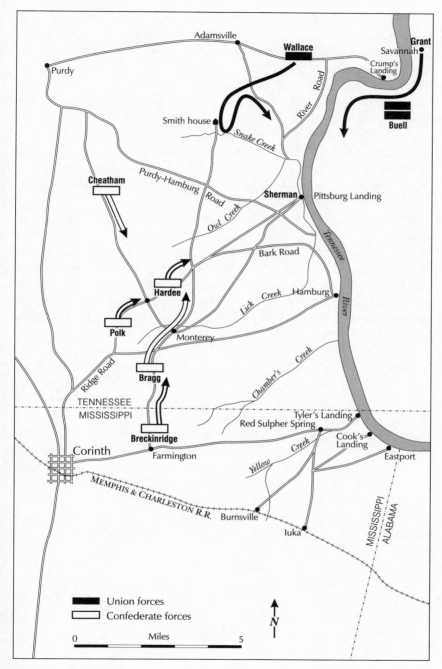

The Shiloh campaign

Maj. Elbridge G. Ricker's Fifth Ohio Cavalry set out for the twenty-mile excursion toward Eastport and the railroad bridge. The area crawled with Confederate sympathizers, and while the rain poured, Sherman waited anxiously for the quick return of Ricker's men. To support the cavalry in case it was ambushed, the general marched his infantry out around 5 A.M. on the morning of the fifteenth, but a few miles into the movement they came upon an impassable bayou that stalled the advance. What made matters worse was that Ricker called off the raid due to the inhospitable conditions of flooded creeks and the continuous rain. The Ohio horsemen returned to the transports later that morning. Disappointed but determined to gain something for his energies, Sherman directed the steamers to dock at the first available location.

Sherman reported on March 15, "I await the general's further orders at Pittsburg Landing." There, awaiting him aboard transports was Stephen A. Hurlbut's Fourth Division. Smith replied that Sherman's division should go ashore and that he and Hurlbut should encamp their divisions far enough inland to make room for the rest of the Army of the Tennessee. As Illinoisan Thaddeus Capron settled into camp in a planter's peach orchard, he could hardly believe he was in Tennessee. "Little did I think one year ago," he wrote, "that instead of singing, 'I Wish I Was in the Land of Cotton,' that I should be here, but so it is." He reasoned that it was "beginning to look as though there was something to be done."[10]

The stir of Union activity alarmed Beauregard. The Creole knew that over a hundred Union transports had steamed upriver from Fort Henry, but he was unsure as to their destination. Confederate intelligence also reported on Sherman's landing at Yellow Creek, but the following day, it was reported that thirty thousand Federals had gone ashore at Crump's Landing. The fact that a sizeable Union force had arrived on the west side of the river convinced a befuddled Beauregard that the entire army would surely follow and most assuredly attack. Thus, he decided to arrange his forces to receive the anticipated assault. Beauregard sent for Bragg, who had already determined to go to Bethel Station on the Mobile and Ohio Railroad some twenty miles north of Corinth and about an equal distance from Pittsburg Landing, to hurry. The general also ordered Leonidas Polk's and Jones Withers's divisions to follow. From what information he had, Bragg determined to unite Polk's command, moving south from Humboldt, Tennessee, toward Bethel Station, with Daniel Ruggles's division, moving north from Corinth, and drive the

Federals into the river. This concentration of forces, however, proved too slow. Consequently, Bragg and Beauregard both began to rethink their strategy as they traveled to Corinth to await Johnston.[11]

The spring rains played havoc with the gathering of Confederate forces. Though it had been a delayed and difficult march from Murfreesboro, Johnston's army arrived at Decatur, Alabama, on March 10. From there to Corinth, the march deteriorated as his men became stretched out along the Memphis and Charleston Railroad for some ninety miles, though the Texan was less concerned than Beauregard over the need for haste. Still, he was cautious and recognized his army's vulnerability, particularly since there were strong indications that Buell was advancing south and southwest. Though the Confederates would be bogged down at the Duck River, if Buell moved swiftly overland, he could threaten Johnston by arriving at Florence, Alabama, and securing the bridge there as a crossing. Convinced that such a dash could be made, Johnston ordered the bridge destroyed if Buell approached. Still, nearly a month would pass from the time Johnston decided to move until he reached Corinth.[12]

The inhospitable weather that hampered road travel was not the only deterrent to Johnston's juncture with Beauregard. The Confederate stalwart continued to be blinded by Buell's potential advance, which delayed his departure from Decatur. Though Beauregard had wired him of an imminent battle near Iuka, Mississippi—referring to Sherman's raid—Johnston either refused or failed to make use of the interior lines available to them. The high command failed to make arrangements to utilize the railroads effectively, and consequently, when they needed to transport large numbers of troops quickly, the Confederates lacked the necessary rolling stock. What cars they had available had been used to transport Bragg's and Ruggles's troops from the Gulf Coast and Polk's men from Humboldt. The prospects for a quick junction with Beauregard, which had seemed relatively easy to make on paper, were plagued by poor planning.

In the meantime, Davis broke his month-long silence about the Donelson fiasco and wrote to General Johnston. "We have suffered great anxiety because of recent events in Ky & Tenn," he confided, "and I have been not a little disturbed by the repetitions of reflections upon yourself. You have been held responsible for the fall of Donelson and the capture of Nashville, [and] a full development of the truth is necessary for future success." The Confederate president closed by supposing that the "Tenn.

or Miss. rivers will be the object of the enemy's next campaign, and I trust you will be able to concentrate a force which will defeat either attempt." Johnston was hoping for just such a conclusion.[13]

By the third week of March, Johnston's army dotted the northern Mississippi and Alabama countryside from Corinth to Decatur. But what had seemed a glacier-like movement ended when two of Hardee's brigades, Sterling A. M. Wood's and Thomas C. Hindman's, arrived at Corinth by the twentieth. William Statham's brigade arrived at Iuka, while John S. Bowen's brigade halted at Courtland, Alabama, and Patrick Cleburne's and William H. Carroll's brigades were at Tuscumbia. John Breckinridge brought up the rear at Decatur. The cavalry continued to scout on the north side of the river and collect supplies. The arrival of the army's vanguard at Corinth greatly relieved Johnston. Bragg, however, was hardly impressed, for he found "disorder and confusion" in Corinth, particularly with Beauregard's troops. Weeks of preparation would be needed, Bragg thought, before the army could launch an offensive of any effectiveness. He wired Beauregard the reasons for his change in attitude regarding an offensive. "The troops," he concluded, "arrived too slowly, were poorly supplied, and too badly organized, instructed, and disciplined, to justify a hope of even carrying them to the point desired, much less a success against a well-organized foe."[14]

Corinth was calm when Johnston rode in on the night of March 22 and made his headquarters in the home of William M. Inge, a local attorney. The following morning, he called a meeting of Beauregard, Hardee, Bragg, and Polk to discuss the newly combined army's next move. Upon greeting Bragg and Beauregard, Johnston extended gracious appreciation for their efforts in concentrating forces at Corinth. Almost embracing Bragg, Johnston remarked: "Your prompt and decisive move, Sir, has saved me, and saved the country. But for your arrival, the enemy would have been between us." A discussion of strategy followed, and although striking at Smith before Buell could arrive and moving the army in a better position to do so appeared the most logical of all decisions, Johnston and Beauregard could not agree on what their next move would be. Neither commander was completely certain of the enemy's position and strength, nor could they be certain that Buell intended a junction of Union forces. After all, Buell had already started a column for northern Alabama, and the bulk of his army continued to be stalled at Columbia, Tennessee. From the crossroads at Columbia, no one could be sure which route, east or south, Buell would take.[15]

During the next few days, the Confederate army continued to trickle into Corinth from all directions, though its ranks had thinned considerably during the past two months. Johnston's entire force, pathetically undermanned though it was, had numbered roughly 55,000 men, but at Corinth he had less than 40,000 effectives. Polk's corps, which had 14,000 effectives at Columbus, could report only 9,000 now, and Hardee's old Army of Central Kentucky could report only 13,000 of the once 24,500 men present for duty. To ensure that the concentration could be made uninhibited by enemy resistance or scouts, Beauregard fanned out small forces around the area to keep watch. Bethel Station, to the north of Corinth and west of Pittsburg Landing, was of particular significance. To guard that station, he sent Frank Cheatham's division, and Beauregard dispatched scouting parties toward Pittsburg Landing around Monterey and Lick Creek. Still, spring rains complicated the Confederates' ability to obtain reliable information.[16]

In March 1862, Corinth, Mississippi, was more than the crossroads of the Southern heartland, it had become the literal crossroads on the vertebrae of the western Confederacy. Before the war it was an indistinguishable hamlet made important only because it was a railroad nexus. Though it had few businesses or shops, its modest character belied its newfound strategic importance. The gathering of the western Confederate army there signaled in many ways what soldiers had come to believe would be the great and epic battle to end the war. It would be the chance for those soldiers whom the Federals had forced into submission and retreat to redeem themselves and their honor. The Confederate army in the West was truly a force of diverse regional and cultural origins from across the western Confederacy. Kentuckians, Tennesseans, Alabamians, Arkansans, Mississippians, and those from the Gulf Coast gathered to form a new community of citizen-soldiers. The accumulation of battle flags, uniforms, and equipment reflected the diversity of the states from which the soldiers came and the experience of war they had already endured. Volunteers and veterans alike marched into Corinth carrying flintlocks, muskets, shotguns, and some unidentifiable weapons that had never been fired. Indeed, it was a grand spectacle, though revealing the army's insufficiency of supplies.[17]

Certainly Johnston had never witnessed such a sight as that taking shape at Corinth. The great advantage he thought in massing his army also proved a great difficulty. The soldiers' morale and enthusiasm had diminished after the losses of Henry, Donelson, Columbus, and Nashville.

The long and torturous march across northern Alabama simply added to the army's fatigue and frustration. The rate of stragglers and desertions increased, and the undisciplined and disorganized mob resembled anything but an army about to embark on an offensive campaign. Worse, the very sight of the retreating soldiers had demoralized the residents in their path, and the barren countryside of abandoned homes, depleted winter harvests, and a pillaged landscape left a sobering impression on the men as they marched. "The advent of an army is . . . to be dreaded by any people," wrote one Tennessean, "for wholesale destruction is sure to follow in its wake. The mere passing of an army renders a country almost worthless for at least one or two years."[18]

Several officers shared in feeling deflated by the early setbacks in the West. Bragg was quick to lay the blame on Beauregard for poor discipline and plundering, but Bragg had spent the last weeks in March hastily equipping and bringing the army together to fight. The fact that he was forced to arrest Maj. Gen. George B. Crittenden and one of his brigadiers, William H. Carroll, for drunkenness and incompetence solidified his view of Beauregard's command. Bragg also considered Johnston and Polk lax in disciplining their soldiers. To say the least, there were grave problems in the Confederate high command.[19]

Perhaps the mere sight of the men at Corinth confirmed for Johnston that he had lost confidence in the army, and perhaps even himself. A few days after arriving at Corinth, Johnston surprised Beauregard by offering him command of the army for the coming offensive, but the Creole graciously declined the offer. The reason for giving command to Beauregard has attracted significant speculation. It was obvious that Johnston believed that the soldiers and the Southern populace had lost confidence in his leadership. The Confederate army, he thought, would be better served with Beauregard at the helm. But Johnston continued to enjoy support and high praise from friends who urged him not to give up. Even President Davis, whose recent letter had demanded some explanations, and his new military advisor, Gen. Robert E. Lee, encouraged General Johnston by expressing confidence in his judgment for the planned offensive. Pleading with him not to turn over command, Confederate governor of Kentucky George W. Johnson concluded that the Confederate cause would otherwise "sink under the curse of Heaven."[20]

Offering supreme command to Beauregard and having it refused was a clear, though embarrassing, sign that Johnston was not confident in his chances; perhaps he just finally realized he had a military theater to command rather than a field army. For that matter, Beauregard may not have been all that enthused about leading the army either. Still, he agreed to be named second in command, to design a plan for the army's organization, and to supervise the task; Bragg was named chief of staff. For Beauregard, it was an opportunity to take charge of the army without being in sole command. Recognizing that regardless of the arrangement he decided upon the conglomeration now known as the Army of the Mississippi would still be significantly outnumbered by a combined Union army under Smith and Buell, Beauregard structured the army to give it the appearance of a larger force. This took the form of creating corps, which typically number about 20,000 soldiers, though none of those planned would come close to that number. Polk commanded the First Corps, totaling roughly 9,000 men. Bragg was assigned the Second Corps with 13,500 men, or about one-third of the army. Hardee took charge of the Third Corps with 6,700 men, and the Reserve Corps of approximately 6,400 men came under the command of Breckinridge, who, although having no military training and little combat experience, proved more suitable than the drunkard Crittenden.[21]

Though Beauregard was confident that the gathering of forces at Corinth would be completed as expected, Johnston, at the urging of Beauregard and Bragg, requested that Earl Van Dorn's trans-Mississippi army at Van Buren, Arkansas, be ordered to Memphis. A Mississippian, Van Dorn had intended to march east toward the Mississippi River and unite his forces with those already assembled at Pocahontas, Arkansas. From there he could head toward New Madrid or Cape Girardeau, Missouri, and attack the Federals, perhaps striking farther north toward St. Louis. Whatever he decided, Van Dorn thought, Halleck would be compelled to shift troops from across the Mississippi River to meet his advance, which would hopefully relieve some of the pressure on Beauregard and Johnston. In mid-March, Beauregard thought it wise to have Van Dorn join his army at Corinth, and he pressed Johnston, who finally ordered Van Dorn to advance east of the Mississippi River. Unfortunately, the two-hundred-mile distance would prove too far and troublesome for a speedy concentration; Van Dorn did not even receive the order until March 27. The whole idea to use these troops seemed based on their ability to cover a terrain more than twice the distance Johnston had traversed since leaving Decatur under the same conditions. President Davis was willing to allow this transfer of troops because the war west of the Mississippi River was simply not as important to him as other regions.[22]

Sherman's operations unnerved Johnston. From Pittsburg Landing, the aggressive commander had decided he would send a courier back to Savannah and convince Smith that the site would provide the most suitable point for the concentration of Smith's and Buell's armies, particularly since he learned that the Confederates considered Corinth the location of the next great battle. In the meantime, his division waited for permission to make a feint toward Corinth while a detachment of cavalry attempted another raid on the Memphis and Charleston Railroad in the vicinity of Farmington, Mississippi. Sherman received approval on March 16. After returning to the landing and making a personal reconnaissance of the Bethel Station area, the commander concluded that Pittsburg Landing was secure.[23]

That evening, Sherman sent the cavalry toward Monterey and Farmington, while his soldiers made their way ashore, a task that took all night. The scouting patrol alerted the Confederates to the possibility that the Federals were out to do more than simple scouting. Early on the morning of March 17, Sherman ordered his infantry forward in the swampy terrain from the landing to protect the cavalry, which was making its way out for another attempt on Burnsville to sever the railroad. Meanwhile, he moved his division two and one-half miles southwest of the landing to a crossroads near a small Methodist church made of logs, "where but lately gaunt clergymen had called upon half-literate farmers to defend the South and slavery as God's special creations." The church was positioned about equal distance in a three-mile expanse from Snake Creek to the north and Lick Creek to the south. Surrounded by a terrain of dense woods with thick undergrowth, small ridges, and ravines, the church's undistinguished features blended naturally with its surroundings. Its name was Shiloh, roughly translated from Hebrew as "place of peace," and it stood like a pillar of tranquility as Sherman's men pitched their tents nearby. DeWitt Clinton Loudon, colonel of the Seventieth Ohio, encamped his men next to the meetinghouse, what he characterized as a "hard looking structure."[24] Hurlbut's division came ashore but remained close to the landing.[25]

While Sherman was making his reconnaissance of the terrain, Halleck restored Grant to command of the army. Interestingly enough, though Grant had busied himself preparing for the campaign, the atmosphere of controversy forced him to request to be relieved of command until he could be "placed right in the estimation of those in higher authority." Apparently, Lincoln and Stanton by now had set things right since Halleck, unable to produce any damning evidence warranting dismissal, refused to accept his resignation. "Instead of relieving you," wrote a chagrined Halleck on March 15, "I wish you, as soon as your new army is in the field, to assume the immediate command & lead it on to new victories. The power is in your hands, use it, & you will be sustained by all above you."[26]

The problem for Grant, however, was that a portion of his army was in the field on the west bank of a swollen Tennessee River. Nevertheless, on March 17, Grant arrived at Savannah with his aide Capt. John A. Rawlins for an inspection, making his headquarters in the same mansion as Smith, who by this time was still hobbling about. That evening he penned Sherman a short note to say that he had arrived and had begun "to feel better at the thought of again being along with the troops."[27]

Grant found the army at Savannah totally in want of discipline and, more importantly, learned that three divisions were actually on the west side of the Tennessee. He concluded that a "better state of discipline than has been maintained heretofore with much of this command, is demanded, and will be enforced."[28] It would be hard to imagine that Grant's characterization of the army pleased Smith.

All that remained for Grant to do was to unite his army. Based on Sherman's report that indicated the terrain at Pittsburg Landing was sufficient to camp all of his divisions and that the enemy at Corinth was no larger than twenty thousand men, the commanding general decided to concentrate the Army of the Tennessee there and move on Corinth quickly. Moreover, Sherman assured him that his own division, encamped in the clearings around the Methodist meetinghouse, was ready for an attack. Still, on March 19, Grant went to the landing to see Sherman's position for himself. Contrary to his friend's observations, Grant was encouraged by the "strong manifestation of Union feeling in this section," which was supported by reports from Phelps and the fact that "some 500 have come in voluntarily and enlisted to prevent being drafted on the other side."[29]

To justify his crossing the river, Grant dispatched Capt. William S. Hillyer to Halleck's headquarters to secure authority to strike at the railroad before the Confederates concentrated. Halleck had previously consented to such a move, but as usual, Grant's swiftness and confidence caught him off guard. The army was moving too quickly for the department commander's liking, and a telegram from the ever-cautious Halleck caught up with Grant on the eighteenth stating that he was to wait for

Buell's army en route from Bowling Green and not allow himself to be drawn into a general engagement. This "must be strictly obeyed," declared Halleck. After all, Grant already had stolen the war in the West from him, not to mention significantly more fame, once. Halleck now was the supreme commander in the West, and he would not want his subordinate to eclipse him once again. When the time came and the armies were joined, perhaps Halleck would go the front himself.[30]

Grant managed to function successfully despite the poor command relationship he had with Halleck; Buell too managed to avoid such suffering, even though Halleck was his superior as well. Though Halleck promised him latitude in commanding the Army of the Ohio, the first sign or fear of a Confederate concentration caused Halleck to use the army as he saw fit. From Nashville, Buell had considered striking the Memphis and Charleston Railroad in northern Alabama and had dispatched Ormsby Mitchel's eight-thousand-man division toward Murfreesboro and then south to Fayetteville. Halleck's new mission for Buell was to march to Savannah, 120 miles distant from Nashville, to avoid allowing the enemy to get between the two Union armies. On March 17 he wired Buell to start west immediately, and in case Buell thought otherwise, Halleck punctuated his orders by remarking: "Don't fail to carry out my instructions. I know I am right."[31]

Fortunately for Halleck, Buell was prepared to march when the message arrived. He had spent his time in Nashville preparing for such a move, though the destination had now changed. Mitchel would be used to cover Buell's flank. To quell the possibility of a Confederate attack from the east and pacify East Tennessee politicians, Buell dispatched Brig. Gen. George Morgan's division to Cumberland Gap. He left a sizeable garrison at Nashville under the command of James S. Negley. The rest of the army, thirty-seven thousand strong, marched out of Nashville on March 16–17 along the Central Alabama Railroad toward Columbia on the south bank of the Duck River forty-two miles distant. The countryside in this region exhibited the scorched-earth policy implemented by the retreated Confederates. To be sure, Buell's soldiers encountered an increasingly hostile reception with every mile they traveled.[32]

Although Buell sent the First Ohio Cavalry forward to secure the Rutherford Creek Bridge and the two Duck River bridges, when the troopers arrived in the early morning hours of March 16, they found the Duck River bridges in flames and the river running out of its banks. Buell wired Halleck that his march would be delayed five days until the bridge could be repaired or pontoons brought forward and used to cross the river.[33]

The Army of the Ohio arrived at the Duck on March 26 only to find that the work involved far more effort than Buell anticipated and had earlier projected to Halleck. He wired his superior the unfortunate news that the bridge construction would require some additional days, hoping that it would be completed by March 31. What made the work all the more crucial was that Buell either ignored, did not himself receive, or simply gave little credence to, a note delivered to him on his way to the Duck River. Grant had sent this message on March 19, received March 23, that his army was gathering at Pittsburg Landing. Thomas J. Bush, a staff officer recalled after the war that Buell was surprised to learn that Grant had concentrated his army on the west side of the Tennessee.[34]

When Buell actually received Grant's message is not as significant as what he did with the information once it arrived. At least he did not deny the ungovernable Brig. Gen. William "Bull" Nelson the chance to move across the bridgeless river and head to Savannah as quickly as possible. As he had in getting to Nashville, Nelson now wanted to have a hand in this looming crisis. On the evening of March 29, Nelson came upon one of his brigade commanders, Col. Jacob Ammen, and told him that the division would be crossing the river the next morning. When the baffled colonel inquired if the bridge had been completed, Nelson replied that it had not. "Are there any boats?" Ammen asked. "No," Nelson answered, "but the river is falling, and damn you, get over, for we must have the advance and get the glory." The river was two hundred yards wide with a swift current. As dawn broke the next morning, Nelson's men stripped to their drawers and waded into the frigid waist-deep water. By sunset, the entire division had crossed, and the following day Crittenden's division forded as well. After a ten-day delay, the army was moving again, inspired by the Kentuckian's example. Just as he wanted, Nelson, who obviously had the "go" in him that Buell lacked, was a half-day's march ahead.[35]

As the rest of the Army of the Ohio regrouped for the march along an eighty-mile country pike toward Waynesboro and Savannah, Crittenden's division led the way followed by the divisions of Alexander McCook and Thomas Wood along with an enormous wagon train several miles long. George H. Thomas's division, some forty miles back, brought up the rear. To make up for the lost time, Buell set a pace of twelve to fifteen miles per day. Still, the delay at the Duck River actually worked slightly to his favor, since the roads at Columbia fanned out in three directions—

south to Decatur, southwest to Florence, and west to Savannah. The longer Buell delayed, the more uncertain the Confederates were about his destination.[36]

During the weeks of late March and early April, Pittsburg Landing, like Corinth, underwent a metamorphosis, as a sea of tents littered the ninety-square-mile area between Snake Creek and Lick Creek. What had been just weeks before an indistinguishable little landing had become the central gathering point for Grant's Federals. By March 31 he submitted a report that gave his present-for-duty strength at 34,500 men exclusive of Lew Wallace's division. During the first week in April, additional units arrived, ballooning the army strength to roughly 45,000. In addition, Grant had twenty-one batteries with 102 guns and three cavalry regiments dispersed among the divisions.[37]

While the concentration had its advantages, it also presented some debilitating problems. Not only did it lead to the accumulation of sickness, but it also revealed the deteriorating health of Charles F. Smith, Grant's most experienced division commander. Smith's obvious absence for the expected fight forced Grant to appoint recently promoted Brig. Gen. William H. L. Wallace, a former Illinois attorney, in his place. More than sickness plagued the Army of the Tennessee, though. The army lacked professional officers, which was revealed in the poor discipline of some of the troops. Perhaps the worst example was Stephen Hurlbut, commander of the Fourth Division, who not only lacked military experience but also a strong deterrent to drink. The concentration of forces also brought together commanders who possessed little except a dislike for one another. The relationship between Grant and McClernand, recently promoted to major general for his performance at Fort Donelson, had deteriorated into a bitter jealously on the part of McClernand. He was still stewing over the fact that Grant had not sufficiently recognized him or his troops for the Donelson victory. Another Illinois lawyer turned commander was Brig. Gen. Benjamin Prentiss, who led the Sixth Division and was not particularly fond of Grant either. Sherman was the only professional commander and was loyal to Grant.[38]

The Union soldiers converging at Pittsburg Landing were mostly from rural areas, but a significant portion of them did come from cities. A few ethnic regiments, comprised mainly of Germans, were spread through the divisions too. Though the men generally lacked the soldierly discipline that Grant expected, they compensated for this by possessing superior initiative and self-reliance. Lincoln recognized this resolve earlier in February after the fall of Fort Donelson. Upon signing Grant's promotion to major general, the president commented to Stanton that "[i]f the southerners think that man for man they are better than our Illinois men or Western men generally they will discover themselves in a grievous mistake."[39]

Most soldiers had never traveled beyond their own state, and this was the first time they had been so far south. "Many of us for the first time behold a cotton field," wrote Ohioan George Botkin to a friend, "and we begin to realize truly that we are in the 'land of cotton.'" They were pleased with the change of climate in Tennessee and northern Mississippi, though the weather continued to be unpredictable and fluctuated between mild temperatures and cold, snowy weather. As the Federals marched deeper into the Confederate heartland, however, they came to see up close what the war had done to Southern citizens. While the cotton plantations were impressive and the countryside around them "splendid," as Cpl. Alexander Varian of the First Ohio in Buell's army remarked, the farther south the army marched, the more disillusioned the soldiers became. The dark realities of war had made tremendous impressions upon the Northerners, many of whom traversing the bleak countryside by land or water concluded that slavery was the chief cause of the poverty that was so apparent. They saw large magnificent plantations reflecting the life of the genteel master contrasting with the unflattering poverty of the small farmer. Northerners were appalled by the underdevelopment and destitution of western Kentucky and Tennessee. "I must tell you something about this country," Pvt. John Sharp of the Second Iowa wrote to his wife, Maria. "I was disappointed in it. From the mouth of the Tennasee it is low along the river and the river being high it was overflowed for miles back and the inhabitants gone. Where they were not they cheered us and made great profession of union." Sharp went on to say that although the peach trees were in full bloom and the weather was warm and pleasant, "the country here is entirely laid waste and there will be little or nothing raised this season. There is no preparation for cotton and things look hard for the people here. The country seems to be ruined for years for any kind of business and the people are discouraged."[40]

Much of this led to a hardening of attitudes toward Southerners. W. H. L. Wallace spoke for many when he surmised that the Union needed to thoroughly whip the Confederates "before they will have respect for us."[41] Some considered that the "peculiar institution" was the chief cause of both the region's underdevelopment and the war. A Wisconsin soldier wrote that from the looks of things, "I should judge that the people of the western part of Tennessee are 175 years behind the people of Jackson County in agriculture."[42]

Still, it was spring in Tennessee and northern Mississippi, and the soldiers spent their time drilling and preparing for the inevitable, many hoping to "see the elephant" soon. Confident though many of them naturally were, the anticipated battle at Corinth was to be the grand battle to end the war. Indeed, many assumed like Col. Cassicus Fairchild of Wisconsin that "the Waterloo of the war will be fought between this place and the [Mississippi] river in the course of two weeks."[43]

The Federal concentration at Pittsburg Landing was sure to be discovered, but Albert Sidney Johnston needed to know the exact deployment of the units and camps, not to mention if Buell was expected to arrive and if so, when. Rather than giving his attention to preparing his own soldiers, Johnston simply secured local reputable citizens to be used to guide his columns along the confusing road network toward Pittsburg Landing and into their attack positions. He also attempted to raise an additional brigade of troops by turning the army's teamsters, cooks, and support personnel into soldiers, replacing them with local slaves. If the planters in Mississippi had given up their bells for cannon, they might be persuaded to give up some slaves as well; however, they refused to part with their human property. Perhaps the fact that, on March 6, the Confederate Congress passed an act making it military policy to destroy all cotton and tobacco and other property that could be useful to the enemy convinced planters to keep the slaves to help fend off enforcers of such legislation. A perplexed and frustrated Johnston concluded to a friend, "these people do not seem to be aware of how valueless would be their negroes were we beaten."[44]

Instead of accepting an offer from some locals to raise an independent guerrilla company to destroy Union communications, Johnston compensated for his lack of reliable information by dispatching Col. Randal Lee Gibson to Monterey to monitor Federal movements in the region. Kentucky-born and Yale educated, Gibson had a distinguished prewar career as a lawyer and a diplomat in Madrid. He had been raised in his family's home state, Louisiana, and during the secession crisis became an aide to the governor. Gibson's brigade arrived on April 1. To bolster his information-gathering force, Johnston gave readiness orders to the First and Third Corps. Later in the day on April 1, Confederates ascertained that some Federals had docked at Eastport and Chickasaw, attempting to undertake an expedition before high water convinced them to abandon it. Nonetheless, Breckinridge hastened several hundred infantry by railroad from Burnsville to Iuka.[45]

More alarming than the fact that the Federals had attempted to go ashore south of Pittsburg Landing was the news in Confederate head-quarters that Buell had crossed the Duck River and was heading swiftly to Savannah. At the same time, north of Pittsburg Landing, Beauregard ordered Maj. Gen. Benjamin Franklin Cheatham, in command of a division posted at Bethel Station on the Mobile and Ohio Railroad, to secretly reconnoiter the area around Purdy, a small hamlet west of Adamsville and Crump's Landing in the direction of the Tennessee River. The activities of Tennessee cavalrymen near Adamsville alerted the Federals that the Confederates were in the area. Knowledge of the incident compelled Lew Wallace to move the rest of his division to Adamsville. Thus, on the morning of April 1, Confederate wires transmitted the news that an entire Union division threatened to unite in the vicinity. Beauregard learned of Wallace's move to Adamsville and of the approach of Buell late on the night of April 2. Though several possibilities could be inferred from the situation, the news alarmed him into concluding that the Federals had divided their force for an advance on Memphis. The time had come, he thought, to strike the enemy at Pittsburg Landing.[46]

Late that same night, Beauregard sent a message to Johnston about these reports. "Now is the moment to advance, and strike the enemy at Pittsburg Landing," he scribbled on the telegram before giving it to Thomas Jordan to take to Johnston. So startled by the message was Johnston, recalled Jordan, that he darted to the Curlee house down the street and awoke Bragg to get his opinion. Bragg agreed with Beauregard, but according to Jordan, Johnston feared his army was not ready to assume the offensive. Despite the considerable inconsistencies in recounting what actually transpired, Johnston was prepared to assume the offensive, and he instructed Jordan to compose orders to Polk, Hardee, and Bragg to be ready to move at 6 A.M. on April 3. Throughout the night the buzzword was the preparation to move. At dawn Beauregard, Johnston, and the corps commanders conferred over operational plans. Afterward, Jordan penned battle orders from Beauregard in the form of Special Order No. 8, which emulated the model of Napoleon's battle plan for Waterloo (appropriate for a battle that would become characterized by many soldiers as an "American Waterloo").[47]

Beauregard's design for marching was an elaborate set of maneuvers too complicated for ill-trained soldiers unfamiliar with the terrain to execute properly. Despite the short distance from Corinth to Pittsburg Landing, roughly twenty miles, he failed to consider the difficulty of the country in between. Moving across the state line into Tennessee, soldiers discovered a terrain of thick woods traversed by creeks, ravines, swamps, and narrow dirt roads recently turned to muddy streams by spring rains. Even with the most cooperative weather, the road system was baffling enough to frustrate the most seasoned scout. Moreover, Beauregard sent more than half of the army by the longest designated route. Nonetheless, the general ordered Hardee's corps to advance on the Ridge Road, which ran north and then turned northeast toward Pittsburg Landing, until he approached the Federals, when he would deploy for battle. Polk, who had placed Cheatham's division at Bethel Station, would depart Corinth with the remainder of his corps shortly after Hardee and head out along the same pike. Bragg's corps would assemble at Monterey and advance in two columns on the Purdy and Savannah Roads, converging at the intersection of the Ridge Road at a place called Michie's (Mickey's), James Michie's farmhouse, some eight miles from Pittsburg Landing. Breckinridge's Reserve Corps would depart from Burnsville and march to Monterey and then to Michie's. As the troops advanced toward Pittsburg Landing, they all marched almost simultaneously, fanning a three-mile line.[48]

Certainly time was of the essence—at least the battle plan made it appear so—but Beauregard's plan would prove impossible to effect. Whether Johnston agreed with the formation and orders is insignificant compared to the fact that he allowed Beauregard to make such elaborate preparations. Besides, he had almost two weeks with which to put into motion a better plan if he had conceived of one.[49]

Thursday, April 3, dawned clear, but Corinth was a picture of chaos, bustling with the sounds and sights of combat preparation. The army remained in ranks well after the designated time of 6 A.M.; administrative disarray (to put it mildly), a lack of appreciation for the density of the terrain, and insufficient guides all combined to delay the march until late afternoon. Special Orders No. 8 assumed that every commander would receive instructions with time to spare to ready their men. It was not until 3 P.M. that Hardee's corps finally marched out of Corinth. An hour and a half later Bragg's corps filed out on the Monterey Road. Johnston waited in Corinth until the next morning to depart for Monterey, where he arrived sometime after midday.[50]

By the night of April 4, the Confederate Army of the Mississippi, containing many new troops, had reentered the state of Tennessee approximately where Beauregard intended them to be. It had not been an easy march. After midnight, the weather turned inhospitable and torrential rains fell upon the tattered and struggling soldiers, severely handicapping the movements of the army. Artillery constantly sank in what seemed like bottomless muddy roads, and the men were fatigued from the extra effort of marching in the muck. Given these circumstances, Johnston called a conference with Beauregard and Bragg. They concluded that it was all the army could do to get to their assigned destinations and that the attack would be postponed until the following morning, April 5. Breckinridge's column trickled in after sunset and was notified of the change of plans. As if to make matters worse, a cold rain continued to fall. For a march of only twenty miles, the Confederates sure made it seem longer.[51]

At dawn on April 5, Hardee's corps, which was encamped at the Michie farm, advanced to within three miles of the Federal line, but not until midmorning were his men deployed for battle. Johnston arrived at the farm about 7 A.M., conferred with Polk briefly, and then rode ahead to meet Hardee. The army was to strike the Federals at 8 A.M., but confusion between Polk's and Bragg's corps delayed the deployment. Bragg had lost Daniel Ruggles's division on the road, but Johnston urged him to hasten his preparations despite the delay. Just after noon, a frustrated commanding general, with some staff members, rode back along the road in search of the division. Thinking that Ruggles's brigades had already passed—Ruggles's men actually had been delayed by Polk's wagons and artillery, which had jammed the Ridge Road—Polk had set his corps in motion, dividing Bragg's corps. Not until 2 P.M. was Ruggles able to file his men onto the road and advance. They finally came into line to the left of the Pittsburg-Corinth Road and deployed for battle around 4 P.M., but by this time it was obvious to the commanders that no attack would be made that day.[52]

What had become painfully apparent to Beauregard was that his battle orders proved far more complicated than he had imagined. The combination of raw troops and rough, unfamiliar terrain proved a burden to the strategic design. Thus, after he arrived at Bragg's temporary headquarters at the intersection of the Pittsburg-Corinth and Bark Roads late in the afternoon, Beauregard and Bragg decided to cancel the attack and return to Corinth. When Polk arrived, Beauregard blamed the bishop for the army's delay. Instantly, tempers flared into a heated argument over who was responsible for the problems. Polk turned on Bragg and censured him for not forming his line promptly. Bragg simply reiterated his earlier concerns, citing bad weather, poor discipline, and poor planning as the causes for the delay. When Johnston rode by, he heard the commotion and inquired about it. Beauregard, second in command, told him that the offensive must be canceled. He argued that given the delay, the Federals could hardly be ignorant of their position. In fact, all that the maneuvering had accomplished was simply to alert the enemy to such an attack, especially given Hardee's skirmishing the day before. "Now they will be entrenched to the eyes," the Creole pessimistically concluded. Besides, the army was short on rations, many of the new recruits having eaten in three days what was to have lasted them for five, and Breckinridge had not even arrived at his designated place.[53]

The discussion turned to alternatives, and as luck would have it, Breckinridge arrived to join in. To get a fresh idea on the matter, the Kentuckian was asked his opinion, to which he replied that a retreat was out of the question. Polk agreed. But Beauregard and Bragg dissented. Johnston listened for a few moments and then interrupted before the conversation went any further, declaring with an uncharacteristic display of firm resolve: "Gentleman, we shall attack at daylight tomorrow." The meeting ended with the commanding general inviting the others to his tent later that evening.[54]

When the generals came together at Johnston's tent, the discussion over the army's situation reopened. Though each maintained his same perspectives from earlier, Bragg now openly supported Polk, Breckinridge, and Johnston by arguing in favor of an attack. Though Johnston earlier had stood alone from the other commanders, Beauregard was now the only one advocating withdrawal. The officers retired about 10 P.M. and the fire was extinguished. Though Johnston hoped his army might still pull off a surprise against the Federals, as he walked away, he turned to a staff officer and remarked, "I would fight them if they were a million." Johnston said to another officer, "Tomorrow at twelve o'clock we will water our horses in the Tennessee River." The night grew still and quiet, no fires were lit. All that could be heard were the drums beating tattoo, closing out the day. Though the rain had ceased, the men lay down again on damp ground.[55]

Fortunately for Grant, Sherman, the only professionally trained division commander in his army, was deployed closest to the advanced Confederate line and covered the main roads leading to Pittsburg Landing. Grant had instructed him to partially fortify his position to withstand a superior force should the Confederates attack. The problem was that Sherman's division was comprised mostly of green recruits, and many of the brigade commanders had little if any military experience. Col. David Stuart's Second Brigade was encamped along the Hamburg-Savannah Road about a mile and a half from the landing. The bulk of the Fifth Division was encamped around the Shiloh Church area near the Corinth-Pittsburg Road. Col. Ralph P. Buckland's Fourth Brigade camped to the west. Col. Jesse Hildebrand's Third Brigade was positioned east of the church. On Sherman's right was Col. John A. McDowell's First Brigade. To the left of Sherman's brigades was Prentiss's Sixth Division, about a third of a mile away.[56]

More significant than the lack of experience was the Sherman's failure to fortify his position. Neither he nor Grant thought that the Confederates would fight in the open away from their own prepared defenses. Sherman wrote to his wife on April 3 that although his men were constantly in the presence of enemy pickets, "I am satisfied that they will await our coming at Corinth." The Federal generals underestimated the enemy and simply neglected preparations that should have been rudimentary. Still, the officers had trained the men well overall. Col. DeWitt Clinton Loudon of the Seventieth Ohio Volunteers was one of those officers and remarked to his wife from the front, "There are a great many troops here—Iowa, Illinois, Missouri, Ohio, Indiana, Michigan, Wisconsin & Minnesota," and "finer *material* never filled the ranks of any army in Christendom."[57]

As the Union army remained on the west side of the Tennessee River, Halleck was desperate for information about the Confederates' strength and position. On the morning of April 4, Sherman ordered Buckland's brigade to head out on the Ridge Road and scout around while some of Hildebrand's units did the same. Capt. William B. Mason of the Seventy-seventh Ohio came in view of a line of enemy infantry, but when he informed Sherman of this development, the stern-faced commander dismissed it as nothing more than a reconnoitering party. The same afternoon, a company of the Seventy-second Ohio, Buckland's brigade, ventured out along the Ridge Road and skirmished with about two hundred cavalry. After an hour the Federals drove the horsemen away and captured a dozen Confederates. When the affair was reported to Sherman, it was stated that the Federals had seen about two thousand infantry, but Sherman dismissed the information. When an anxious Lt. John T. Taylor, Sherman's new aide-de-camp, queried the general about the possibility of simply marching out after the enemy, Sherman replied: "Never mind, young man, you will have all the fighting you want before this war is over; it will come fast enough for you after awhile." When Buckland mentioned the likelihood of a Confederate advance, Sherman glibly remarked: "Oh! tut; tut. You militia officers get scared too easily."[58] Still, something was about to happen, and as the soldiers waited in suspense to give battle, Colonel Loudon spoke for many when he concluded, "our men don't count on any thing else than thrashing them [the Confederates] soundly."[59]

On April 5 Sherman received reports throughout the day that the Confederates were in the vicinity and that Union pickets were being driven back. Intelligence accounts also concluded that enemy cavalry detachments were spotted in the area. As reports came in, Sherman became increasingly irritated by what he considered unsubstantiated assessments of the situation in his front. At one point during the night, when a courier reported that Col. Jesse J. Appler of the Fifty-third Ohio had run into a line of Confederates, Sherman responded by telling the courier to tell Appler to take his regiment back to Ohio. "There is no enemy nearer than Corinth," he barked.[60]

What proved more alarming to Sherman, however, was the enemy activity in Prentiss's and his own front. On the night of April 5, Lt. John W. Rumsey told Sherman that while on the picket line, they had seen squads of enemy cavalry in front of both divisions. Sherman acknowledged their presence but responded that he was under orders not to bring on a general engagement until Buell arrived.[61]

Though Halleck's messages to Buell contained no hints of urgency, the Ohioan should have known that Grant's situation remained precarious, despite Sherman's nonchalance about the enemy. Grant went to the front daily and conferred with his friend each time, but like Sherman, he remained confident that the enemy would not leave a fortified position at Corinth to attack the Federals at Pittsburg Landing. Besides, Buell was expected very soon, and the presence of his army alone would be enough to deter the enemy. What troubled him was the news that Cheatham's Confederates at Purdy just west of Crump's Landing were reportedly more numerous than Lew Wallace's division could withstand if the enemy decided to strike. On the afternoon of April 4, Grant heard a distant thunder of artillery, and he hastened to Pittsburg Landing. Once he learned of the situation in Sherman's front, he rode to Crump's Landing and discussed the situation with Wallace, who assured him that all was quiet. Grant recalled that the night was one of "impenetrable darkness, with rain pouring down in torrents, nothing was visible to the eye except as revealed by the frequent flashes of lightening." On his way back to the landing, Grant's horse slipped from under him and fell on his leg, severely injuring the general's ankle. For the next few days, he would be forced to get around on crutches.[62]

On the morning of April 5, Nelson's 4,500-man division arrived at Savannah, despite Grant's remarks not to hurry because it would be Tuesday, April 8, before the division could be transported to Pittsburg Landing. Fortunately for Grant, Nelson pushed forward anyway. Around 1 P.M., the Kentuckian reported at Grant's headquarters at the Cherry mansion, asking if he could continue on to Pittsburg Landing and camp. "Not immediately," Grant replied, "you will encamp for the present at Savannah." When Nelson expressed concern about Beauregard, Grant answered that he could hold his own. Charles Smith, still struggling with his leg injury, commented confidently that the Confederates were at Corinth: the Union army would have to go there "and draw them out, as you would a badger out of a hole."[63]

Nelson's division bivouacked just outside of Savannah along the Waynesboro Pike. Later that afternoon Grant paid a visit to his old friend Col. Jacob Ammen, a brigade commander under Nelson. In the course of the conversation, Ammen asked about pressing on to just opposite the landing. Grant remarked that the terrain along the east bank of the river was swampy and assured the colonel that all was under control. In answer to Ammen's remark that his troops were not fatigued and could continue to Pittsburg Landing, Grant replied, "You cannot march through the swamps; make the troops comfortable; I will send boats for you Monday or Tuesday, or some time early in the week." He added confidently: "There will be no fight at Pittsburg Landing; we will have to go to Corinth, where the rebels are fortified. If they come to attack us, we can whip them, as I have more than twice as many troops as I had at Fort Donelson."[64]

True, some 240 miles downstream at Paducah reinforcements were departing for Pittsburg Landing. "Here are plenty of soldiers and several boat loads of old muskets and spoils of war of war brought down from Donelson and Henry," wrote Cyrus Boyd of the Fifteenth Iowa. Aboard the *Minnehaha,* "an old shaky tub," he penned in his diary, "Here we enter the dark land of secession and the enemies home."[65]

About the same time that Grant was returning to the Cherry mansion, Buell himself rode into Savannah. Grant was unaware that the general had arrived, but later when he knew he notified Buell that he would meet with him early the next morning. Before turning in for bed, Grant confidently wrote to Halleck that the main enemy force was at Corinth: "I have scarcely the faintest idea of an attack (general one) being made upon us, but will be prepared should such a thing take place."[66]

Col. Everett Peabody, commander of Prentiss's First Brigade, camped in Spain Field west of the Eastern Corinth Road, did not share Grant's or Sherman's sentiments that the enemy was at Corinth. On Saturday afternoon, April 5, he assumed responsibility to satisfy his curiosity as to whether or not the reports coming in from the field were accurate, deciding to survey his immediate front. The colonel ordered a reconnaissance for later that afternoon and evening, dispatching some infantry companies under the command of Maj. James E. Powell to undertake the mission. In the wooded darkness of the early morning of April 6, the Sabbath, about 250 soldiers of the Twenty-fifth Missouri and the Twelfth Michigan returned to Seay Field. One Union veteran recalled years later that Peabody had remarked to one of his officers before the move was made "that he would not live to see the result of it."[67]

Meanwhile, Jacob Ammen, commanding Buell's lead brigade, asked his men if they could march faster. "[W]e want to the see him [the elephant] once anyhow," they complained.[68] In a few days, they would never again be so anxious.

CHAPTER SIX

Bloody Shiloh

Almost sixty years after the battle of Shiloh, Joseph Ruff, a German veteran of the Twelfth Michigan, remembered that the night of April 5 was warm and the "stars were shining." As nearly as he could judge, it was about 3 A.M. when Maj. James Powell's three companies patrolled the vicinity south of the church. As the soldiers passed through Seay Field and crossed the Pittsburg-Corinth Road, they advanced into a forty-acre cotton patch known as Fraley Field. At one point, Ruff recalled, "we came near opening fire on our own men." There in the darkness, as the troops heard the "crowing of fowls," they stumbled upon Brig. Gen. Sterling A. M. Wood's brigade of Hardee's corps deployed in the southeast corner of the field. It was approaching 5 A.M. when Confederate pickets fired at the approaching Federal line. In the dawn before sunrise, the soldiers fought a spirited engagement. Standing behind a tree hardly large enough to cover him, Ruff had his right ear clipped by a bullet. As the musketry became thicker and faster, Powell realized that he had incited more Rebels than his small force could withstand and called upon his bugler to sound the retreat. In thirty minutes, this opening skirmish was over.[1]

Up before dawn, Johnston and his commanders sat around a small campfire eating breakfast and discussing the planned attack when they heard musket fire. Interestingly enough, it had been just over two months since Johnston first predicted where he might meet the Federals. According to one source, in late January, while studying a map prepared by an engineer who had returned from a survey mission of the Tennessee River, Johnston pointed to the spot marked "Shiloh Church" and "quietly but impressively" said, "Here the great battle of the Southwest will be fought."[2] Now, rising to his feet, Johnston remarked, "The battle has opened gentlemen; it is too late to change our dispositions." Mounting his thoroughbred, the general turned to his staff and, hoping to stir the soldiers, remarked: "Tonight we will water our horses in the Tennessee River."[3] Johnston then rode to the front, encouraging the officers as he passed by. The battle of Shiloh had begun whether the Federals had realized it or not.[4]

Col. Everett Peabody was just about to eat breakfast when Brig. Gen. Benjamin Prentiss rode into brigade headquarters and inquired about the firing coming from the direction of Fraley Field. Peabody replied that it was the result of a reconnaissance he had ordered. Angered by the colonel's unauthorized actions and nonchalant attitude about the affair, Prentiss accused him of bringing on an attack. Instantly, he ordered reinforcements to the field to assist Powell, and soon the clattering of musketry increased. Peabody jumped to his feet and ordered the brigade to form. The colonel was preparing to mount his horse when Prentiss galloped up and again accused him of precipitating an attack. Peabody brazenly remarked, "If I brought on the fight, I am to lead the van." Prentiss rode off to inform the Second Brigade as Peabody's Missourians and Michigan troops deployed.[5]

While Peabody and Prentiss readied the Federals for the battle, the Confederates forced back Powell's patrol. Col. David Moore advanced with five companies of the Twenty-first Missouri to the front, where they passed the withdrawing soldiers of Powell's party, berating them as cowards for retreating. Infuriated by the major's carelessness in bringing on the attack and watching his men fall back, Moore ordered Powell and his retreating patrol to the rear. Moore was convinced he could turn the tide with some additional men, so Prentiss dispatched the remaining companies of Missourians to strengthen the Union line. Within minutes of taking command and positioning his Federals, however, Moore was struck in the leg and forced out of action. Powell resumed command, but soon afterward the firing decreased. Concluding that the affair had ended, he ordered his force to retire.[6]

Had the Confederates been prepared to attack at dawn as expected, they might have been able to sustain the element of surprise they had planned. The advance and deployment, however, took longer than expected. Brig. Gen. Thomas C. Hindman's two brigades, commanded by Wood and Col. R. G. Shaver, managed to advance only a few regiments to the southwest corner of Seay Field, while the rest of the brigade was stalled by a breakdown in regimental and company alignment. Meanwhile, the rest of Hindman's force advanced northward astride the Pittsburg-Corinth Road. By 7 A.M. the Confederates had forced the Federals to retire. As daylight came streaming through the dense woods, the glowing sun on the eastern horizon presented a colorful scene of the Hardin County landscape in full bloom. As the sun rose higher, the soldiers "passed word from lip to lip that it was the sun of Austerlitz."[7]

About a half-hour later, a long gray line appeared in Peabody's front. Hindman's brigades advanced to within 125 yards before the Federals opened fire and threw the extreme right flank of Wood's brigade into confusion. The Confederates approached to within 75 yards and then opened fire with a severe volley, forcing the Federals back. Prentiss soon withdrew the entire line slowly back toward camp, and the Confederates, their bayonets flashing in the morning sun, launched an all-out assault. Hindman galloped back and forth between brigades waving his cap and cheering on his men. Peabody tried to locate Prentiss, and when he returned to the front he was shot in the mouth and killed as the ball passed to the back of his skull, slain nearly four hours after making a prophetic remark about his death to an officer. Powell took command briefly before he too was killed. The Federals broke into chaos and scattered like "wild turkies" while falling back to the trees at the edge of the field. An hour had passed, and Hindman's brigades had advanced to where Peabody's troops had been camping the night before.[8]

While the Confederates were driving the Federals back, Prentiss ordered Col. Madison Miller's brigade to form battle lines in the southern portion of Peter Spain's field. The batteries of Capt. Andrew Hickenlooper and Capt. Emil Munch deployed on the right flank. Within minutes, gleaming bayonets signaled the approaching Confederate brigades of Brig. Gen. Adley H. Gladden and Brig. Gen. James Chalmers, positioned somewhat chaotically astride the eastern Corinth Road. Gladden's soldiers made their way across a shallow branch of Locust Grove and struck at Miller's line around 8 A.M. As they closed in, the Federals opened with a severe artillery and infantry barrage. Meanwhile, Chalmers brigade had also come under fire but managed to press forward. At one point, the Mississippians and Louisianans caught Hickenlooper's Ohioans repositioning their guns and completely destroyed the battery. By 9 A.M. the Confederates had routed the Federals, driving Miller's men through their camps.[9]

For days since coming ashore at Pittsburg Landing, Sherman had listened to the wild rumors about large bodies of troops in his front.

Despite the sighting of enemy scouts and cavalry on April 5, he still remained unsatisfied that the Confederates posed any threat. Shortly, however, Sherman received intelligence that Confederates were overrunning the Federals in Fraley Field; his division was located to the right and behind Prentiss's camps. Sherman sent readiness orders to Col. Jesse Hildebrand's brigade, and shortly the soldiers attempted to get in battle formation. Suddenly, Confederate skirmishers emerged from the woods on the right flank and threw Jesse Appler's men into chaos, forcing many of them to retreat. The long gray line that appeared was the brigade of young, Irish-born Patrick Cleburne. The Southern brigadier marched his men to the swampy thickets of Shiloh Branch, where he divided his regiments and pressed forward. His Mississippians ran into a tremendous fire from Appler's men but soon swept over them, wreaking havoc on their untrained adversaries.[10]

George Ruff had been in the thick of the fighting since before daylight and during the retreat was carrying a wounded soldier in search of water when he came upon Shiloh Church. As he dipped up a pail of water from a nearby spring, it was obvious that Sherman's men, watering their horses and mules, were not in line. As he turned to head back to his camp, he saw in the distance "men, horses and mules on a run, a perfect rout." When word of the fighting between Hardee's and Peabody's pickets finally reached Sherman, he and his staff rode a few hundred yards in front of the division and into Rhea Field. Suddenly, a volley of enemy fire came whizzing by, killing one of the general's aides, Thomas Holliday, and wounding Sherman in the hand. Still refusing to believe what was happening, the cantankerous commander grabbed his binoculars and peered out across the field. At first, he saw what he thought might be a skirmish, but when an officer called his attention to the right, a line of Confederate skirmishers came into focus, and the stunned general exclaimed, "We are attacked!" Sherman then galloped off with his staff to bring up reinforcements.[11]

Because Appler's men protected the left flank of the division, Sherman shouted to him to hold his position while he sent for support. Instantly, the general turned and sent couriers galloping off to inform McClernand, Hurlbut, and Prentiss of the situation. Sherman then rode off to survey the rest of his command. Soon, drums sounded the long roll and soldiers jumped into line, ready to march into combat. It was a sharp contrast from the previous Sunday, recalled Ruff, when he and others had stacked a couple of hardtack boxes and gathered around to hear a chaplain from an Ohio regiment give a sermon. It was an impressive service that deeply touched the soldiers with a feeling of awe. "What a change from that Sabbath evening's hour of divine service," he remembered the following Sunday morning, as the crack of musketry and the roar of heavy artillery swept across the landscape.[12]

At 7 A.M. the clear sky and fresh air gave way to the smoke and dust of combat. The intensity of the firing had increased so much that it could be heard nine miles downriver at Savannah. Grant had just sat down to breakfast at the Cherry mansion when an orderly rushed in and reported that artillery fire could be heard in the direction of Pittsburg Landing. Grant rose to his feet, his ankle still swollen and painful, hobbled down to the landing, and boarded his headquarters boat, the *Tigress*. Before departing he scrawled two messages. With one, Grant canceled the scheduled meeting with Buell, though he mentioned nothing about the sounds of battle upriver. With the other, he gave orders for Nelson to commandeer the services of a local guide and advance his division to the riverbank opposite Pittsburg Landing (without mentioning this to Buell).[13]

At the time, Buell was on his way to Grant's headquarters, arriving only in time to see the *Tigress* pulling away from the dock. Inside the Cherry mansion, he found C. F. Smith, who though still laid up, was in fine spirits. When Buell inquired where Grant was going, Smith replied that he had gone to Pittsburg Landing to survey the situation. The old general confidently declared that the noise was nothing more than skirmishing. At first, Buell thought the same thing, since it mirrored the previous day's firing. Nelson soon informed his superior that Grant had ordered his division to march upriver opposite the landing, which gave Buell reason for concern. For one thing, Grant was ordering a division of the Army of the Ohio forward, and for another Grant himself recognized the swampy conditions along the river bottom Nelson would have to use; the roads were so waterlogged that artillery and wagons would have to be left behind and carried forward by steamers. In the meantime, Nelson sent his staff into Savannah in search of someone who could guide them to the crossing site. Buell waited. The sounds of the battle carried across the Tennessee countryside to Buell's other units spread up to thirty miles away. "Thinks I to myself," wrote Samuel B. Franklin, "now pretty soon we will know what war is."[14]

About half past eight, an agonizingly slow *Tigress* neared Crump's Landing and steamed alongside the *Jesse K. Bell*, where Lew Wallace, hearing the artillery, was standing in expectation of orders. Grant and

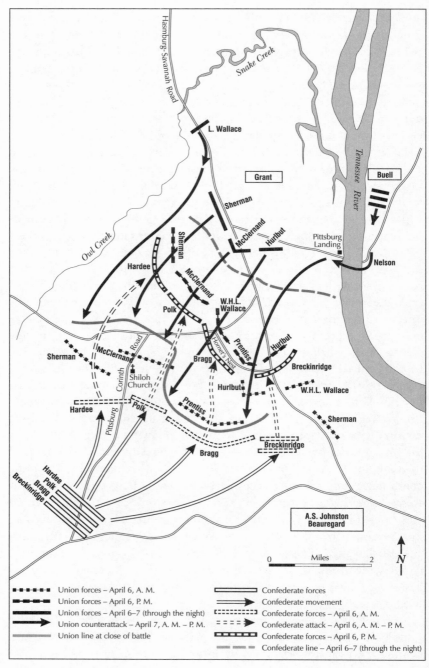

Snake Creek

Hasmburg-Savannah Road

Owl Creek

Tennessee River

L. Wallace

Grant

Buell

Sherman

McClernand

Hurlbut

Pittsburg Landing

Nelson

Sherman

Hardee

McClernand

Polk

W.H.L. Wallace

Prentiss

Hurlbut

Sherman

McClernand

Corinth Road

Hornet's Nest

Bragg

Breckinridge

Shiloh Church

Hurlbut

W.H.L. Wallace

Hardee

Pittsburg Corinth Road

Polk

Prentiss

Sherman

Bragg

Breckinridge

Hardee
Polk
Bragg
Breckinridge

A.S. Johnston
Beauregard

0   Miles   2

N

Union forces – April 6, A. M.
Union forces – April 6, P. M.
Union forces – April 6–7 (through the night)
Union counterattack – April 7, A. M. – P. M.
Union line at close of battle

Confederate forces
Confederate movement
Confederate forces – April 6, A. M.
Confederate attack – April 6, A. M. – P. M.
Confederate forces – April 6, P. M.
Confederate line – April 6–7 (through the night)

The Battle of Shiloh, April 6–7, 1862

Wallace discussed the situation as the *Tigress* slowly steamed past. The commanding general told Wallace to ready his division, and he would send orders once he reached Pittsburg Landing and surveyed the situation. Wallace shouted back that he was already on standby and was anxious to move. Nonetheless, Grant reiterated that Wallace should wait for orders, and with that, the steamer slowly pulled away. Shortly, the *John Warner* appeared steaming downriver, when it came upon *Tigress*. A lieutenant came aboard with a message from W. H. L. Wallace informing Grant that the army was under a general attack from a large enemy force and had been driven back. Grant was unmoved, confidently informing the young officer that when he arrived at Pittsburg Landing, he would take care of the situation.[15]

By the time the *Tigress* arrived at Pittsburg Landing, it was around 9 A.M., and the deafening storm of the raging battle made it seem to be just above the river bluffs. The scene at the riverbank was one of total pandemonium as thousands of wounded soldiers, teamsters, and stragglers were already cowering below the bluff for protection. Some were attempting to swim across the river but found the current too swift, others simply floated downstream on whatever they could find. Attempting to bring the confusion under control, Grant mounted his horse and rode off the steamer to the top of the bluff, where he tried to stop soldiers who were running away. The general wanted to direct those under the bluff to reform as a reserve force and even positioned an artillery unit to deter others from fleeing. Grant then rode about a mile up the Corinth Road and came upon W. H. L. Wallace, who informed him of the situation. Wallace's news confirmed for Grant what the commander had suspected, and the panic at the riverbank was evidence that the Confederates had launched a full-scale attack from Corinth (rather than Crump's Landing). Grant quickly sent messages to Lew Wallace to march his division to the battle and to Nelson to hurry his division to the river.[16]

An hour had passed since Grant arrived at the landing, and about 10 A.M. he found Sherman, covered with dust and powder, mirroring the battle's intensity, at Jones Field. Sherman remarked that although the situation was not desperate—he had steadied his line for a countercharge—his division might soon run out of cartridges; the men used weapons of sixteen different calibers. Impressed with Sherman's vigor, Grant praised his friend, encouraged him to continue the fight, and rode on to visit McClernand. The Illinois politician was in a near panic, and Grant attempted to calm the distressed commander by ordering up his only reserve regiments—the Fifteenth and the Sixteenth Iowa—to reinforce the First Division. Riding along the lines, Grant found Prentiss, whose division was deployed in a shallow wagon trace in a densely wooded area about a half-mile to the rear of his former headquarters. (Years after the battle, the trail would become known as the Sunken Road.) Positioned on Prentiss's right along the trail and bent back toward the north was W. H. L. Wallace's division. In his front was a large open field, an advantageous firing range for Wallace's soldiers against any enemy charges. Hurlbut's division was positioned on Prentiss's left, and some of his men occupied the fringe of a peach orchard slightly ahead. Together, these 10,200 Federals, supported by eight batteries, held the Union center.[17]

Grant believed that in this critical situation, Prentiss would need to remain steadfast and hold the position "at all hazards." He then rode on to meet briefly with Hurlbut and Col. David Stuart on the extreme left. Stuart's brigade was posted near the river and had already fought bravely during the morning against a larger Confederate force, holding his ridge-top position.[18]

About noon, Grant returned to the landing, where the situation had worsened since his arrival. He found several thousand combat-frightened fugitives beneath the bluff. Reports soon indicated that, having been driven back from their original lines, Sherman's and McClernand's positions were continuing to deteriorate. Grant knew that if either division broke and ran, complete disaster would prevail; he had already sent his reserve division to the front and had not managed to form another. Nothing had been heard from Lew Wallace, Nelson, or Buell. Thus, a desperate Grant sent the Kentuckian another message to hasten him forward. Buell had just left Nelson, who had finally obtained the services of a local guide and was just heading out. Tired of waiting around and knowing that Nelson would head out shortly for the riverbank opposite Pittsburg Landing, Buell decided to head to the landing himself. As he steamed upriver, his boat met a vessel descending the river. It chugged alongside, and a sailor handed Buell a letter. Here, for the first time, he learned of Johnston's attack. Relating that the Confederate attack was "very spirited," Grant wrote, "The appearance of fresh troops on the field now would have a powerful effect both by inspiring our men and disheartening the enemy." Furthermore, he added that if Nelson could get upon the field, it would "possibly save the day to us." Certainly, from the estimated one hundred thousand troops that Grant told Nelson he faced, the army was experiencing more than a spirited attack.[19]

Buell's steamer pulled up to the landing about 1 P.M. The scene there must have been the most shocking he had ever witnessed to that point in his military career. "Seeing the elephant," as contemporaries called the experience of combat, must have seemed more like seeing a stampede of elephants to many. As some soldiers of Grant's army fled to the rear and cowered under the bluffs, others swam across the mouth of the Snake River. Buell was absolutely stupefied. "[A] confused mass of various regiments," as he remembered, numbering between four thousand and five thousand men, swarmed the riverbank. Buell found Grant aboard the *Tigress,* where the two commanders consulted briefly. The general's physical appearance gave the impression of a horrific fight, and Buell never forgot the relief on Grant's face at seeing him. He "appeared to realize that he was beset by a pressing danger," Buell remembered, and lacked the "masterly confidence" credited Grant after the battle.[20]

Indeed, it was a nasty predicament, a sight not easily forgotten. Buell and Grant debarked together, and the soldiers under the riverbank captured Buell's attention. The grime of several hours of fierce fighting masked their faces. The Ohioan's reaction impressed Grant, so much so that he recalled in his memoirs that Buell must have concluded that "a line of retreat would be a good thing just then." As the commanders parted, Buell attempted to stir the fugitives of Grant's army back to the battle, but all efforts to form the troops and move them forward to the fight failed.[21]

Seeing Buell certainly relieved Grant, but the appearance of Nelson's division across the river at that point would have been more heartening. About the time Buell arrived, the Confederates had succeeded in driving back both Union flanks. The Federal defensive line along the Pittsburg-Corinth Road had been smashed, and Stuart's brigade near Lick Creek was rapidly breaking apart. By early afternoon, both armies had called up their reserves, but most units were divided and intermingled all over the battlefield. The inhospitable terrain, cut with deep gullies on its boundaries and covered with broadleaved trees, made it difficult to effect orderly and rapid troop movements. Moreover, soldiers frequently attempted to use the topography to protect themselves rather than maneuver in large formations, which usually exposed them in open fields. This made unit cohesion difficult to maintain, and the battle's outcome depended on the individual soldier's decision to stay with his regiment. Because of the limited tactical options, the fight became a series of frontal assaults and counterattacks. Under the dense undergrowth, the soldiers fought desperately amidst their dead, dying, and wounded. The sharp crash of thousands of rifled muskets firing was joined by the roar of cannon and the explosions of shells. As the day progressed, frightened riderless horses came thundering through the woods in increasing numbers.[22]

As the Federals redressed their lines, Johnston and Beauregard had been encouraging their troops all morning. The Creole had been riding over the field collecting reports from the front, supervising the rear, and forwarding reinforcements to the front lines mainly by listening to the sound of the heaviest fighting. Shortly after midday, he established his headquarters at Shiloh Church and was reinforcing Hardee on the left. Johnston, meanwhile, had been riding along the front lines, reconnoitering enemy positions and consulting with his corps commanders. He spent most of the morning monitoring the Confederate center, where Bragg had directed the assaults. Still, he thought it imperative to observe Patrick Cleburne's spirited attack and rode to the right in time to witness the advance against Stuart's brigade. Thomas Jordan, Beauregard's chief of staff, was also up front with Col. Jacob Thompson. Together, the officers rode the lines gathering information. It was clear to them that the terrain and lack of communications inhibited the corps commanders from managing the lines effectively. The units were chaotically intermingled, and the commanders were forced to make independent decisions about battle deployment, resulting in the inability of the entire army to sustain any significant advance.[23]

The site of the most severe combat was the same old wagon road that comprised the center of the Union line, where the Federals under Prentiss, Wallace, and Hurlbut held firm. Sheltered by woods, the Federals peered out across the thirty-acre farm belonging to Joseph Duncan. Shrouded by a densely wooded area filled with thick, entangling underbrush, the centers of both armies found some protection. The position that Grant ordered Prentiss to hold to the end was elevated in favor of the Federals, whose line consisted of infantry anchored with batteries strategically deployed between the regiments. Throughout the day, the Confederates attempted to overrun this stronghold, charging across the open fields in front and through the woods on either side with fixed bayonets. As the Federals forced the Confederates to retreat each time, someone likened the intensity of buzzing projectiles to a "hornet's nest," and as historian James McDonough observed, "the name stuck."[24]

By late Sunday morning, Braxton Bragg was commanding the majority of the Confederates making repeated attempts to break the Union center.

An old-army stalwart, he believed that a bayonet charge would bring the Confederates victory. The Union soldiers, equipped with rifled muskets, raked the attacking Southerners repeatedly with severe volleys, defeating charge after charge. The slaughter that took place from late morning until late afternoon bore testimony to the intensity of the struggle and the tenacity of the soldiers on both sides. None of the commanders on the field that day, though, knew how much the rifle had trumped conventional tactics. As Confederate units broke against the strong Union position, Bragg stubbornly rallied the troops and simply ordered them back to the underbrush.[25]

About 4,300 Union soldiers out of the total 10,200 along the wagon trail held the Hornet's Nest, and although the Confederates ultimately committed about 18,000 soldiers strung out opposite the Federals, the bluecoats managed to hold out for most of the day. Bragg reported that it was "here [where] we met the most obstinate resistance of the day," a fact confirmed by Hurlbut on the other side, who reported that "for five hours these brigades maintained their position under repeated and heavy attacks."[26] Throughout the afternoon, thousands of Southerners all along the line launched a series of separate assaults, resulting in scores of dead and wounded who littered the ground between the two forces. Still, the uncoordinated and unsuccessful charges had the overall effect of wearing down the Union defenders.[27]

Bragg observed wave after wave of futile assaults he ordered and did not appreciate the difficulties his soldiers faced in the thicket. Still, he remained convinced that the Federals could be taken by bayonet. He ordered Col. Randal Gibson's brigade to storm the Federal line in yet another charge. The young colonel led his Arkansans and Louisianans at the Union line and came to within sixty yards of the old wagon road before being forced to retreat. Immediately, he sent his aide-de-camp to Bragg for artillery support, but the general was relentless and ordered the brigade to immediately assault the Federal line again. Gibson's bloodied Louisianans would storm the Union line four times that early afternoon, but the Federals held firm. Bragg believed the failure to break through was due to Gibson's mishandling of his regiments, a charge the colonel vehemently denied. It is generally recognized by historians that Bragg might have been successful had he decided to send the entire Confederate line at once instead of in "driblets," as the general's biographer Grady McWhiney characterized the piecemeal assaults.[28]

But Bragg was not the only one attempting to overwhelm the enemy

with successive bayonet charges. Farther to the right, General Johnston
was also looking to cold steel for victory. About 2 P.M., Breckinridge,
who had been assaulting Hurlbut's line in and east of the peach orchard,
complained to Johnston that he could not persuade a Tennessee regiment
to advance again. "Oh, yes, general, I think you can," Johnston replied,
and he sent Gov. Isham Harris of his staff to encourage the troops
to undertake another assault. At that point, Johnston decided to assist
Breckinridge in rallying the men forward. While riding in front of the
reluctant regiment, Johnston touched the Tennesseans' bayonets with
a tin cup he had picked up from Prentiss's camp. "These will do the
work," he confidently remarked. "Men, they are stubborn; We must use
the bayonet." When he reached the center of the line, he shouted, "I will
lead you," suddenly swung his horse around, and spurred it forward. Col.
William S. Statham's men raced down a slope, across a ravine, and up the
crest of a hill. Other regiments followed, forcing the Federal line back to
the cover of Prentiss's batteries. Breckinridge pursued, yelling, "Charge
them, Tennesseans! Charge them!"[29]

Whether Johnston actually led the charge is not as significant as what
happened to the commander during it. When the Federal battery opened
up on the advancing Confederates, Johnston had ridden within easy range
of the enemy's musketry and was struck by a bullet in the back of the leg
below the knee. "In the ardor of the moment," recalled one participant,
"he probably did not realize that he had been hit, or if he did, thought
the wound a mere trifle." When the injured commander returned from
the field, his clothing had been ripped and torn and his boot sole cut in
half. Governor Harris was elated at what he himself had done and came
galloping back only to find Johnston alone and swaying in his saddle. He
asked the commander if he had been wounded. "Yes," Johnston replied,
"and I fear seriously." Harris guided the general's horse to cover away
from the fighting and helped the commander to the ground. Johnston had
dispatched his medical staff earlier, and Harris was unable to administer
medical aid to stop the bleeding. By this time, staff member and kinsman
Col. William Preston Johnston arrived, dismounted, kneeled beside the
general, and attempted to revive him. "Johnston," he asked "don't you
know me?" No response came. Albert Sidney Johnston had expired at
half past two in the afternoon. Perhaps his dying on the battlefield had
redeemed the Texan as a commander in the estimation of his critics.[30]

At the time of Johnston's death, the Confederate flanks to the right and
left of the Hornet's Nest began to press forward with some success. When

Beauregard learned of his commander's death, the entire Union army was dependent on the Federals of Wallace's, Prentiss's, and Hurlbut's divisions in the center holding off another assault. Grant was back at the landing in the midst of complete chaos, struggling to assemble Sherman's and McClernand's disorganized and overwhelmed troops, many of whom had just fallen back from around the Hornet's Nest, into a defense line. Ambulance details were carrying scores of wounded soldiers back from the front, confirming the intensity of the battle. Still, Grant never lost confidence and persisted in pulling together the stragglers from the rest of the army into a defensive line. As the day was closing, he waited for Buell's men and Lew Wallace.[31]

Grant had sent out a search party at about 2:30 to locate the seven thousand men of Wallace's division and Capt. William R. Rowley, whom Grant had dispatched hours before to hurry Wallace to the fighting. Though there is considerable controversy over why Wallace failed to show on the battlefield that day, the fact was he set out on the wrong route. When he finally departed Crump's Landing, Wallace directed his division toward Purdy. After about seven miles of marching, Captain Rowley caught up and informed him that Grant needed him immediately. Wallace turned the division around and headed back to where it could take a shortcut to the River Road. About this time, Grant's search party caught up with the division and directed it to Pittsburg Landing. It was nearly dark when Wallace's troops finally took their position on Sherman's right behind Tilghman Branch, about two and one-half miles from the position it had occupied when the battle started.[32]

Grant was also concerned over the whereabouts of Nelson, who he had ordered to march to the river before he left Savannah in the morning. He followed up these instructions with another message later to hurry Nelson's division along, which Buell read on his way to Pittsburg Landing. Buell and Nelson waited for several hours before starting out, and many of the soldiers, particularly those in the Fifty-first Indiana, were indignant about Buell's apparent negligence during the morning as he listened to the distant guns without prodding Nelson on. One Ohio soldier in Nelson's division recalled that the Kentuckian "chafed like a lion caged." Finally, after obtaining the services of a guide, which Buell in later years claimed was the reason for the delay, the division set out at about 1:30 through the seven-mile "labyrinth of roads" toward the river. The division would not make it across to the landing until late in the day.[33]

Beauregard, meanwhile, took command of the Confederate army and positioned six brigades as best he could to overwhelm the Federals in the Hornet's Nest. He ordered Brig. Gen. Daniel Ruggles's regiments to attack on the left and center, while Bragg left the troops he had been with and rode toward the right flank. There he found the divisions of Brig. Gen. Jones Withers and Cheatham and the corps of Breckinridge "without a common head," and Bragg decided to throw all of these troops forward as well. Ruggles strengthened his line with nearly sixty cannon, a line of guns extending about one-fifth of a mile along the western side of Duncan Field. Firing for well over an hour, the Confederate cannoneers bombarded the Hornet's Nest with roughly ten thousand projectiles. Bragg wrote that the descending sun, though hardly noticeable through the smoke, warned the soldiers to press their advantage and "finish the work before night should compel us to desist."[34]

The artillery barrage was overwhelming. In the midst of the flurry of shell, grape, and canister, Hurlbut's command broke and fell back, though "quietly and steadily," the general later reported. His center rested near a shallow pond, where wounded men had crawled to quench their thirst, many for the last time. A number of soldiers died at or near this pond, and their blood stained the water; soldiers from that day forward dubbed it the "Bloody Pond." As if things could not get any worse, the continuous iron hail that ripped through the woods felling trees and limbs made even retreating dangerous. Prentiss and Wallace conferred and, remembering Grant's earlier order to hold the line "at all hazards," determined to stand their ground and prevent the army from being completely routed. At about 5 P.M. both commanders dispatched orders to retreat, and while leading part of a brigade of Iowans to the rear, Wallace was shot in the head, and the mortally wounded general was taken from the field; many of his men thought he was dead. As the Confederates converged around them, the Federals attempted to cut their way back toward the landing. Prentiss remained steadfast for a little longer while other units attempted to get away. Finally at about 5:30, seeing that further resistance was futile and would result in the "slaughter of every man in the command," he yielded the fight and surrendered the remaining 2,200 soldiers, all of them from Wallace's division. Prentiss would be delivered to Confederate headquarters as a prisoner.[35]

Though the Confederates forced the surrender of the defenders at the Hornet's Nest, the Federals, in truth, had staved off a much more significant defeat. Their gallant efforts had delayed the Confederate advance throughout the day, inflicting a terrible toll on the Southerners. Some

4,300 soldiers had essentially occupied the entire Confederate army in repulsing multiple attempts to take the Hornet's Nest with bayonet assaults when there were clearly other points the Confederates could have targeted and stormed with greater ease and much less destruction. Combined with soaring casualties, the unbreakable resistance of the Federals sapped the strength and momentum of the Confederates. The stand saved the Army of the Tennessee from complete destruction. An opportunity that the Federals had given the Confederates by landing on the west bank of the Tennessee River had now been overcome.

By the time Beauregard received the news of the surrender, it was approaching 6 P.M., the sun was fast descending, and hundreds of troops, fatigued from the day's fight, hungry, and scattered across the battlefield, were already making their way back to the enemy camps in search of food. From his headquarters at Shiloh Church two miles to the rear, Beauregard concluded that not much more could be effectively accomplished, so he refused to authorize a final assault and instead ordered the troops to retire to the captured enemy camps for the night. Prentiss's surrender yielded over two thousand prisoners, one division and several brigade commanders, thousands of small arms, and an immense supply of subsistence, forage, and munitions. The Creole was confident. He had practically driven the Union army into the river, and as he later reported, he had acquired "all the substantial fruits of a complete victory."[36]

Beauregard had no idea he had given the Federals an advantage by halting the attack, and he would spend the rest of his life dodging criticism for it. In giving up the Hornet's Nest, the Federals were actually afforded a formidable position. As the soldiers fell back toward the landing, they found themselves in possession of slightly higher ground than they had held throughout the day. Moreover, the line was not as extended as it had been, running westward in a shallow semicircle protecting the route leading up from the landing to the Hamburg-Savannah Road, which was protected in anticipation of Lew Wallace's arrival. They were also afforded other advantages of terrain. On the left the line was protected by the mouth of Dill Branch, and on the right by Tilghman Branch. Artillery was planted on the left, which would strengthen that end in case the enemy crossed Dill Branch and advanced through a deep ravine, heavily timbered and thickly covered with undergrowth. To anchor the line at the other end, Grant called upon the gunboats *Tyler* and *Lexington* in the Tennessee.[37]

Besides being forced back to a more formidable position, the Federals were strengthened by the arrival of Nelson's troops at 5 P.M. As soon as the first steamer docked, Nelson rode through the stragglers on the riverbank and to the top of the bluff. The landing and the bluff above were covered with terrorized men from Grant's army. The transports were ordered to pull away from the landing to keep soldiers from running on board. Jacob Ammen, commander of the arriving Tenth Brigade and a devout Episcopalian, witnessed a chaplain haranguing the mob in what another soldier characterized as the "whangdoodle style." Ammen shouted, "Shut up, you God damned old fool, or I'll break your head!" New York correspondent Henry Villard, one of the few reporters actually with the army at the landing, accompanied Nelson's division and found himself amid thousands of "panic-stricken" and "uncontrollable" soldiers, "all apparently entirely bereft of soldierly spirit, with no sense of obedience left, and animated by the sole impulse of personal safety." Another New York correspondent, William Shanks, wrote that when Sherman's soldiers finally realized that Nelson's men had arrived, they shouted, "Buell! Buell!—here come Buell's veterans." After the horror of the days' fight, surely this was a sight to behold.[38]

Though Nelson's arrival did little to determine the outcome of Sunday's fight, Buell's soldiers (and many in Grant's ranks) at the time believed that the Army of the Ohio had arrived just in time. Postwar posturing by the commanders and later historians, however, cannot do justice to what the thousands of men surely felt with the arrival of a fresh division boosting considerably the confidence of all who had witnessed the destruction of the day.

Beauregard had confidence too, but ironically it was in the belief that Buell had not arrived, the day's battle had been won, and the next day would belong to him as well. He wired Richmond that "after a severe battle of ten hours, thanks be to the Almighty, [we] gained a complete victory, driving the enemy from every position."[39]

The fact that Beauregard penned these words from Sherman's vacated tent confirmed for him the completeness of the victory. The next day's fight would simply complete the victory that Johnston had started. Without knowledge of Buell's or Wallace's arrival, the Confederates naturally concluded that the Union army would retreat during the night. In fact, a cavalry report from northern Alabama led Beauregard to believe that Buell was heading away from the Tennessee; apparently Buell's decision to send Mitchel east as a diversion had paid off. Beauregard, however, did not have Grant's good fortune of fresh troops. Wallace's seven thousand men and about seventeen thousand of Buell's soldiers would be in the Federal line by morning. Grant had every reason to be confident. Though his army had been driven back, its position was stronger and considerably strengthened by reinforcements.[40]

The only reprieve soldiers on both sides enjoyed was darkness, and lightning flashes and the ceaseless firing from Union gunboats in the Tennessee disrupted even that. The *Tyler* and *Lexington* lobbed shells throughout the night to keep the Confederates from sleeping. All across the battlefield, tentless soldiers attempted to find relief from the sickening sights that lay around them. Cyrus Boyd of the Fifteenth Iowa recalled that the "struggles of the wounded horses as they floundered upon the ground and came running through the darkness made the situation one of almost as much danger as during the day in battle. . . . No pen can tell, no hand can paint[,] no words can utter the horrors" of that night.[41] Patrick Cleburne reported that the naval shells fell chiefly among the wounded Union soldiers "strewn thickly between my camp and the river," leading him to conclude, "History records few instances of more reckless inhumanity than this."[42]

The rain came down slowly at first, then steadily, and at times heavily, drowning out the wailing sounds of the wounded and dying men who literally covered the ground. Unlike Beauregard, who enjoyed the comforts of Sherman's tent, Grant walked the lines in a poncho. When Col. James B. McPherson rejoined Grant after helping conduct Wallace's men to the battlefield, he asked the general if he should make preparations to retreat. "No," replied Grant, "I propose to attack at daylight and whip them."[43] Later that night, Sherman came up to Grant, who was standing under a tree, his hat and poncho turned against the pelting rain, and said, "Well Grant, we've had the devil's own day, haven't we?" "Yes," replied the soaking commander, "lick 'em tomorrow, though."[44]

Buell also walked the lines that night, and the scent of cigar smoke no doubt drew him to a spot where he found Sherman standing against a tree. Buell had not seen Sherman since the general had left Louisville under charges of insanity. Though having been in the thick of the fighting all day, Buell remembered, "Sherman never appeared to better advantage." Buell asked him for information about the ground in front, and the division commander, handing Buell a small map, related what he knew about the enemy's position and strength. He also remarked that Grant intended to attack in the morning and that Buell was expected to position his army to the left of the Corinth Road. Sherman remembered that Buell was

nervous, "seemed to mistrust us," and "did not like the looks of things."
Buell recalled, however, that Sherman's explanations on that occasion
were briefer than "would ordinarily be expected from him." And while he
indicated he was glad to see Buell, Sherman also hinted that victory would
have been certain even without the Army of the Ohio. Twenty-two years
after the battle, Sherman would go even further in his assessment of the
affairs of Buell's arrival, privately charging that he and Grant both thought
Buell was "derelict" in coming to the battle so "slowly and deliberately."
A few days later, however, Sherman admitted to his wife: "One thing
pleased me well—On Sunday we caught thunder and were beaten back,"
but "Buell arrived very opportunely."[45]

During a night when it rained incessantly and was as "dark as a stack
of black cats," the men rested on their arms. After walking Nelson's front
line, Buell made his way back to the landing and found the advance of
Crittenden's division arriving by steamboat. He then led the men to a
position in the woods one-half mile from the landing and then later to
the right of Nelson's division, where they peered out toward the ominous
Hornet's Nest and Bloody Pond. Meanwhile, McCook's division had
poured into Savannah, and his soldiers were waiting to be transported
upriver. From the look of things at the landing and at the front, Buell
expected to carry the weight of the battle the next day. Besides, he and
Grant did not discuss any coordinated attack, and the Ohio commander
decided to lead his own divisions. There was no tactical plan, simply an
understanding that both armies would advance and that Buell should
take the left of the field.[46]

The command situation on April 7 was peculiar, though not when
viewed in the context of command relations in the West. Halleck dwarfed
Grant, and only by taking Forts Henry and Donelson had Grant partially
redeemed himself with higher authorities as a commander. Buell was Mc-
Clellan's favorite, and he had maintained a senior and favorable position
since coming to the West in large measure because of his Washington
friend. Grant, however, had been too busy to be impressed by either
Halleck or Buell. Although he may have been discouraged by the first
day's chaos at the landing and being pushed back, in Buell's presence
Grant refused to appear weak or vulnerable. He would attack the next
day aiming to pull off a victory in a battle he had already come close to
losing.[47]

The field was littered with dead, dying, and wounded soldiers exposed
to the incessant rain. The afterlife must have seemed more pleasing than

the hell they endured that night, as the groans and cries of the wounded echoed in the woods. North of the peach orchard, where Hurlbut's men had been, soldiers attempted to drag themselves to Bloody Pond for a drink. Earlier in the day, an Illinois surgeon had established a field hospital nearby, and the discarded remains of human flesh still covered the ground. The dead bodies of soldiers who had earlier sought relief also remained. In addition, the wounded who made it back to the landing presented a gruesome picture to the arriving soldiers of Buell's army.[48]

For the Confederates, who thought that the only unfinished business was to bury their dead, they enjoyed the fruits of what they thought had been a victory. Many soldiers, hungry and in search of whatever might make them more comfortable during the night, looted the Union camps, while others, thinking the battle was over and that Grant's troops were surely retreating across the river, started back toward Corinth. Beauregard had attempted to hastily reorganize for the morning's final blow, organizing an entirely different plan from the deployment of troops on Sunday. He appointed Braxton Bragg as his second in command and ordered him to oversee the left flank, incorporating a division of Polk's command into his own corps. Hardee shifted from commanding the left to leading the right, with Breckinridge on his left flank positioned somewhat in advance of the Hornet's Nest. Beauregard then ordered Polk to the left of Breckinridge. Though there was considerable confusion in undertaking this speedy rearrangement, Beauregard still remained confident he would carry the day.[49]

Close to Sherman's vacated tent, a captured General Prentiss conversed with prewar friends. Despite Confederate intelligence indicating that Buell was heading toward Decatur, Alabama, the captured general provided information to two of Beauregard's staff officers, Jacob Thompson and Thomas Jordan, to the contrary. Prentiss and Thompson knew each other before the war and openly discussed Union plans. The prisoner boasted to the aides that Buell was expected during the night and the combined Union armies would go on the offensive in the morning. Neither officer believed him. Still, Prentiss insisted he was right.[50]

Nathan Bedford Forrest could have corroborated Prentiss's claims. Disguised as Union soldiers, Forrest's scouts had earlier crept down near the landing, where they observed Buell's men arriving. Forrest understood fully what was transpiring and the consequences if he did not inform the Confederate high command. Roaming the battlefield late at night looking for an officer who could authorize a surprise attack, Forrest finally came across Hardee. He told the general what his scouts had seen and that the Confederates should attempt to either drive the Federals into the river or plan a retreat, if not, he concluded, "We'll be whipped like Hell tomorrow." Hardee told Forrest to return to his command and remain watchful. The piqued cavalryman galloped away, taking a major portion of a division with him. He would not fight the next day.[51]

As the light of Monday morning broke the darkness, Beauregard's illusions of an easy victory abruptly ended as Grant ordered seven divisions, forty-five thousand soldiers, to advance and reclaim the Union camps. On his left were Buell's divisions of Nelson, Crittenden, and McCook; on his right were Hurlbut, McClernand, Sherman, and Lew Wallace. In their front were the twenty to twenty-five thousand Confederates who had managed to regroup during the night. The Federal offensive began as a general advance, driving back Confederate pickets, but some of the units became badly intermingled, slowing what would otherwise have been a swift assault to a crawl. On the extreme left, Nelson had initially advanced easily and rapidly, though apparently too fast as he exposed his flank and was forced to halt and wait for Crittenden to come up. When he attempted to renew the advance, he found that the Confederates had massed in his front and with the aid of artillery stubbornly resisted his progress, forcing the division to a halt around 8 A.M.[52]

The Southerners were in no position to counter the overwhelming Union assault on the morning of April 7 largely because they expected to go on the offensive themselves. To be ready to attack at daylight, Beauregard had reorganized his command during the night. Bragg wrote to his wife that the soldiers were "disorganized, demolished, and exhausted" and that "not one officer in ten [had] supplied his men, relying on the enemy's retreat."[53]

Several divisions experienced confusion due to a combination of factors. Throughout the night, the shelling from the Union gunboats had aided in disrupting Confederate attempts to regroup. An incessant rainstorm drenched the terrain, making it difficult to reposition artillery. Meanwhile, in the pitch dark, soldiers attempted to find their brigades or divisions, some of which were shifting or gathering supplies for the next day. Some brigades became separated from the army during the night. To make matters worse, Beauregard's overnight repositioning of commands—Hardee to the left and Bragg to the right—had created a hole in the line that had been assigned to Polk, who with Frank Cheatham's Second Division had gone back to Hardee's campsite the previous night some four miles from the landing. Polk and Cheatham would be late to arrive on the field the next morning. The next day, their soldiers were handicapped by the fatigue of closing the distance from the combat area and by attempting to make their way through the mass of troops falling back from the front.[54]

By the light of the morning, all along the Confederate line, officers frantically tried to maintain some semblance of order, but they could not overcome the confusion. Several commanders who managed to keep control of their regiments simply did not have enough soldiers in the ranks, and many of these men lacked sufficient ammunition. Patrick Cleburne reported the pathetic news that his 2,700 men had been "sadly reduced" by the battle's first day to about 800 available on Monday morning. When they realized the Federals were staging a counteroffensive, many soldiers simply ran off before the fight—"some through cowardice and some loaded with plunder from the Yankee encampments." Hardee tried to rally some of his men back to the front, but the attempt was futile. The Second Texas, reported Hardee, "seemed appalled, fled from the field without apparent cause, and were so dismayed that my efforts to rally them were unavailing."[55]

Although it was quite a struggle, Confederate commanders managed to pull together enough men in a line and to put up a hardy resistance. The Federals' vicious assault, however, struck Hardee's flank on the far right of the Confederate line. Soon, Breckinridge and Bragg also came under attack. Breckinridge fought against Thomas L. Crittenden, his former commander and closest friend during his youth. It was 10:30 A.M. before Polk's men finally came up, and he was given a portion of the line between Breckinridge and Bragg. "Wherever Kentucky met Kentucky, it was horrible," wrote a Confederate cannoneer. Bragg wrote to his wife the following day, "We fought them with . . . success for eight hours, our generals having to lead in person one half the troops."[56]

On the Union left, the men of Nelson's division were having a hard fight. Buell was at the front when the Confederates stalled Nelson's advance, and he directed two rifled batteries to deploy immediately. Between 9 A.M. and 10 A.M., there was a lull in the artillery duel, and the Federals of the First Kentucky and the Ninth Indiana charged the Confederate guns, driving the cannoneers away. However, they were quickly repulsed by a regiment of Louisianans. The Confederates forced the Federals back elsewhere, and soon they were swarming through the underbrush west of Wicker Field. Union batteries held firm, though, and forced the Confederates back several times. Seeing the chance at a counterstrike, Col. William B. Hazen shouted to his men to fix bayonets and his brigade of Indiana, Kentucky, and Ohio volunteers stormed forward, overtaking the Rebel artillery.[57]

As Nelson's and Crittenden's men fought over this ground, they came upon horrendous scenes of the dead from the previous day's fighting. The men of Col. Jacob Ammen's brigade, who during the march through the swamp the previous day had been concerned that the fight might be over before they arrived, encountered horrible destruction. An Ohio soldier recalled, "The gory corpses lying all about us, in every imaginable attitude, and slain by an inconceivable variety of wounds, were shocking to behold." Hoosier Thomas Prickett wrote, "I saw some awful sights on the battlefield that day," remarking that he hoped to bring himself home as a living "trophy."[58]

Although the Confederates repeatedly managed to stage counterattacks, which at times forced portions of the Union left to falter and fall back, by noon the Northerners had forced the Southern line back to a position along the Hamburg-Purdy Road. Beauregard had worked desperately to hold on to this line because he needed the intersecting Corinth Road in case he was forced to retreat. But the commands of Wallace, Sherman, and McClernand had fought successfully, pressed Beauregard's left back, and now were converging in the general direction of Shiloh Church. On two occasions earlier in the day, Beauregard himself grabbed the colors of regiments pressing forward and led them on. From his headquarters, though, Beauregard received word of the futile attempts and observed the stream of stragglers heading south, quite difficult to restrain. He had been studying the situation and knew the only option was to retire to safety. Shortly after 2 P.M., aide Thomas Jordan, watching the fighting, recalled that he said to the Creole: "General, do you not think our troops are very much in the condition of a lump of sugar, thoroughly soaked with water, but yet preserving its original shape, though ready to dissolve? Would it not be judicious to get away with what we have?" Beauregard replied, "I intend to withdraw in a few moments."[59]

The Confederate commander then ordered Jordan to retrieve what units he could and post them as a rear guard so others could withdraw. At the same time, staff officers galloped off with orders for commanders to commence a slow and orderly retreat. John S. Jackman of the Ninth Kentucky saw Beauregard and his staff ride leisurely back to the rear "as cool and unpreterbed as if nothing had happened."[60] Meanwhile, preparations were made to depart the battlefield and retire to Corinth.

Jordan collected roughly two thousand infantry and a battery of twelve guns, positioning them on an elevated ridge just to the south of Shiloh Church. For the next hour and a half, the Confederates pulled back to their previous lines and then headed south. By this time the rains had come again, and the road back to Corinth, littered with discarded wagons and artillery, became almost impassable. Many of the Confederates had had enough of the war. "I shall never forget how I felt that day," penned a Tennessean in his diary early on the seventh, "as we lay there listening to the incessant roll of the federal drummer in our front often lying on the ground I would look at the bright fleecy clouds . . . and think of all I loved and all I feared in life . . . knowing that with the early tomorrow many of us would likely pass away." He closed, "[T]hen I would think of Tennessee and of the South."[61]

Many Union soldiers had also seen enough of the elephant. They were too exhausted to pursue the vanquished Confederates until the following day. Grant had not prepared for a pursuit of the enemy; indeed, it was all he could do to defeat them on the battlefield. Two raging days of fighting had thoroughly expended Grant's men, and Buell's soldiers, weary from a grueling march, sleepless night, and a hard day's battle, had no desire to chase after an enemy. The following morning Sherman moved out toward Corinth with two brigades and a regiment of cavalry. Buell sent Thomas J. Wood's division, which had arrived on the battlefield late in the afternoon on April 7, to support him. Still, it was not much of a pursuit. Sherman had no intention of advancing farther toward Corinth; he simply wanted to make sure that the Confederates did not linger nearby. On a patch of ground littered with trees from a prewar logging operation (appropriately called Fallen Timbers), Sherman and Forrest, in command of the rear guard, clashed. When the Southerner saw the Federals advancing, he charged the blue column and drove the pickets into the main line, causing considerable confusion. Seeing this, Sherman called for more troops to stabilize the line, but it disintegrated and the Federals retreated. In the heat of the moment, Forrest galloped ahead of his men into the enemy ranks and soon found himself surrounded by Federals shouting, "Shoot that man!" Realizing the danger, he reared his horse around and slashed and shot his way out of the blue swarm.[62]

The now-quiet battlefield revealed the horrific nature of the two-day fight: dead bodies massed in certain sections demonstrated the result of the initial surprise attack and later tactical blunders. One Ohio soldier concluded that the scenes after the battle "would have chilled the blood of the most cold hearted."[63] Cyrus Boyd wrote in his diary, "War is *hell* broke *loose* and benumbs all tender feelings of men and makes them *brutes.*"[64] Sherman and Grant were among those significantly affected by the battle. Although scenes from the fighting may have convinced soldiers that the war was nearing its close, it convinced Grant and Sherman that only total conquest would end the conflict. Why Buell did not see for himself Grant's conclusion reflected the Ohioan's inability, or refusal, to learn from the war.[65]

To those who fought at Shiloh, it was hard to do justice to its ferocity. Even for a seasoned veteran like Bull Nelson, the battlefield was a *"shocking sight,* a *heartrendering sight,"* as he related the battle to Treasury Secretary Chase. "War is an emanation of Hell," he concluded.[66] In the days following the battle, the rest of Buell's army arrived at what Andrew F. Davis of the Fifteenth Indiana called "the Waterloo field of the American Continent."[67] The grisly sights of bodies churned into the ground by artillery and wagons and burned-to-death soldiers pinned under fallen leaves caught even those officers who had become accustomed to seeing the dead after battle completely unprepared.[68]

For a week or so afterward, Richard Pugh, a soldier in the Army of the Mississippi, observed that a certain numbness had come over the whole army. "Everything was quiet as if the whole country was one church," he remarked.[69] Indeed, the Methodist meetinghouse had proven the inspiration for noted author Herman Melville to compose an elegiac memorial to those who perished beside the humble country church. In "Shiloh: A Requiem," Melville attempted with poetic words to return Shiloh Church to the quiet refuge it had once been. As though nothing had transpired, "Shiloh" represented the healing land as it was before the carnage.[70]

After the battle that gave the Union its first taste of large-scale fighting in the West, the soldiers hailed Buell as the savior of Shiloh. William H. Clune of the Sixth Iowa concluded that "General Buell [was] the hero of Pittsburgh, and from [what] they say of his management yesterday [he] could go to bed and forget more generalship in one night than Gen. Grant ever knew."[71] Because he remained with his men at the front, like Sherman, busily barking out orders and positioning his brigades, the men gloried in Buell's presence. Though usually modest, Buell wrote his wife that a great battle had been fought and that his army had "saved the army of General Halleck, commanded by General Grant, which otherwise was doomed to destruction."[72]

It would have been difficult for Buell to conclude anything other than Grant's army was in trouble. The scene at the landing made it appear as though the Army of the Tennessee had been completely overwhelmed by a larger Confederate force or completely surprised. Of course, some officers were more adamant than others about who won the battle and the cause for the overwhelming casualties. Thomas L. Crittenden's aide-de-camp, Louis M. Buford, was quick to render his verdict. "Grant was badly whipped," he wrote to his brother, "and if we hadn't have come to his relief when we did [,] his entire army would have been taken prisoners or [drowned] in the Tennessee River."[73] Lovell Rousseau, a division commander in Buell's army, wrote Secretary Chase a several-page-long letter arguing that what Grant allowed to transpire was not simply a blunder but "the most stupendous crime of this age," asserting that "this battle has blown to the winds, all our admiration for Gen. Grant."[74]

Shiloh had a tremendously sobering impact on both soldiers and civilians alike. Newspaper correspondents sped the news of the battle to their editors before the smoke had even rolled away. "The great battle of Pittsburg will stand forth in bold relief upon the page of future history," claimed one New York correspondent, "as one of the most bloody and obstinate of the century, and by far the greatest our young republic has ever known. . . . Everywhere was mad excitement, everywhere was horror."[75] New York journalist Henry Villard spent hours after the battle trying to pull together some facts and information from the participants to give his editors as complete an account as possible. He had been one of the few correspondents who actually witnessed the fighting. Many Northern reporters who wrote about the events of April 6–7 never came closer to the battlefield than Cairo, Illinois. On April 9 Villard's report reached Washington, and in the morning the U.S. Senate was temporarily interrupted as Illinois senator Orville H. Browning read Villard's account in the *New York Herald*. It began: "The bloodiest battle of modern times just closed. . . . Slaughter on both sides immense." Later in the day, the article was read before the House of Representatives. As Washington politicians read the details of the battle, they began searching for answers.[76]

In the weeks and months following Shiloh, when Americans were attempting to draw conclusions about what happened during those two

days in April, critics from the secretary of war down to the lowly private
considered Grant careless and completely to blame for the debacle. Ethan
Allen Hitchcock agreed with the dismal assessment in Washington of the
general's performance, remarking that Grant had been "little better than
a common gambler and drunkard for many years." The number of Union
casualties alone caused Massachusetts senator Charles Sumner to fume
that some of the Union generals "ought to be shot—according to all the
laws of war." Timothy Blaisdell, a soldier in the Army of the Tennessee,
complained that Grant was an "imbecile" who "had caused the whole
thing." Charles Tompkins lamented, "Our Genl [Grant] ought to be
compelled to serve as a private for the rest of his life."[77] Nelson, never at a
loss for harsh words, also dashed a letter off to Treasury Secretary Chase
informing him that Shiloh was a "blunder on our part arising from the
sheer stupidity of our Generals." Though he praised Sherman, on Grant's
role Nelson wrote, "I say XXXXX-XXXXX. Consider it said."[78]

Although Grant reported to Halleck that Buell had arrived and fought
the second day of the battle, he failed to comment further on Buell's
contribution, though later commending both the general and his army.
Grant praised Sherman highly and rightfully so. Sherman had impressed
Grant by his willingness to earlier waive his seniority and come up to
Donelson from Paducah. The two had developed a friendship before the
battle, and Shiloh deepened it.[79]

By the time the news of the battle filtered eastward, the Lincoln administration was trying to decipher fact from fiction. Among the more
prominent reports that held wide currency with the public was that of W.
C. Carroll, an enterprising young reporter whose dispatch to the *New York
Herald* on April 10 contained a gross overstatement of casualties. According to his brief account, the Federals lost between 18,000 and 21,000 men,
and the Confederates suffered between 35,000 and 40,000 casualties.
Town and village newspapers reprinted this article, thus spreading the
misrepresentations throughout the West. For the residents of Mishawaka,
Indiana, "the shock to the community was one never to be forgotten."[80]

Whatever rumors existed, Lincoln demanded to know if "any neglect
or misconduct of General Grant or any other officer contributed to the
sad casualties that befell our forces on Sunday." To be sure, Congress,
particularly the Joint Committee on the Conduct of the War, would come
down hard on those found guilty of either neglect or misconduct. Halleck,
who had hurried to Shiloh, found it expedient to remain quiet until he
had all the facts and had discussed the battle with the generals in charge.[81]

The Confederates had suffered more than the Federals, though the sheer numbers of killed and wounded overwhelmed both sides. With a combined force of about 65,000 men, Grant's and Buell's casualties numbered just over 13,000 killed, wounded, and captured or missing. Despite the prebattle estimates that Johnston's army was 60,000, 80,000, or even 100,000 men strong, he really had roughly 45,000 engaged and suffered nearly 11,000 casualties. An eager Northern public, anxious for victory, had a combat-tested hero in the West. No longer would McClellan and grand maneuvers dominate the front pages of the Northern press, but fighting—brutal fighting—would be the new standard by which to gauge success. Two days after the battle, Illinoisan George Carrington learned through camp gossip and from prisoners that Beauregard had said at the beginning of the battle: "I'll water my horse in the Tennessee River that night or in h— —" (though Johnston reportedly spoke those words). "Well," penned Carrington in his diary, "I guess he did not reach the drinking place that day." Other opportunities would come to prove such predictions true.[82]

Because it happened on the way to Corinth, Shiloh represented the end of the Confederate counteroffensive in the West to undo the losses of Mill Springs, Forts Henry and Donelson, Columbus, and Nashville. The battle's significance to the Confederacy was felt west of the Mississippi River as well, as Van Dorn's twenty thousand troops, attempting to get to Johnston's aid, abandoned Arkansas and never returned. Yet it also represented the beginning of something larger militarily and politically for the Union. As Sherman attested to his wife shortly afterward, the scenes on the battlefield of Shiloh would "have cured anybody of war. . . . I still feel the horrid nature of this war, and the piles of dead Gentleman & wounded & maimed makes me more anxious than ever for some hope of an End but I know such a thing cannot be for a long time."[83]

CHAPTER SEVEN

A Siege from Beginning to Close

On Friday, April 11, a group of Federal officers walked down to the landing where just days before sheer pandemonium reigned as thousands of panic-stricken soldiers cowered under the bluffs during the fighting. All was calm now and a steamer was approaching. It pulled up to the landing and docked. After a few moments, a rather striking figure appeared. He stood five feet, nine inches tall, weighed about one hundred and eighty pounds, and he was a man of purpose. One officer recalled, "He was carefully dressed in a new uniform, wearing his sword, and carrying himself erect, with a distant and somewhat austere manner, presenting, as he walked down the gangplank, altogether a striking contrast to General Grant." The man was Henry Halleck. Here was the master theorist and overall commander of the West coming to learn the details of the two-day battle of Shiloh. He had written Grant two days before, ordering him to avoid another battle until he arrived; "we shall then be able to beat them without fail."[1]

For Halleck, however, seeing the battlefield was a startling revelation, and beating "them" without fail was a premature notion. The site and the official reports perhaps confirmed for him that his decision to restore Grant as commander of the Army of the Tennessee had its consequences. Scores of rumors circulated through the armies for weeks after the battle, and Old Brains had difficulty deciphering for himself what was truth and what was fiction about the Confederate surprise attack. The fact that Buell had arrived in what many soldiers concluded was the most opportune time to save Grant did little to diminish Halleck's animosity for the whole affair. Of all the commanders he liked less than Grant, Buell was at the top of his list.[2]

As officers prepared their official reports shortly after the battle, it became clear to Halleck, as well as to Grant, that there was considerable debate about the details of the battle. About the only thing soldiers could agree on was that Sherman had performed remarkably during the fighting and consequently emerged as a hero. Thus, whatever problems Grant created for Halleck, Sherman's behavior, at least during combat, had reflected well on Halleck's assistance in restoring the general's emotional stability. Old Brains was so impressed that he requested Sherman be promoted to major general of volunteers. Several officers concluded that Grant was not responsible for the victory, and in fact, many thought that it was his ineptitude that had led to near defeat. Whether or not these accusations were true, soldiers and politicians came to believe them based on the rumors among the ranks that Buell's army should have been credited with the victory. Ohio governor David Tod declared that his citizen-soldiers had been surprised as a consequence of the "criminal negligence" of their generals.[3]

Because of the fog of rumor, debate, and controversy, Halleck was forced to delay his own official report for almost three weeks. In the meantime, Sherman defended Grant, arguing to Secretary of War Stanton that his friend was not at fault. Still, the debate was played out in the press for weeks after the battle, and Buell was credited with saving Grant from the jaws of defeat. Had any other commander allegedly saved Grant, Halleck might not have been so quick to dismiss the accusations. But Buell had been on Halleck's last nerve for several months, and he did not want to believe that his adversary had acted so superbly, while Grant acted so recklessly. Although he thanked Buell for his bravery and for his army's part in the battle, Halleck wired Stanton that the casualties were "due in part to the bad conduct of officers . . . and in part to the numbers and bravery of the enemy."[4]

Moreover, he fumed, "the newspaper accounts that our divisions were surprised are utterly false. Every division had notice of the enemy's approach hours before the battle commenced." Besides, he informed Washington, as if to eclipse the most significant issue of justifying the long list of casualties, "the enemy suffered more than we did."[5]

Over a month and a half later, when he submitted an official topographical map of the battlefield, Halleck would modify his tone, though still refusing to comment on either Grant's or Buell's conduct. The department commander privately knew of Ethan Allen Hitchcock's displeasure at Grant's performance—although Grant was "brave and able on the field," he had "no idea of how to regulate & organize his forces before a battle or how to conduct the operations of a campaign."[6] Benjamin Prentiss, who had every reason to be angry about the battle, perhaps said it best when he perceptively observed that although "we were not surprised . . . , we were not prepared." Nonetheless, Halleck stood by Grant as protector and grew tired of the criticism. After all, he had given Grant the command.[7]

Whatever Halleck's personal views were about Shiloh, Grant, or Buell, he knew he had to finish what his subordinate had begun, and now with such an enormous army, he also wanted the spotlight, which he believed was twenty-five miles south at Corinth. Just as the Confederates came to realize the town's significance as a gathering point for its forces before Shiloh, so too had the railway junction impressed Halleck as the location of the next great battle. Southern poet turned special correspondent to the *Charleston Mercury* Henry Timrod arrived at Corinth in late April, when the Confederates were tending to their wounded, and was surprised to find that it was "quite a place." He had expected to find an insignificant railway junction.[8] On the contrary, it was the most important junction on the Memphis and Charleston Railroad, a line Leroy Walker had characterized in mid-February as the "vertebrae of the Confederacy."[9] There was no question that it had to be defended, and Beauregard was preparing to do just that, or at least Halleck thought so, by marching regiment after regiment into town to recover from the devastating losses at Shiloh. In addition to casualties, what made the defeat even more significant was that, after the battle, a Confederate locomotive would never again run from Chattanooga to Memphis.[10]

Halleck nonetheless remained frustratingly focused on making the war bend to his philosophical Jominian premise: in this case, to capture and occupy the town without fighting. As one soldier put it, "Genl Halleck intend[ed] taking Corinth without firing a musket."[11] Halleck reasoned that the Confederacy could not endure without its strategic cities or railway junctions. Thus, he set out to simply capture Corinth and would be happy to leave Beauregard to maneuver at will. In the days after his arrival at the battlefield, Old Brains began preparing for the advance.[12]

Halleck's shift from his St. Louis headquarters as departmental commander to field commander attracted national attention, and it heightened the public's expectation for success. Naturally, the officers welcomed his presence, not only because his leadership was needed to organize the army but also to quell the continuing animosity between Grant and Buell, a relationship one New York reporter characterized as having "much ill feeling."[13]

Soldiers of the two armies continued to pass campfire gossip, and Halleck's arrival did little to diminish it. But it did provide another topic for discussion. Few soldiers in either Buell's or Grant's army had ever seen Halleck, they knew him only through rumor and a series of rudimentary orders. The general had limited combat experience, and his cautious nature compelled him to be even more deliberate in preparing for what he thought would be a grand battle. Halleck's physical appearance made a lasting impression on the soldiers, who came to understand why he earned his nickname Old Brains. His large frame, protruding eyes, high forehead, and emotional intensity certainly impressed the soldiers that he was a man of determination. Rather than distancing himself from the rank and file, however, Halleck attempted to endear himself to them by sharing the modest lifestyle of the foot soldier, which was not an easy transition. New to field command and a born engineer, anyway, he had little in common with the average infantryman. Newspaper reporters were less impressed. *"He is a Cabinet General,"* wrote the correspondent of the *Boston Traveller.* "There is not the slightest particle of magnetism, of fire, in the man's composition."[14]

Still, he camped in a tent and shared the food of the enlisted. "Living out this way," he wrote his wife, "is not very comfortable in rainy weather, but it always agrees with my health, and I rather like it, notwithstanding the inconveniences." Besides, "it will have a good effect upon the soldiers to camp out with them." Not surprisingly, he blamed the field rations for the mounting sick list. There would be less illness, he concluded, if the meals were properly prepared. Thus, he directed company officers to forage more liberally and to see to it that each meal was inspected. Despite his attempts, soldiers came to view Halleck as the military intellectual that he was, and the moniker Old Brains stuck.[15]

To undertake the offensive against Beauregard's army, a force he mistakenly considered equal in size to his own, Halleck made organization, discipline, and size his immediate priorities. Besides the armies under Buell and Grant, he called on John Pope's services for the move against Corinth. Pope had recently overrun Island No. 10 on the Mississippi River, which thoroughly impressed Halleck and had completed the Union's dominance of the rivers in the Upper South in the West, opening the Mississippi all the way to Vicksburg. Newspapermen were equally impressed by the fruits of that victory, referring to Pope's capture of Brig.

Gen. William C. Mackall's nearly seven thousand men, including three generals, more than 270 officers, and over a hundred artillery pieces—without sustaining any Federal casualties—as "one of the most important and brilliant achievements of the war."[16] Illinois governor Richard Yates immediately recommended to Lincoln Pope's promotion to major general. What made Pope even more pleasing to Lincoln, however, was that he was a prewar friend and a Republican, neither politically ambitious like McClellan nor as tenacious as Buell. Still, Lincoln hesitated to promote Pope, reasoning that while he appreciated the general's grand achievement, "Major Generalships in the Regular Army [were] not as plenty as blackberries."[17]

Halleck ordered Pope to Pittsburg Landing, and on April 22 the four infantry divisions and single cavalry division of his Army of the Mississippi joined those of the Army of the Tennessee and the Army of the Ohio. Combined, Halleck's fighting force ballooned to roughly 105,000 men. Being a subordinate was a new situation for Pope, accustomed to fighting independently in the field, like Buell and Grant before Shiloh. The strain of organizing such an overwhelming force after Shiloh must have taken its toll on Halleck. Years later, Pope would recall that on arriving and reporting to Halleck, he saw the commander "in a tent planted in the mud and lying on a cot with as woebegone a countenance as I ever saw."[18]

Halleck's was the largest concentration of Union forces in the West, indeed on the entire continent, to that time. To ensure that Grant, Pope, and Buell shared his priorities, he made each commander responsible for his own army's organization, discipline, and preparation for service. To help with logistics, Halleck sent for Capt. Philip Sheridan at St. Louis. Sheridan would be more helpful, Halleck thought, coordinating supplies and expediting wagon trains across the virtually bottomless swampland from Pittsburg Landing to Corinth. He designated John McClernand commander of the reserve.[19]

Although it had taken Johnston's army two days to march from Corinth to Shiloh, Halleck was determined not to be caught by surprise. Consequently, he kept his command tightly concentrated and allowed his generals little independence. He emphasized that pickets should be posted well in advance of the camps and that direct communication between army commanders and himself must be maintained. Moreover, roads were to be repaired and constructed as the troops advanced, since there were no railroads or rivers, and entrenchments built when encamped. Thus, swords, bayonets, and muskets were turned into ploughshares, picks, and shovels in the overland crawl to Corinth. On paper, of course, Halleck's vision for the campaign was idyllic, but the weather, typical of spring in the region, was wet, severely hampering operations. When it rained, the narrow roads flooded, bridges washed away, and the whole countryside turned into one huge quagmire. Oddly enough, what proved to be Halleck's logistical curse had for decades allowed the region's agricultural production to flourish (giving credence to its characterization as the Southern heartland).[20]

Besides logistical and organizational difficulties, Halleck had to deal with the political situation in his command. He "promoted" Grant to second in command, which confirmed that the appalling casualty list ultimately forced Halleck to believe that the Army of the Tennessee had been surprised by the Confederates. Too, the resentment of Grant's actions at Shiloh permeated the camps. "Genl Grant is hated and *despised* by all the men and cursed ever since the 6th of April," grumbled one Iowan.[21]

Already concerned over Grant's previous recklessness at Forts Henry and Donelson, Halleck replaced him in command of the Army of the Tennessee with George H. Thomas of Buell's army. Naturally, this made Sherman uncomfortable, since he was now a subordinate of Thomas, whom he had commanded eight months earlier. Despondent over the change, Grant considered resigning from the army altogether. Lew Wallace remembered that shortly afterward he came upon Grant at his tent, and after a brief conversation the general remarked to Wallace that despite all he had done for Halleck, "I was ignored."[22] To his wife Grant wrote, "I have been so shockingly abused that I sometimes think it almost time to defend myself."[23]

Sherman also visited Grant, who was intending to depart on a thirty-day furlough, at his tent one day and convinced him to remain in the army. Though there was enough work to keep Grant busy as second in command, he soon tired of the position, and his desire to leave the army returned, particularly because Halleck had proved that he was capable of managing the armies alone. Part of Grant's frustration, he later wrote, stemmed from the fact that he had earlier thought the Federals should have seized Corinth after the fall of Henry and Donelson. Moreover, to wait for Pope's troops was simply an unnecessary delay. All of this led him to later conclude in his memoirs that Halleck's campaign was a "siege from the start to the close."[24]

Halleck would not have cared much how Grant's memoirs characterized his campaign to Corinth had he lived long enough to read them. At the time, it was all he could do, Halleck wrote Grant, to protect his subordinate from criticism. In fact, Halleck was surprised to learn that Grant found cause to complain about the recent assignment of commands. "For the last three months," he chided, "I have done everything in my power to ward off attacks which were made upon you. If you believe me your friend, you will not require explanations; if not, explanations on my part would be of little avail."[25] This was Halleck's real character.

Though Old Brains gave Buell suspiciously little recognition for his role at Shiloh, he must have been impressed with the Army of the Ohio's performance. The fact that he had three fresh divisions perhaps influenced Halleck to give Buell command of the center wing of the newly christened Grand Army of the Tennessee; either that or he feared putting Buell in charge of one of the flanks. Though Buell was content with his new title and duties, he resented the fact that Halleck transferred Thomas's division to Grant's former army. This irritated Buell because he viewed Thomas as his best division commander, and it left him with only three divisions (eighteen thousand men), one of which was composed almost entirely of new regiments. For Buell, however, the irritation went deeper than simply having his army reduced. He calmly voiced his indignation to Halleck. "You must excuse me for saying that, as it seems to me, you have saved the feelings of others very much to my injury."[26]

The fact that Ormsby Mitchel's division had reached Huntsville, Alabama, in mid-April and severed the Memphis and Charleston Railroad complicated Buell's command arrangement. Mitchel was 125 miles deep in the Confederacy with uncertain connections to his Nashville base. His telegraph line was frequently cut and his decision, on Buell's orders, to destroy the bridges near Stevenson inflamed Stanton, who was anxious that the railroad carry the army east toward Chattanooga. Mitchel was ready to move east, and he bypassed the reluctant Buell and instead wrote Stanton, whom he knew would be sympathetic to his wishes of campaigning aggressively; "The entire war has been moved too slow," Mitchel had griped to a friend. What made matters worse for Buell was that many soldiers in Mitchel's division came to share their commander's sentiments. Buell's conciliatory General Orders 13a, issued after the capture of Nashville, had proven ineffective in northern Alabama, and several officers came to believe that Buell was interested in preserving constitutional guarantees even at the expense of his troops' safety. With this attitude, Mitchel and his subordinates were sure to impress upon

Stanton the need to change war policy or eliminate Buell from command. In the meantime, politicians and the Northern public failed to appreciate the difficulties of occupying a region about the size of France.[27]

The loss of Thomas's and Mitchel's divisions would render more difficult Buell's ability to keep Tennessee's military governor, Andrew Johnson, pacified. It was an odd situation for Buell, since Halleck was in command of the entire West but refused to involve himself in the disputes with Johnson regarding the government's reconstruction efforts and the army's advance to Corinth. Halleck simply allowed Buell to continue to suffer the annoyances of the governor and his wishes to see Nashville securely defended. Although the department chief limited Buell's discretion in other aspects, the fact that he refused to get involved here was curious, particularly since he knew Buell was torn politically and militarily between Johnson's demands and the Corinth campaign. The governor consistently lamented his problems to Washington to get Lincoln's attention, often arguing that Buell's lack of military support in defending Nashville amounted to "substantially surrendering the country to the rebels." Feeling the pressure from Washington, Buell at one point confessed to Halleck that Johnson's views regarding the disposition of troops in Tennessee were "absurd." Old Brains probably took some perverse pleasure in allowing Buell a free hand in the matters Buell knew least how to handle. His refusal to get involved was just another example of the continued unproductive command relationship in the West.[28]

Buell did the best he could with the military governor, and Halleck even made a supportive gesture for Buell's efforts, remarking to his general that he was right in focusing on the advance to Corinth, particularly since, he metaphorically argued, "to accommodate Governor Johnson would be releasing our grasp on the enemy's throat in order to pare his toe-nails."[29] Still, Halleck left the bickering to Buell, which ultimately forced Johnson to engage President Lincoln directly about the situation. "Petty jealousies and contests between generals wholly incompetent to discharge the duties assigned them have contributed more to the defeat and embarrassment of the Government than all other causes combined," he complained.[30] Lincoln simply passed on Johnson's concerns to Halleck, who in turn forwarded them to Buell. Thus, the merry-go-round continued.

The enemy's throat, as Halleck characterized Corinth, had become the center of the Confederate armies and the focal point for Washington officials anticipating an enormous battle. Many political leaders around the country thought as did Assistant Secretary of War Thomas Scott, who concluded that "Beauregard will fight at Corinth."[31] Thus, Halleck settled into a deliberately cautious mental framework and prepared. On the afternoon of May 3, the grand army departed Pittsburg Landing destined to fulfill its commander's prediction that the Federals would be before Corinth, some twenty-two miles away by the nearest road, the following night. "There may be no telegraphic communication for the next two or three days," he warned Stanton.[32] Heavy rains, suffocating heat, and waterlogged roads quickly disabused Halleck of his optimistic schedule. Still, Washington waited daily to hear that the eminent battle of Corinth had commenced.[33]

After plodding for two days over unbelievably inhospitable terrain—what he called a "wilderness" with underdeveloped roads—Halleck's army advanced to within six miles of their goal. Another half-day's march and the army would complete its journey. On the night of the fourth, however, the rains commenced, damaging bridges and flooding roads, and the advance ground to a halt. Halleck prepared earthworks all along the enemy lines to lay siege to Corinth, essentially settling down to wait to see how Beauregard reacted. Each day began with the soldiers standing watch until ordered forward for less than a mile, where they watched and waited throughout the day. After a day of inching forward, the soldiers exchanged their muskets for shovels and dug in during the evening; Halleck was not about to be surprised by a Southern attack. It was a fatiguing march that not only frustrated the soldiers but also made for unhealthy conditions in the poor weather. The large concentration of soldiers certainly afforded advantages, but it provided numerous complications during an advance over rough terrain in soggy conditions. Sheridan, who was appointed colonel of the Second Michigan Cavalry during the campaign, recalled that of his regiment's twelve hundred members, camp fever had stricken nearly two-thirds. Such sickness compelled some Northern governors such as Indiana's Oliver Morton, who was visiting the camps, to bring the deplorable condition of their states' troops to the administration's attention.[34]

Beauregard did not endure the problems of the Union command, but he was not without troubles of his own. President Davis's military advisor Robert E. Lee, writing from Richmond, alluded to these in a message shortly after Shiloh. "Beauregard is pressed for troops," he telegraphed Maj. Gen. John Pemberton at Pocotaligo, South Carolina, "if [the] Mississippi Valley is lost [the] Atlantic States will be ruined." Though the loss of Corinth did not mean losing the Mississippi Valley, it

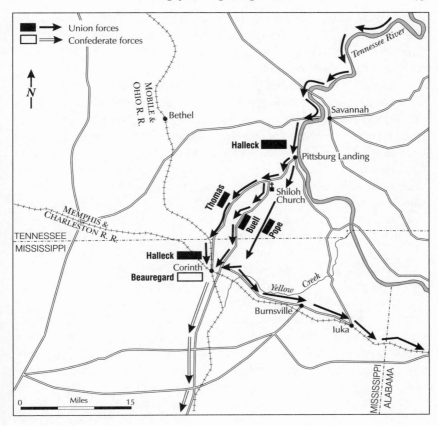

The Corinth campaign

certainly was a vital nexus in that region. It was during the Confederate's retreat from Shiloh that Beauregard was informed that Pope had taken Island No. 10, which doomed Memphis to Union capture. The fact that New Orleans had fallen on March 24 made it apparent that the Mississippi was being lost at both ends; Vicksburg in between was the only Confederate stronghold. He realized that the Memphis and Charleston Railroad was no longer useful, but the Mobile and Ohio ran south through Mississippi, providing shorter communications and the possibility of defensive concentration. On April 29 he ordered the majority of railroad stock at Memphis transferred to Grenada, Mississippi.

The fall of the river cities was made more significant because they were home to several thousand potential recruits. The Confederacy had

lost over thirty thousand men in the West since the fall of Fort Donelson, and most of this was due not so much by fighting armies as by
defending fortified places. Still, Halleck's painfully cautious preparations
gave Beauregard the resource he most needed—time. The Creole had to
contemplate his next move, and Halleck's slow advance gave him more
than enough time to decide about possibly going on the offensive. Still, he
desperately needed more troops. Richmond authorities transferred units
from New Orleans and Charleston to Beauregard, and state governors
drained their resources to increase his force. Earl Van Dorn's veteran army
from Arkansas, which had once been nearly twenty thousand strong, had
been reduced to roughly fourteen thousand men, and they were pathetically armed. It was patently obvious, even to journalists, that Beauregard's
goal was simply to "delay the advance of the enemy."[35]

Though he estimated the size of the Federal army at somewhere between eighty-five and one hundred thousand men—and his own army,
with Van Dorn's troops, at just over fifty thousand effectives—Beauregard
was still hopeful about his offensive prospects, particularly diversionary
strikes into Middle Tennessee and western Kentucky to harass the Federals. The ground at Corinth was particularly strong. The town stood
on a ridge in the fork of two streams that ran parallel to each other,
almost connecting. It was protected to the front and on both flanks by
swampy valleys through which ran flooded streams. A patch of dense
thickets obstructed the swamps from view, and along the highland ran
Confederate earthworks concealed by a stretch of timber.[36]

To defend Corinth, Beauregard used the corps of Polk, Hardee, and
Bragg to configure an arc of works three miles north of Corinth. He positioned Van Dorn on the army's east flank and designated Breckinridge's
corps the reserve unit. Beauregard was not about to wait passively for Halleck's blue wall of Federals to converge on the railroad junction, though.
He would try to lure a portion of Halleck's massive grand army away from
the main advance and into the Tennessee countryside by sending cavalry
detachments out to raid Federal communications. But handicapped by
insufficient manpower on horseback, the small number of detachments
did little to deter Halleck. Beauregard also watched Halleck's advance
carefully enough so that when any one of his army's wings separated
from the main force, he could pounce on it immediately.[37]

Fortunately for the Creole, he did not have to lure the aggressive
Pope much. Acting independently, Pope moved out on the Federal left
from Hamburg and carelessly led his army dangerously far away from

the main column. On May 3 he advanced to Farmington, Mississippi, just four miles east of Corinth, where a virtual swamp and thick jungle divided him from Buell's wing. Pope was nervous, and he wired Halleck to make sure that Buell would keep pace with his own advance. Seeing the opportunity to catch Pope unsupported, Beauregard ordered Bragg to attack the Federals from the front while Van Dorn attacked from the flank. "You are again about to encounter the mercenary invader who pollutes the sacred soil of our beloved country," Bragg proclaimed to his soldiers. "We have, then, but to strike and destroy . . . and redeem Tennessee, Kentucky, and Missouri at one blow" and "open the portals of the whole Northwest."[38]

The Confederates' opportunity to take advantage of Pope's aggressiveness failed because while Bragg did attack, Van Dorn was unable to get to Pope's flank. Beauregard was convinced that Bragg had forced Pope back, and Peter Alexander, a reporter for the *Savannah Republican* in Corinth, telegraphed his paper that the Federals had broken and run "like the Union troops at Bull Run to avoid the capture of the greater part of their command." Pope, however, interpreted his brief encounter as his own victory and was chagrined to find that Halleck ordered him back to main line. When the general again ventured out to Farmington on May 4, Halleck simply ordered him back to his former position before the Confederates attacked. He implored Pope not to advance, saying that it was "dangerous and effects no good." Buell was holding back, which frustrated both Halleck and Pope. Beauregard, also fearing that his flank was exposed, ordered Bragg back to his original line. On May 8 Pope again pushed into Farmington and almost to the Confederate entrenchments, but again Halleck informed him that Buell was not ready to move. Not surprisingly, where Pope saw an opportunity to strike, Buell remained passive, cautious and concerned, like Halleck, about the obstacles in his front.[39]

The Federals continued to advance slowly during the next few weeks, and nothing of particular significance transpired. Halleck's excessive digging-in began to attract considerable criticism from the same reporters who had criticized Grant's failure to entrench at Shiloh. Some soldiers, however, though growing tired of digging, remained committed to the army's purpose "if this rebellion lasts fifteen years." Still, others such as C. Mitchell, who had survived Shiloh, were not anxious for another battle. "I a'nt particular whether I see any more of the elephant or not."[40]

Soldiers such as Lewis Mathewson of the Eleventh Ohio Battery, though, were more affected by the pathetic consequences of the war. Writing to his parents, Mathewson captured a scene frequently observed by the soldiers passing south. While on a brief respite, the artillerist came upon a knoll with a house "occupied by a family of the class known as poor whites, too [proud] to work, living from hand to mouth, and in fact it was very hard for me to see how they lived at all as there was nothing outside except a small peach orchard." He continued: "The old woman said her husband had been dead 10 years, yet she had a family of 8 or 10 ranging in age from 3 days to 18 years. All, save the youngest, chewed tobacco; and they were very anxious for the war to end so that it would not cost them so much."[41] Such scenes no doubt served to reinforce the thinking of Northern soldiers that slavery had produced such a class.

During the second week of May, the army moved to within two and half miles of Corinth, where they dug in and remained for several days. The armies were so close to each other, recalled one soldier, that the pickets were within speaking distance. Lincoln had written Halleck on May 11 that Federal forces had taken Norfolk, Virginia, and that a campaign was under way up the James River. "Be very careful to sustain no reverse in your department," he warned Halleck, which justified the general's decision to remain entrenched for an entire week. On May 18 he wired Stanton that Beauregard was apparently waiting for an attack. Nevertheless, Halleck reported that the Confederates not only outnumbered him but were also being reinforced daily. "Richmond and Corinth," he concluded to the secretary of war, "are now the great strategical points of the war, and our success at these points should be insured at all hazards." Toward that end, Halleck needed more men, fifty thousand more to be exact. Thus, he would continue to wait until reinforced from the East. On May 21 he advanced his works to within one and three-quarter miles of Corinth.[42]

Meanwhile, the Federal command relationships deteriorated. Grant still brooded over essentially being put on the shelf (again) by Halleck, Pope could not believe the grand army moved so slowly, and Buell resented being Halleck's subordinate, though the pace of the advance suited him just fine. In the span of five months, Buell had gone from departmental commander with tremendous latitude in decision making to commander of the smallest wing in a combined army.

It did not help Halleck and Buell's relationship when Pope arrived, since Halleck feared Pope was too aggressive and Buell was too slow. Nor did the situation improve when Buell twice offended Halleck. On

May 17 Halleck sharply criticized the Ohioan for a delay in keeping up with Pope to protect his flank. "You were ordered to move at 8 o'clock this morning. . . . I do not understand the reason for the delay." Buell argued back that he had to examine the ground in his front before moving and thought Halleck would have approved. Old Brains lashed back that Buell was "entirely mistaken" if he thought he could assume such independence. After reading the dispatches from an annoyed Pope and Sherman, whose division had kept up with Pope's pace, Halleck replied chidingly, "Your not moving this morning as agreed upon, has caused great embarrassment." Buell was outraged, particularly since he thought Halleck had allowed him some independence of judgment. "I certainly have intended to carry out your instructions," he insisted, "but where they have not been specific I have supposed that you expected me to exercise my own judgement."[43] As Buell caught up with Pope, Halleck impressed the latter that he should avoid a general engagement.[44]

Halleck had other problems as a result of the pace of his advance. The press began to hound him for the apparent inertia that had characterized the campaign thus far. What made matters worse was that attached to his command was a brigade of some thirty correspondents, the largest such group ever assembled to witness a battle at the time. Not immune to reporters, he handled newspapermen just as Buell and Sherman had as departmental commanders—he expelled them to Pittsburg Landing, where they could get the news from a bulletin board to which officers posted abstracts of dispatches for the Associated Press. This action simply brought on more negative criticism and publicity. Several correspondents of prominent northeastern papers such as the *New York Times,* the *New York Daily Tribune,* and the *Boston Traveller,* called on Halleck for a compromise, provided they professed complete secrecy. Still, the general refused to allow them into camp, which simply added fuel to the journalistic fire against him. Reporters characterized his campaign as a "fiasco," and the dismissed *New York World* correspondent characterized him as an "irritated old maid, a silly school girl, a vacillating coquette."[45]

Moreover, Lincoln himself pressured Halleck for a victory, inform-ing the general that although he meant to cast no blame, each of the Union commanders from Richmond to Corinth "supposes himself to be confronted by numbers superior to his own," which greatly reduced the Potomac line, and that he now felt "justified to rely very much" on Halleck, saying that "the brave officers and men with you can and will get the victory at Corinth."[46]

Some soldiers shared this disillusionment and frustration over what many Americans were anticipating to be the grandest of all campaigns. "A battle is expected everyday," wrote Hoosier Thomas Prickett. If the grand battle was to be, why not get to Corinth quickly and bring it on. But for Shiloh survivors such as Ohioan DeWitt Clinton Loudon, the pace of the advance suited him just fine. He wrote to his wife, Hannah, "we are putting our time in the usual routine of camp, guard & picket duty & drill. There will be no surprise or blundering I think. We sleep on our arms & turn out [in order of battle before day] stand so till after sunrise. Our army is proving the truth of the old saying that large bodies move slowly." Having been at Shiloh Church on the morning of April 6 when the Confederates came screaming out of the woods, Halleck's careful approach seemed necessary to Loudon. James A. Garfield wrote to his brother: "the fate of Corinth must soon be decided. If the enemy still determines to maintain himself at Corinth, there must be one of the bloodiest battles of the war." David H. Thomas concurred, remarking to his parents that if the soldiers ever made it to Corinth, "it will be the greatest battle that has been fought yet." Such foreboding doom caused Loudon to pen what he thought might be his farewell remarks to his dear Hannah and children. "If I should not return," he wrote, "do the best you can for our children. Teach them to love their country & not to forget that their father gave his life for his country that they among others might enjoy the blessing of liberty of law & order & good government." Significantly, Loudon had not written such words before Shiloh.[47]

Governors struggling to meet the increasing demands for men were also annoyed by the slow march to Corinth. What made matters worse was that those whom traveled with the soldiers, such as Indiana governor Oliver P. Morton, made no secret of their ill feelings about the Union high command and Lincoln's handling of the war. Morton was among the most prominent of the Midwestern governors who came to detest the slow pace of the war and had earlier blamed Halleck and Buell for their lack of cooperation in producing a victory. These governors not only kept Washington informed about campfire gossip but also stirred up damaging rumors about commanders. Though insignificant at the time, Buell's capabilities and his noted Southern sympathies would find wide reception among the troops in his wing. Soon, Morton would play a role in turning his Hoosiers against Buell. In the meantime, the governor was concerned enough about the illness in the camps that he wired his state capital that at least ten additional regiments must be sent up the Tennessee River to join the army immediately.[48]

Beauregard was having his share of problems as well. Twice he attempted to attack Halleck's grand army, and on both occasions he found the force too formidable. Waiting for the Federals to give battle was even more frustrating, particularly since the Confederates feared an attack every day and were convinced they could not withstand it. When nothing materialized, the soldiers tried to keep busy. Still, morale was at an all-time low, for the Shiloh defeat continued to cast a shadow on the army. "I am afraid the Confederacy is gone forever," wrote a disillusioned Louisianan.[49]

Worse yet, the condition of Beauregard's army deteriorated from the inhospitable conditions of Corinth itself. Rain and mud made it an uncomfortable and unhealthy campsite. Drinking water was scarce, and in an attempt to obtain it, soldiers dug shallow holes, which quickly became polluted by refuse, throughout the camps. One newspaper reporter commented that the water smelled so "offensively that the men have to hold their noses while drinking it."[50] Even the horses and mules refused to drink from the holes. The misery from lack of good water was compounded by the lack of proper food. The commissary general failed to produce either fresh beef or vegetables. The net result from the ill conditions was that dysentery and typhoid began to take a toll on the army, producing nearly as many casualties as the battle of Shiloh. Beauregard and Bragg themselves began to experience the effects of such conditions. "It is heart sickening to see the poor soldiers in a cold tent on the cold ground without one comfort," complained one disillusioned Confederate.[51]

The Creole began to think he might have to abandon the town due to sickness alone, and he attempted to prepare Jefferson Davis for the inevitable departure. He knew the president was disappointed with the Shiloh defeat, and one more telegram informing him that his forces were falling back again might cost him his command. Still, the options were limited. Beauregard laid out the situation in a letter to Adj. Gen. Samuel Cooper, which began with his determination to hold Corinth at the risk of defeat because of its strategic importance to the Confederacy. He would stand fast until the odds for capture were too great and then pull out and head south along the Mobile and Ohio Railroad to Meridian or Montgomery. Informing Richmond by mail would allow Beauregard about a week to act independently of higher orders. In the meantime, he grew increasingly discouraged by the fact that Halleck had learned through the capture of a Richmond-bound telegram that the Confederates at Corinth were only fifty thousand strong. What made this even worse was that the *New York Herald* printed the dispatch, making Beauregard appear a laughing stock.[52]

The enormous blue mass of troops had moved slowly across the swampy countryside, but it would soon come streaming into Corinth. Beauregard knew he had to act fast, for while he could hold out for a time, the end result must be to give up Corinth, and if he waited too long, his army as well. On May 25 he called a council of war to discuss options. All of the generals agreed that to attack Halleck's well-fortified entrenchments would prove futile. Soon, the Federals might begin bombarding the town, which would make any retreat hazardous. Thus, the obvious decision was to retire, but Beauregard wanted to make sure all of his commanders agreed in order to save himself from the wrath of Davis (once Corinth was abandoned) and to make the evacuation all the more deliberate. He directed all newspapermen out of camp and away from Corinth despite their protests.[53]

Although Halleck was determined not to be surprised during the Corinth campaign, Beauregard devised such a well-orchestrated ruse in carrying out his retreat that it rivaled the Confederate assault at Shiloh in its effect. The Creole devised a false story to leak to the Federals that an advance was about to commence. This was not meant to avoid panic among his soldiers but rather to confuse and freeze the ever-cautious Halleck, whom he feared might attack if he learned that the Confederates were retreating. "[E]verything that is done must be done under the plea of the intention to take the offensive," Beauregard explained. He wrote out carefully detailed orders for his corps commanders to follow in effecting the retreat. The general designated the morning of May 29 as the time of the army's departure; its destination was Baldwyn thirty-five miles south, provided the water was good. Bragg went to the railroad depot to see that the heavy equipment, the sick, and the wounded were put on trains south.[54]

Beauregard's evacuation of Corinth made what was otherwise an obscure and quiet little village appear like Grand Central Station. To disguise his departure as the arrival of a vast force, the general kept trains running throughout the night of May 29, ordering each to stop at certain places and blow its whistle, signaling the arrival of fresh troops, whereupon details of troops would rush to the trains cheering the arrival of reinforcements. Campfires burned all night and drummers from each brigade remained behind to beat reveille at the usual hour. Sentinels remained posted in plain view of Federal scouts, and tree stumps were painted black to make them appear like siege guns and positioned to face the Federal lines. These "Quaker Guns," as they were called, were manned by stuffed "paddies" for gunners and worked quite well in deceiving Federal scouts. Soon, however, crowding at the station became overwhelming, and Beauregard directed Bragg to take charge of all loading operations. "I find trunks enough here to load all trains for a day," Bragg reported. "They are being piled for burning, and great is the consternation." Large numbers of soldiers were so sick, however, that they had to be carried to the station, and the surplus of supplies and shortage of cars compounded his challenge. Still, a more complete evacuation of any Southern city during the war was never accomplished.[55]

While Beauregard was busy creating his deception, Halleck visited Pope's camp, where he learned that the Confederates were concentrating in his wing's front. After midnight on May 29, Pope reported heavy reinforcements arriving in Corinth. The whistling of the trains, the numerous stops, and the commotion of cheering all combined to convince him that the long-anticipated great battle was about to occur. Minutes later, Halleck told Buell that he should be prepared to support Pope immediately. Throughout the night, the Federals waited and listened to the sounds of what they thought was the arrival of more troops. One Ohio soldier wrote to his wife, "One thing certain he [Halleck] will not be taken by surprize [*sic*] as general Grant was at the battle of Shiloh."[56]

The dawn of May 30 broke to the crackling sound of fire burning the supplies the Confederates left behind. Smoke began to fill the sky over the town, and Halleck began to realize that the mystery of the long-awaited enemy attack had gone up in smoke. There was no offensive, no concentration, and as they soon discovered, not even an army. At 6 A.M. Pope rode into town and discovered the completeness of what Beauregard had accomplished. Two hours later the Federals sent some cavalry and artillery in pursuit, but they had no idea where the Confederates had gone. When Halleck rode into Corinth that afternoon, he noticed a blue uniform stuffed with straw hanging by the neck from a scrubby tree limb. Nearby, nailed to a tree, was a pine board inscribed: "Halleck outwitted— what will old Abe say?" After briefly glancing at the dummy and sign, Halleck rode on, only to have his horse nearly throw him after tripping on a telegraph wire. Noticeably shaken and frustrated, Old Brains ordered the wire remounted, supervising the work personally, and then rode out of town.[57]

Lew Wallace, no doubt hoping to redeem himself after Shiloh, had finally made it to a battlefield but was disgusted to learn that there was no enemy army to fight. He was angry over the hollowness of Halleck's victory, griping: "Corinth was not captured; it was abandoned to us. At dawn of May 30th, we marched into its deserted works, getting nothing— nothing—not a sick prisoner, not a rusty bayonet, not a bite of bacon— nothing but an empty town and some Quaker guns."[58] All that remained, wrote a Chicago correspondent, were two or three men with a few women and children gathered around little heaps of furniture that had been swiped from a few burning buildings.[59] The emptiness of the capture had so impressed Pope that years later he remarked, "The enemy was gone . . . and we had nothing to compensate us for our long operations and all the labor the troops had undergone, except an empty little village, dilapidated and dirty."[60]

Halleck was as surprised as Grant had been at Shiloh, which he knew would not bode well in the press or in Washington. To avoid the criticism, he noted for Secretary of War Stanton that the Confederate's position in front of Corinth was "exceedingly strong," the enemy "cannot occupy stronger positions." He went on to further justify why Beauregard left, contending that the Confederate commander "evidently distrusts his army" and that the troops were "much discouraged and demoralized." The fact that Halleck significantly outnumbered Beauregard was not a reason Old Brains wanted to use. If he had, Stanton and Lincoln would have questioned why he failed to bring on a general engagement that would have resulted in both the capture of Corinth as well as Beauregard's army.[61]

Halleck made much of the evacuation and declared the occupation of Corinth a great victory. "Thousands of the enemy are throwing away their arms," he boasted to Stanton; "The result is all I could possibly desire." Of course, Stanton was elated and sent Halleck's dispatch to every state. "The whole land will soon ring with applause at the achievement of your gallant army and its able victorious commander."[62] Halleck rephrased a message from Pope that said not less than ten thousand Confederates were scattered and demoralized and will desert or be captured, which *Harper's Weekly* picked up and disseminated. Though no prisoners materialized, Halleck still used the message to support his claim that the capture was more than the simple occupation of a strategic railroad junction.[63]

The great battle Halleck predicted his army would fight at Corinth proved false because he failed to precipitate it himself. This failure cost Halleck some standing and respect in the press and among his soldiers. Reporters wrote scores of scathing articles focusing on the hollow victory. Halleck had achieved one of the most "barren triumphs of war," wrote a correspondent to the *Chicago Tribune*. "In fact, it is tantamount to defeat."[64] A reporter for the *Cincinnati Commercial* was particularly harsh on the commander, saying he had "been fooled." The writer went on to add that he had previously held a high regard for the conduct of Halleck's advance, convinced that it was reflective of the commander's "deep wisdom." After Corinth, he did not maintain this attitude.[65]

More alarming to Washington, though, was that newspaper correspondents raised significant concerns about how Halleck conducted his operations. Some highlighted the fact that the general had been deceived because he continued to exclude fugitive slaves from his camps, people who might have proven useful to him as informants. Others simply concluded that there had been some gross "mismanagement on the part of General Halleck."[66]

Still, the Union commander had accomplished precisely what he had intended to do, and he would reap the rewards in short order. During the days immediately following the capture, Halleck mounted a modest pursuit after learning that Beauregard had moved south to Baldwyn and then on to Tupelo. On June 5 McClellan emphasized to Lincoln that a campaign to Chattanooga would be rendered much easier now that Corinth was in Federal hands. Chattanooga was important for McClellan because Union possession of that city would force the Confederates to send reinforcements westward by weakening their eastern armies.[67]

From Corinth, Halleck had many options for operations and priorities for the summer, but he would need time to contemplate precisely where his next moves would be. Meanwhile, Beauregard's army marched to the Tuscumbia River, halted, and waited for Halleck. Realizing the Federals were not in full pursuit, the Confederates fell back to Baldwyn, where they halted again to see what Halleck would do. There, Beauregard wired Adjutant General Cooper that the evacuation was complete and the army was heading to Tupelo. It was a "most brilliant victory," he concluded to Cooper, attempting to interpret for Richmond the positive significance of the ruse. Still, news that Beauregard had left Corinth and that the Union army had moved in was anything but pleasing to a Southern public hoping to hear of a battlefield victory, particularly since correspondents reported that it was a Union defeat. President Davis had received the general's previous letter saying that he would hold Corinth until the last extremity. At that time, Davis had Lee respond by saying that the Creole would have to hold out at Corinth, since the military situation was bad elsewhere. Thus, whatever Beauregard said to excuse his evacuation would have to go a long way to satisfy Davis. "The retreat was conducted with good order and precision," Beauregard wrote, "and must be looked upon, in every respect, by the country as equivalent to a brilliant victory."[68]

Whatever doubts Davis had about Beauregard's command abilities before the evacuation of Corinth, the retreat gave him considerable cause for concern. Although he may have saved his army to fight another day, Beauregard had surrendered a significant Southern railroad and all of western Tennessee in the process. The Confederate president had previously sent William Preston Johnston to inspect the western army, and his report confirmed for Davis that Beauregard's actions had done irreparable damage to the Confederacy's position in the region. "I fear Beauregard has thrown away the campaign in the West," Johnston wrote to his wife.[69]

CHAPTER EIGHT

The Promise of Summer

If Beauregard had not actually thrown away the war in the West as he was criticized for doing, the loss of Corinth undeniably diminished his credibility as a commander. Many Southerners came to believe he was responsible for the recent setbacks, and most certainly in Jefferson Davis's estimation, the general was to blame. For months after the battle of Shiloh, the Southern press stirred controversy over the Creole's handling of the second day. The loss of Corinth inspired the press to step up its criticism of Beauregard, which further disheartened his soldiers who read the avalanche of condemnation and listened to camp gossip.[1]

The loss of the Confederate heartland might have been overlooked, as historian Thomas Connelly contends, had Beauregard been able to hold the Mississippi Valley. But like Albert Sidney Johnston, he had no alternative but to concede the region to the Federals because his responsibilities far exceeded his resources. Like the Confederate administration, Beauregard discovered that he could not fulfill all of his strategically important commitments. Indeed, it looked to many Southerners as though the Union might soon conquer the Confederacy west of the Alleghenies, particularly after Halleck's massive army wedged itself deep in the heartland between the Mississippi River and Middle Tennessee. Since the fall of Fort Henry in February, the Federal armies had managed to overwhelm the Confederates in the West by precipitating a domino-like collapse of Southern defenses. Despite Union command problems, the armies made great use of the natural highways afforded by western rivers and had successfully occupied militarily and economically important regions.[2]

Although the Corinth campaign was filled with what seemed like endless days of intense anticipation, capturing the railroad junction represented another significant step in the Union's attempt to thrust a harpoon into the very heart of the Confederacy. It brought closure to the long-awaited battle that never came—a confrontation that both Northerners and Southerners feared would make Shiloh a bloody sideshow. Significantly, the possession of Corinth added yet another dimension to the Union's reconsideration of its war aims by highlighting the realization that complete conquest meant the occupation of territory, the destruction of Southern resources, and the annihilation of Confederate armies. If the resources of the occupied region remained available to Rebel forces, it was simply a matter of time before their leaders tapped these reserves and attempted to recapture what had been lost. Now in northern Mississippi and northern Alabama, Halleck's Federals were positioned to strike harsher blows at the Confederacy's most vulnerable commodity, its people and (most importantly) their slaves. Since Congress convened in December 1861, civil and military authorities continued to assess the significance and value of military occupation in regions that contained hostile citizens and large numbers of slaves. Politicians had decided how to deal with occupation in political terms, but the desire to end the war more quickly focused their attention on broadening the targets of the armies. The experience of Federal forces as they moved south to Shiloh and to Corinth confirmed that half-hearted campaigns were certainly not going to end the war sooner than later.[3]

No matter what civil authorities thought of Corinth's capture, military leaders in the West continued to bask in the glory of accomplishing much with little or no loss. Sherman, for example, shared Halleck's elation over the occupation of Corinth. In an address to his soldiers thanking them for their services, he made some important assertions: "They boldly and defiantly challenged us to meet them at Corinth. We accepted the challenge and came slowly and without attempt at concealment to the very ground of their selection and they had fled away." The occupation of the railroad junction, he concluded, was "a victory as brilliant and important a victory as any recorded in history." Sherman no doubt was just as surprised to find Corinth abandoned as Halleck was, but he de-emphasized the hollowness of not bringing Beauregard to battle and instead highlighted the importance of occupation.[4]

Still, the war was far from over and Sherman knew it; a fact confirmed for him earlier by the fight at Shiloh. He was skeptical about the fruits of the conciliatory policy, stressing to his men that the Confederates must be obedient to the laws of their country and "not attempt its overthrow by threats, by cruelty and by war." To accomplish this, argued Sherman: "They must be made to feel and acknowledge the power of a just and mighty nation. I contend we are fighting for the supremacy of *Written Law* as against the Rule of mere party and popular prejudice."[5] By late spring Sherman had come to believe that it was time for a necessary change in attitude toward the enemy, which he thought would inevitably shorten the conflict.[6]

Indeed, the war in the occupied regions, like the rest of the Confederacy, began to assume a fundamentally new character politically. From a military perspective, the needs of the war and of the Confederate armies had alarmingly exceeded the resources provided by the original volunteering spirit of Southerners. Military setbacks during the winter of 1861 and the spring of 1862, culminating with the horrific battle of Shiloh and the capture of Corinth, combined with the routine severity of camp life and the burdens and hardships of families at home stifled the enthusiasm for soldiering. It was not significantly revived by the lure of a fifty-dollar bounty and a two-month furlough to those who would reenlist for three years or the duration of the war. Thus, prodded by Robert E. Lee and other generals, President Davis recommended and the Confederate Congress enacted the first conscription law in American history nearly two weeks after Shiloh. Conscription made all able-bodied white males between the ages of eighteen and thirty-five eligible for three years of military service, and the terms of those soldiers already in the army were extended to three years from the date of their original enlistment unless the war ended sooner. Given the Confederacy's adoption of measures in February that authorized Davis to suspend the writ of habeas corpus and declare martial law, conscription seemed an appropriate war measure. At the time, Davis remarked to his brother Joseph E. Davis that "this will give [us] men & if you can get arms all will be well."[7]

Conscription represented a political counteroffensive of sorts by the Confederates. Though Davis did declare martial law and suspend the writ of habeas corpus, he was judicious by doing so only in regions that were generally untouched by Federal occupation. Not surprisingly, the very concept of conscription dramatized a fundamental paradox in the Confederate war effort. As Jefferson Davis took the role of loosely interpreting the Confederacy's "necessary and proper" clause of its constitution, which made conscription possible, state representatives fashioned themselves once again in favor of state liberties over national authority. Conscription, they argued, was military despotism and unconstitutional.

Southerners in Virginia, western Tennessee, northern Mississippi, and northern Alabama probably agreed with Davis about his interpretation of the constitution when it came to conscription, for they were most threatened by invasion and occupation.[8]

As an act designed to strengthen the Confederate armies, conscription actually commenced a massive and forced removal of white labor from the countryside at the worst possible time. On small farms, for example, young white males between the ages of eighteen and thirty-five, generally both heads of households and agricultural laborers, were unable to plant spring wheat and corn, thereby leaving families at the mercy of local markets for foodstuffs. Simultaneously, planters of large holdings who were exempt from the draft directed their slaves to plant corn, wheat, and beans instead of cotton, which ensured that not only would there be subsistence for slaves but also a large marketable crop that would command premium prices among the poor during the next fall and winter. Moreover, Southern business leaders guilty of not complying with the law would find themselves without laborers until they conformed to the Confederacy's military priorities.[9]

Confederate conscription was a radical and comprehensive war measure, and it aroused considerable popular resentment. In addition, these actions indicated to Federal leaders that the Richmond government possessed an ardent desire to carry on the war even at the risk of alienating the citizens on whom they placed the burden to fight. Obviously, Confederate officials had concluded from the Union's penetration into the heartland that desperate measures were necessary to win the war. So too had the army's advance south opened the way for Union authorities to implement new policies in dealing with the people and countryside they now occupied. Federal success in the West bolstered the position taken by many congressmen that policies regarding civilian property would have to be modified.[10]

In this regard, politicians as well as military commanders learned not so much from policy decisions but from the experience of trying to police the occupied regions where enemy resistance had escalated beyond conventional warfare. Soldiers and journalists traveling with the armies provided the Northern populace with the evidence that a change in policy was necessary based on their experiences in the Southern countryside. Not only did the press play an important role in generating public support for such changes, but editors also published bitter editorials aimed at discrediting commanders unwilling to adopt harsher measures. Generals, like Buell, who continued to favor conciliation as the most expedient and safest way to end the war particularly received such attention.[11]

Now that the Union occupied a significantly larger and strategically more important region of the Confederacy, administration officials believed that it was time to continue what Lincoln had begun by appointing Andrew Johnson military governor of Tennessee and make a broader statement about how Federal troops should treat Southern civilians who resisted them. Although some commanders opposed expanding war aims and abridging the constitutional rights of civilians, Federal soldiers were becoming increasingly aware that conciliation would have to end before the Union army could effectively be used as an instrument of civil policy, both in terms of confiscation and emancipation.[12]

Several commanders had already tested the constitutional waters of living off the countryside and of responding harshly to civilian opposition precisely because of where they were marching. The experience of Col. John Beatty of the Third Ohio was representative of numerous experiences and similar feelings within the Federal ranks. The condition of the countryside itself and the destruction of war had made lasting impressions on the men. Beatty's Third Ohio was moving through Murfreesboro, Tennessee, and across the Alabama line at about the time of the battle of Shiloh. By mid-April his regiment, part of Brig. Gen. Ormsby M. Mitchel's division, had made it to Huntsville, Alabama. As the troops marched out of Tennessee and into the Deep South, they witnessed "fewer, but handsomer houses; larger plantations, and negroes more numerous." The men saw "droves" of women working in the fields, certainly a consequence of war, according to Beatty.[13]

In late April, while Mitchel's division was operating near Stevenson, Alabama, Colonel Beatty reported that his troops were short on provisions. The owner of a nearby gristmill claimed that the mill was broken and in need of machinery. When Beatty inquired into the man's loyalty, he found that the owner was a Rebel and that the machinery had probably been hidden. Tired of conforming to the administration's limited conception of war, Beatty took matters into his own hands and informed the man that if he did not have the mill going by noon, the colonel's men would "burn it down." By mid-morning the man had his mill running, and the soldiers of the Third Ohio had plenty of cornmeal.[14]

Beatty was involved in early May in another significant episode that highlighted the need to take matters into one's own hands despite Union policy. On May 2 he reported that at Paint Rock, Alabama, several of his troops were wounded when Confederate bushwhackers fired on a passing train. Beatty called the local citizens together and informed them "that this bushwhacking must cease. The Federal troops had tolerated it already too long," he scolded them. "Hereafter," the colonel warned, "every time the telegraph wire was cut we would burn a house; every time a train was fired upon we should hang a man; and we continue to do this until every house was burned and every man hanged between Decatur and Bridgeport." He told the residents that if these partisans wanted to fight, they should join the army and "meet us like honorable men, and not, assassin-like, fire at us from the woods and run." Beatty concluded, "We proposed to hold the citizens responsible for these cowardly assaults, and if they did not drive these bushwhackers from amongst them, we should make them more uncomfortable than they would be in hell." After his speech to the residents, he set fire to the town of Paint Rock, took three prisoners, and continued on to Huntsville. When Mitchel learned of the colonel's actions he was pleased. "The burning of the town has created a sensation," Beatty remarked, "and is spoken of approvingly by the officers and enthusiastically by the men. It is the inauguration of the true policy, and the only one that will preserve us from constant annoyance."[15]

These kinds of reprisals were winning the endorsements of soldiers and commanders, all stemming from the Federal invasion inaugurated by the river victories in February. Still, some commanders such as Buell wholly disapproved and chastised Mitchel for allowing his subordinate officers to abuse the residents for actions in which Buell was convinced they probably had no part. But Brig. Gen. James Garfield, like some other officers, completely approved, convinced that the Union had carried out the conciliatory policy for far too long. He wrote his brother in May that he felt the Union government had been mistaken in believing in a "suppressed Union sentiment in the South," at least in the regions of Tennessee where he had campaigned. "It is my opinion, formed against my will," he concluded, "that there is not enough Union (unconditional) feeling south of Kentucky to plant the seeds of public faith in. The fact can no longer be denied that the white slave interest is inveterately hostile to the Union, and I am most thoroughly persuaded that the Union can never live in these states, except upon the 'broken body and shed blood' of slavery."[16]

In the same letter, Garfield highlighted another dimension of the Union's attitude toward noncombatants. There was a growing dissatisfaction within the ranks toward commanders who continued to protect the institution of slavery and the rights of masters. "A command in the army is a sort of tyranny and in a narrow and ignoble mind engenders a despotic spirit, which makes him [the commander] sympathize with slavery and slaveholders." According to Garfield, this resulted in soldiers feeling abused by the power of tyranny.[17] It had become patently obvious to those soldiers who were doing the actual occupying that a change must come about before the Union could ever be completely successful in winning the war.

There is no question that the Federal advance into the Confederacy's heartland had opened numerous opportunities to test the validity of the Union's policy toward Southern civilians, slaves, and slavery. The arrival of Federal troops in areas with heavy concentrations of slaves certainly stretched the practice of excluding "contraband" from the camps and dramatized the need for a more forthright commitment to harsher war measures. Though in February the Union faced questions about the political dimensions of the conflict, by June their armies had experienced enough actual warfare to persuade Radical Republican leaders to seriously consider revising the war aims to include confiscation and emancipation.[18]

The cumulative effects of the Union's occupation in the West had inevitably disrupted slavery and provided numerous opportunities to escape bondage, slaves believed. Still, black expectations that the war would make a difference in their condition at first led not to insurrection but to restlessness and confusion. They reacted cautiously to the disruptions of war, but discipline deteriorated along with daily routines. When slaves heard that the Yankees were approaching, they became restless with anticipation. But the Union's initial refusal to allow fugitives to fight as soldiers persuaded slaves in Middle Tennessee, for example, that life in the Northern army held no more promise of freedom than what they had on the plantation. When, for example, Buell arrived in Nashville, he strictly forbade slaves into the ranks and, in fact, made it among his top priorities to return them to their masters simply to encourage their masters' loyalty. While the city was under his control, Buell vowed not to interfere with Nashville's enforcement of the slave code and assisted the local police in eliminating vagrancy by fugitives and free blacks. Consequently, slaves in Nashville came to believe that they should avoid Union troops.[19]

Interestingly enough, at a time when the Federals needed friends in the South, they were wedded to a policy of exclusion, which proved more of a curse than a blessing in the long run. Some soldiers came to believe that slaves should be "disposed of" in such mysterious ways that neither their masters nor the commanders would hear from them again. Beatty thought that it was possible that the "two saw-bones, who officiate at the hospital, dissect, or desiccate, or boil them in the interest of science, or in the manufacture of the villainous compounds with which they dose us when ill."[20] Thus, it should hardly be surprising that, as historian Stephen Ash argues, many slaves during this early occupation "readopted their habitual masks of insouciance, and resumed their accustomed toil, to the profound satisfaction of their masters and mistresses."[21]

Still, the Union's occupation of Middle Tennessee and the Mississippi Valley had a liberating impetus; over time soldiers simply reacted to the presence of slaves by routinely employing the men and sending women and children away. Some able-bodied men who fled their masters readily found work in the Union army, first as field hands in the employ of Northerners who captured estates and later with the army itself. Beatty commented from Huntsville, Alabama: "We have in our camp a superabundance of negroes. . . . All the colored people of Alabama are anxious to go 'wid yer and wait on you folks."[22]

The arrival and departure of Union troops certainly affected the mood of the nearby slave population. Beatty concluded shortly after arriving in Nashville that because the Union troops had obtained the reputation of being abolitionists, every slave would desert his master if he could get away with it. Increasingly, more did get away with it because the Union army needed laborers and teamsters to maintain the enormously long supply lines and wagons needed to operate in a countryside where the troops were forbidden to confiscate provisions necessary for their survival. Union soldiers also found that slaves frequently possessed useful information at a time when the loyalty of white civilians was becoming more suspect, and they increasingly harbored fugitives who provided military information. Writing from Jackson, Tennessee, Col. John Kennett of the Fourth Ohio Cavalry concluded: "The white people are treacherous and unreliable, all lying to deceive us. We can only depend on the statement of negroes." Some slaves concluded that working for the Union army was perhaps better than working the plantation, and they gradually left the perimeters of bondage. Many slaves who ran away from their masters, but did not burden an indifferent army by coming into Union camps, simply wandered about. Whatever the case, the death of slavery in the heartland was clearly the result of the Union's occupation of the region.[23]

The penetration south had not only significantly disintegrated slavery in the Upper South but also the policy of conciliation, as the exclusion of slaves appeared not to be a practical solution to a delicate but growing problem. By June 1862 the Union occupied Middle and West Tennessee, the state's two plantation regions, and had advanced temporarily into northern Alabama. Although in February commanders had uniformly promised to protect the property of peaceable citizens, which would keep the Union armies safe as they moved through the Confederacy, now not only had the policy changed but so had the view of some of the commanders engaged in carrying it out. In March a Congressional mandate had prohibited Union officers from returning fugitive slaves to their masters. The initial Federal advance along the sparsely populated Tennessee and Cumberland Rivers masked the difficulties inherent in this policy. For months commanders sought to disentangle the army from disputes about slavery and eliminate the logistical and supply problems created by fugitive slaves, which they thought might encourage masters to reaffirm their allegiance to the Union.[24]

With the West under one command, any alteration in political policy would ripple throughout the armies, now moving in three directions in regions with distinctly different attitudes toward the Union. This was particularly critical for commanders unwilling to deviate from the administration's initial limited-war policy. One of the enduring qualities of Buell, for example, was his refusal to accept the departure from limited to broader war aims having to do with confiscation and slavery. Brig. Gen. James Garfield felt such officers were too sympathetic toward planters, even emulating some of their attitudes toward laborers, or in the army's case, soldiers. He explained: "the position of a soldier in the ranks . . . makes him feel the abridgement of liberty and the power of tyranny. I find my reasoning on this subject vindicated by the fact that there is a growing hatred of slavery among the rank and file of the army." There was no question, concluded Garfield, that the "spirit of slavery is the soul of [the] rebellion, and the incarnate devil which must be cast out before we can trust in any peace as lasting and secure."[25] Naturally, the attitude of Buell and his like-minded subordinates, whom Garfield argued would be content to end the war without trifling the liberties of slaveholders, outraged him.

Although General Mitchel's penetration into northern Alabama presented the administration with considerable optimism about holding on to the Memphis and Charleston Railroad and perhaps advancing to Chattanooga, it also created distress for Lincoln. Both he and Secretary

of War Stanton were elated that Mitchel had severed the Memphis and
Charleston Railroad, but in occupying the region his army would clearly
have to depart from the policy of conciliation (even more pronounced in
Buell's army because he enforced this policy as strictly as possible). This
was not easily done because, of all the division commanders in the Army
of the Ohio, Mitchel stood alone in his views with regard to abolition and
broadening the war's aims to include confiscation.[26]

But it was the behavior of Southern civilians and not the intensity of
the attack at Shiloh that proved decisive in changing the minds of Grant
and Sherman, as well as the administration, about the duration and scale
of the conflict. Civilian resistance greatly affected the transformation of
Northern war aims. Worse than losing their slaves to Union troops, many
Southerners thought, was succumbing to the Yankee hordes. "I am a
greater rebel than ever before," Alice Ready of Murfreesboro penned in
her diary in late March. "I cannot feel yet . . . that God has forsaken us."[27]

Even if morale was low in the Confederate ranks as soldiers experienced a crisis of faith, the morale of the civilian population endured the
bludgeoning casualty rates, military defeats, surrender of cities, and loss
of slaves. The sustaining factor behind this spirit of hope was the belief
that the Confederate army would prevail in the end and drive out the
unwanted Yankees. Civilians prayed for redemption and a counteroffensive. The Federals were not simply military invaders but also agents of
change—a change that represented the demise of Southern culture and
the honor that was such a part of that lifestyle. The fear of the humiliation
and emasculation that occupation represented was enough to bring about
civilian resistance to the invaders.[28]

Throughout the late spring, General Mitchel wrote private letters to
Stanton and Secretary of Treasury Salmon P. Chase about changing the
administration's conciliatory policy. He had experienced a significant
degree of guerrilla hostility from civilians, and although a majority of
northern Alabama residents had registered their support for the Union,
it was the occupation itself and the fear of a lasting Federal presence in the
region that gave rise to guerrilla activity. Thus, Mitchel saw himself and
his forces as the protectors of Union soldiers as much as loyal residents.[29]

As Grant and Sherman administered West Tennessee and Buell administered the interior, they each discovered that sympathy for secession
remained strong among the area's residents despite the Union's best
efforts to promote a sense of reconciliation. Civilians proved recalcitrant,
and guerrillas prowled the countryside, attacking Federal detachments.

"The People are as bitter against us as ever," Sherman remarked to his brother John, "and the greatest danger is that they [the Confederate army] will scatter and constitute Guerilla Bands."Years after the conflict, Grant wrote in his memoirs that it was the Confederate counterattack at Shiloh that had caused him to give up "all idea of saving the Union except by complete conquest," adding, "I regarded it as humane to both sides to protect the persons of those found at their homes, but to consume everything that could be used to support or supply armies."[30]

Still, the increasing guerrilla activity forced Grant to conclude that the "masses this day are more disloyal in the South, from fear of what might befall them, in case of defeat to the Union cause than from any dislike to the Government." He continued to his friend Elihu B. Washburne: "It is hard to say what would be the most wise policy to pursue towards these people, but for a soldier his duties are plain. He is to obey the orders of all those placed over him and whip the enemy wherever he meets him."[31] Thus, whatever Grant's attitude about any escalation of the war, the order would have to come from higher up. And until a change of policy came from Washington, Grant would administer the District of West Tennessee under Halleck's orders, though not without adopting some practical measures to curb public displays of disloyalty.[32]

The latent Union sentiment that Lincoln hoped would surface had not done so by June 1862, particularly not where the armies were positioned. Such behavior, especially when it came to guerrilla operations, blurred distinctions between combatants and noncombatants and marked a distinct intensification of the conflict. Though his division was not present at Shiloh or Corinth, Mitchel's experience in northern Alabama perhaps proved more valuable to the Union.[33]

Despite the earlier assessment by the administration regarding the loyalty of Southern civilians, those residents had contributed to the Confederate war effort, and political leaders as well as many Northern soldiers concluded that they should be punished, not rewarded, for their involvement in the war. Moreover, Southerners should not only be punished for unconventional attacks on Union soldiers but also because of their use of slaves in their fight to retain slavery. Soldiers in the occupied areas believed the peculiar institution had to end. Mitchel's advance through Alabama provided soldiers the opportunity to harden their views about slavery one way or the other. The general himself concluded to Treasury Secretary Chase that, although he could not agree with Chase before the war began that slavery would have to be ended, now that the fight had come, "I shall be rejoiced to see slavery driven from the national jurisdiction."[34]

James Garfield was representative of a growing number of officers who had translated the war into a conflict over the liberation of slaves. "Before God," he wrote to his old college roommate Harry Rhodes in May: "I here second my conviction that the spirit of slavery is the soul of this rebellion, and the incarnate devil which must be cast out before we can trust in any peace as lasting and secure. It may be a part of God's plan to lengthen out this war till our whole army has been sufficiently outraged by the haughty tyranny of proslavery officers and the spirit of slavery and slaveholders with whom they came in contact, that they can bring back into civil life a healthy and vigorous sentiment that make itself felt at the ballot-box and in social life for the glory of humanity and the honor of the country."[35]

Joseph Keifer of Mitchel's division echoed Garfield's sentiments that a growing number of soldiers believed the war was about slavery. "There is no disguising the fact," Keifer wrote to his wife, "that slavery is the issue, that has brought on this war."[36] Certainly, it was considerably easier for soldiers to eliminate distinctions between supporters and dissenters and simply confiscate property that would help feed and shelter the army, particularly if the property included slaves. Emancipation, then, had a military usefulness, since the loss of slaves to the Union resulted in fewer laborers for the Confederacy.[37]

Some soldiers, however, simply viewed the institution as a nuisance. They could not bring themselves to accept that the cause for which they had joined the army and sacrificed so much had so dramatically changed. They voiced their contempt and disdain openly in letters home or in discussions with newspaper correspondents. The longer the soldiers lived with the difficulties presented by fugitives, the more hostile some soldiers became in dealing with blacks. For example, John G. Fox, an Ohio soldier in Buell's army, wrote to his wife during the Corinth campaign: "A greater evil could not exist than to free the negro at this time, why they [would become] more and more insulting and would be even more tyrannical than many officers. If this had been supposed for one minute we would not and could not have had half of this Army. I never would have gone to save a Negro and place my life in jeopardy as I have."[38] Fellow Ohioan James Easton shared this opinion, writing to his family that he wished "Congress would let the nigger alone."[39]

By June of 1862, Halleck could not be bothered by thinking about the political aims of the administration. He simply decided it was better for the Federal army to continue to penetrate and occupy more portions of the Confederacy, especially since Rebel armies in the West would offer little resistance during the summer. With railroads fanning out in all directions from Corinth, Halleck's options for where to move his well-equipped grand army of over one hundred thousand men seemed less problematic. Moreover, he concluded that the Confederates would or could do little to stop whatever he intended. He was perceptive enough to realize that Lincoln and several members of Congress had clamored to seize Chattanooga for several months and that the president would certainly reward the architect of such a plan. Thus, when Lincoln asked for just that kind of campaign, Halleck was more than willing to oblige.[40]

With the exception of a short stretch from Vicksburg, Mississippi, to Port Hudson, Louisiana, the Mississippi River was under Union control by June. Flag Officer David Farragut had led the naval assault up the Mississippi in early April, which culminated on April 25 with the capitulation of New Orleans, the largest city in the Confederacy and one of its major seaports. Halleck could now coordinate his attacks to clear most of the Mississippi of Confederate fortifications, concentrating on Memphis first and later Vicksburg, while sending an army east to Chattanooga to satisfy politicians. But, despite the strength the Union possessed in the West, they would soon fritter away an advantage afforded them by the Confederates' withdrawal farther south.[41]

Beauregard was as scattered as Halleck was concentrated. Though he had nearly fifty thousand effectives at Tupelo, they were responsible for defending the Mississippi River from Fort Pillow to Vicksburg as well as the interior of Kentucky, Tennessee, northern Alabama, and Mississippi. Maj. Gen. Edmund Kirby Smith had twelve thousand men at Knoxville, and a few thousand troops in Louisiana were watching Maj. Gen. Benjamin Butler at New Orleans. Though still pathetically outmanned and undersupplied, Beauregard anticipated an opportunity to resume the offensive with a chance for success. In the meantime, he watched Halleck's every move, worrying him almost daily with detachments of skirmishers.[42]

But just as the Tennessee and Cumberland Rivers had proven a great benefit to Halleck in the winter, so now was it time for them to become a great burden, as summer heat shrank these transportation arteries. The railroad, therefore, became the principal line of operation and support. The swampy roads, destroyed bridges, difficulty of getting supplies, and relentlessness of the heat of the approaching Mississippi summer made his decision to rely on the rails all the more judicious. Halleck turned his attention for the first week of June to opening up the railroads for communication and supply, fanning out his three wings, which quickly restored independent commands, for pick-and-shovel duties.[43]

With the Union in control of Corinth, Halleck returned leadership to the armies in the West to their former commanders Buell, Pope, and Grant; George H. Thomas, however, remained in Grant's Army of the Tennessee. Although being a part of the victorious force that now occupied Corinth, Grant was unmoved by the change. It was a thankless task to have been Halleck's second in command, and he continued to feel abused by the general he had served under for nearly two months. Grant decided to leave the army and return to St. Louis for a thirty-day furlough. True to his temper, he refrained from complaining about Halleck and simply went about his business quietly. Still, the Corinth campaign had made an impression on him. Grant had written his wife that there would be "much unjust criticism" of the Corinth affair, but that "future effects will prove it a great victory."[44] More than that, however, was the sense of displacement he felt for the fifteen hundred inhabitants of the town forced to flee. War had rendered Corinth desolate and its families destitute. He remarked to his wife: "Soldiers who fight battles do not experience half their horrors. All the hardships come upon the weak, I cannot say inoffensive, women and children."[45]

In early June, when Sherman overheard Halleck remark that Grant was about to leave, he set off to find his friend. In camp he found the general seated on a campstool sorting letters. Grant looked up and remarked: "Sherman, you know that I'm in the way here. I have stood it as long as I can and can endure it no longer." After listening for a few moments, Sherman responded that he himself had once allowed himself to be overwhelmed by the mere assertion of newspapers that he was crazy, but that he had remained in the army and the battle of Shiloh had given him new life. "Now I am in high feather." Sherman told him that if he left the army, the war would progress and Grant would be forgotten. He convinced an otherwise demoralized Grant to reconsider his position. On June 6 Grant decided to remain in the army and wrote Sherman of the news. His friend replied in a note that he was "rejoiced" at Grant's choice. It was the beginning of a new phase in their friendship, one of the most productive command relationships of the war.[46]

Meanwhile, Halleck remained at Corinth. Sherman was ordered to repair the railroads to Memphis, and John McClernand, commanding the reserve, was detailed to rebuild the bridges on the line to Columbus, Kentucky, which Halleck saw as a main supply route. Pope was ordered to repair the railroads south of Corinth, and Buell was sent east to open the line to Tuscumbia and Decatur. Halleck anticipated that the Army of the Ohio would soon move farther to the east all the way to Chattanooga, and he wanted Mitchel to cross a small force at Decatur to repair the road and communications in preparation for Buell. On paper, at least, Halleck viewed this campaign the least problematic to effect. "The main object now," he lectured Pope, "is to get the enemy far enough south to relieve our railroads from danger of an immediate attack. There is no object in bringing on a battle if this object can be obtained without one." The months ahead would prove his predilections wrong.[47]

Being strategically centered on the rails heading in all directions strengthened Halleck's position, and it made the Confederate stronghold of Fort Pillow on the Mississippi vulnerable. By June 1, Brig. Gen. John B. Villepigue abandoned the fort, throwing residents of Memphis seventy miles south into hysteria. Citizens throughout the river city wondered, "When do you think the Federals will be here?"[48] Five days later Adm. Charles H. Davis, who had succeeded Commodore Andrew Foote in command of the gunboats, appeared and destroyed the Confederate fleet in front of the city. The battle that determined Memphis's fate was fought on the Mississippi River a short distance above the city on the morning of June 6. Thousands of anxious citizens flocked to the bluffs to witness the fighting that would determine the fate of their city. Among the eager spectators who had arrived at the bluff even before dawn was the *Charleston Courier* correspondent Felix Gregory de Fontaine, formerly of the *New York Herald*. De Fontaine, who had been carried from his sickbed to an observation point described how the Federal warships let loose nearly seventy heavy guns against Commodore James E. Montgomery's Confederate fleet, which was armed with less than thirty guns, and won the engagement in less than an hour.[49]

That same day, the Forty-third and Forty-seventh Indiana, two regiments Pope had left with the fleet, entered Memphis. Union gunboats now could steam all the way south to Vicksburg. Though the city's papers tried to put the best face on the disaster, the news of Memphis's surrender thoroughly diminished Beauregard's chances to resume the offensive. Like the residents of Nashville had in late February, so now did the residents of Memphis acquiesce to the Federal occupation. Oddly enough, the most Confederate region of Tennessee was now in Union hands, while the most loyal region—East Tennessee—remained occupied by Confederates.[50]

Though Beauregard had avoided wiring Richmond the reason for giving up Corinth, the surrender of Memphis would demand an immediate explanation. Coming on the heels of Corinth, the loss of the important Mississippi River city compounded the Confederacy's losses in the West. Though the Southern army was intact, conceding the heartland and the Mississippi Valley was alarming to the Confederate cabinet and certainly demoralizing to the soldiers. The atmosphere in the western army was so dreary that rumors surfaced claiming that the Creole had been insane at Shiloh, hiding in his tent. It did not help Beauregard that he assumed command of the second-most-powerful Confederate army by default when Albert Sidney Johnston was killed.[51]

Just when he most needed support from prominent political leaders, Beauregard failed to enlist Jefferson Davis. In fact, the president had not spoken to the general since the battle of Bull Run and had concluded that he was sympathetic to the anti-Davis faction in the army and Richmond. Nevertheless, Davis had increased his efforts to reinforce the western army after Shiloh. He had called on the governors of the states for more troops and arms to support Beauregard's expected battle at Corinth. When it did not happen, Davis concluded that he had unnecessarily badgered state representatives already hostile since the inception of the draft.[52]

While Beauregard had corresponded with Richmond prior to the fall of Corinth, he failed to explain exactly what he intended to do there. On June 12 the general wired a brief message to Davis explaining that he had not time to report either his plans or the reasons for abandoning Corinth. Still, Beauregard had found time to defend his retreat in the Southern press by writing a long-winded letter arguing that the Confederacy should look upon his retreat from Corinth as a "brilliant victory." When he did report the following day, it was too late. Davis, still at odds with the general and no doubt questioning his decision to send him to the West, decided to transfer him elsewhere—after all, it was Beauregard's departure from Virginia months before that set Halleck, or rather Halleck's subordinates, in motion along the rivers. When South Carolina governor Francis Pickens complained that Maj. Gen. John C. Pemberton needed to be replaced and suggested Beauregard as his successor, Davis used the opportunity to make a judicious change. He confided to his wife that "there are those who can only walk a log when it is near to the ground, and I fear he

[Beauregard] has been placed too high for his mental strength, as he does not exhibit the ability manifested on smaller fields." Lamentably, he concluded, "We must make a desperate effort to regain what Beauregard has abandoned in the West."[53]

Meanwhile, the general's health continued to decline, as a throat ailment continued to bother him. Finally, on June 14 he took the advice of his medical staff and traveled to Bladon Springs, a resort north of Mobile. He left Maj. Gen. Braxton Bragg in command during his absence. But Beauregard communicated nothing to Davis, and his departure in the president's mind amounted to little more than desertion.[54]

Beauregard's brief absence from the army provided Davis the opportunity to have Governor Pickens request Beauregard to come to Charleston as commander and avoid having to dismiss the general outright from command. When Beauregard refused to acquiesce, however, Davis decided to replace him with Bragg, charging that the Creole had left his army under improper circumstances. Naturally, Beauregard was personally injured by the dismissal. To his chief of staff, Thomas Jordan, he spoke his mind. "If the country be satisfied," he wrote, "to have me laid on the shelf by a man who is either demented or a traitor to his high trust—well, let it be so. As to my reputation, if it can suffer by any thing that living specimen of gall & hatred, can do—why it is not then worth preserving. . . . I am annoyed to death now by having everybody looking at me, wherever I go, like a wild beast."[55]

Bragg was promoted to full general and made permanent commander of the western department, but it was an embarrassing situation for him. Though he had been jealous of Beauregard, he had nonetheless respected his commander greatly. Still, the situation in the West was in disastrous shape and the army's high command in turmoil. Bragg faced the same challenges as Beauregard, for the mass of problems had not diminished in the least. Food, supplies, and transportation were all as scarce as manpower. The army was in need of reorganization, restoration of morale, and motivation to resume the offensive and reclaim some of what had been lost over the past several months. Davis had been looking for the opportunity to eliminate Beauregard, and now he had done so. The Southern press, however, had generally been favorable toward Beauregard, and when Bragg replaced him, editors accused the president of "gratifying his spleen at Beauregard's expense."[56]

Though Beauregard had suffered the political guillotine and the Confederates had endured the loss of the Confederate heartland, the Federals were not without their problems despite having several laurels of which to boast. Buell's campaign to Chattanooga, for example, proved to be a long, fatiguing march across the countryside that made railroad workers out of soldiers. It attracted the wrath of political leaders, editors, and soldiers alike because of its slow pace and the commander's refusal to consider the prize of Chattanooga worth more than the risks he might have taken to get there sooner. Federal strategy would have to change. The difficulty of getting supplies to the advancing armies would tax the quartermaster, who was forced to rely on the iron rails instead of the rivers. Also, where the soldiers had to live off the countryside, it was in the same region through which the Confederates had retreated, depleting the resources as they went.[57]

Additionally, there was increasing proof that the Southern reaction to Union occupation was no better than it had been six months before. Civilians had decided to defend themselves in unconventional ways such as forming guerrilla groups or as individuals sabotaging resources that might prove useful to the Yankees. But there was reason to believe that the war could be ended before it became all consuming. Writing to his wife from Corinth in mid-June, Grant observed that the citizens were returning to the small hamlet and concluded, "they all seem to think the Yankees a much less bloody revengeful and to be dreaded people, than they had been led to think." He argued, "In my mind there is no question but that this war could be ended at once if the whole Southern people could express their unbiased feeling untrammelled by leaders."[58] Until they did, though, Federal soldiers and politicians came to believe in the need for a harsher policy toward them.

By the end of spring 1862, the advances of the Federal armies convinced political leaders in Washington that the Union had positioned itself to touch the real strength of the Confederacy—the civilian population and slavery. It was in the West and not the East, some leaders were convinced, where the Federals could inflict the most severe damage to what many believed was the cause of the war—the institution of slavery. Significantly, it was in this context that Union forces expanded their objectives as they advanced into the South. For some months, generals had tried to restrain men from living off the countryside, religiously protecting the rights of Southern civilians. By the summer, however, Northern political leaders became convinced that the war would continue indefinitely unless the Union armies engaged in harsher measures. Military gains in the West, according to historian Jeffrey Hummel, "had brought the total area requiring Northern occupation up to the size of France," and the failure on the part of the Confederate army to defend the region's citizens unwittingly resulted in guerrilla warfare. Thus, efforts to expand the war found wide reception among Union soldiers and those politically enlightened commanders eager to live off the country. The experience over the past months allowed them to better comprehend that victory could be achieved only if the Northern people remained committed to an expanded policy.[59]

Once the Union convinced itself that the war could not be won with half-hearted campaigns, Confederate armies in the West could do little more than engage in an uphill fight to reclaim at least part of the Mississippi Valley. This meant that Southern armies would have to go on the offensive. It could be done, but not without great loss, which the Confederacy itself had not the replacement capacity to sustain.

After months of campaigning through the Southern heartland and seeing the desolation of the countryside left behind by war—even one that had been limited to battlefields—Grant was among the most profoundly affected by what he had witnessed. "What the people are to do for the next year is hard to surmise," he penned his wife, "but there must be a vast amount of suffering. I pity them and regret this folly which has brought about this unnatural war and their suffering."[60] An impassioned letter though it surely was, Grant recognized that nothing short of military success would end the war. Thus, when the administration adopted an attitude of severity against the enemy, Grant would become one of the North's leading disciples of harsher warfare against the Confederacy itself, not merely its gray-clad combatants.

By mid-summer the Union's second confiscation act became law, enacting a policy to seize everything in enemy territory that could be used to support the armies. Lincoln sent for Halleck to come to Washington as his military chief of staff. Grant and Sherman policed West Tennessee, while Buell inched his way across northern Alabama toward Chattanooga. It was an eventful summer, even when compared to the past winter and spring, because the struggle to maintain supremacy and perhaps bring about some fundamental change in the occupied regions constituted a form of warfare not easily combated. Union soldiers no doubt reflected on what they had achieved, while the Confederates thought of how to reclaim what they had once possessed. In the meantime, the men of both armies went about their business with great anticipation of what was to come. According to Manning Ferguson Force, colonel of the Twentieth Ohio at the time and later author of *From Fort Henry to Corinth*, it was during the campaigns from Fort Henry to Corinth that the soldiers "had learned something of the business of war and were now ready for campaign, battle and siege."[61]

Notes

INTRODUCTION

1. Review of Manning F. Force, *From Fort Henry to Corinth* (New York: Charles Scribner's Sons, 1882), by Theodore A. Dodge in *The Dial* 2 (1882): 211–14.

2. Larry Daniel, *Shiloh: The Battle that Changed the Civil War* (New York: Simon and Schuster, 1997), 13.

3. Benjamin Franklin Cooling, *Fort Donelson's Legacy: War and Society in Kentucky and Tennessee, 1862–1863* (Knoxville: University of Tennessee Press, 1997), xiv.

4. Cooling, *Fort Donelson's Legacy*, xii.

5. Daniel E. Sutherland, ed., *Guerrillas, Unionists, and Violence on the Confederate Home Front* (Fayetteville: University of Arkansas Press, 1999), 113–32.

1. RIVERS, VALLEYS, AND ARMIES

1. Allen Nevins, *The War for the Union: War becomes Revolution* (New York: Charles Scribner's Sons, 1960), 14–15.

2. Henry Clyde Hubbart, *The Older Middle West, 1840–1880: Its Social, Economic, and Political Life, and Sectional Tendencies before, during, and after the Civil War* (New York: Russell and Russell, 1936), 74–89; Benjamin Franklin Cooling, *Forts Henry and Donelson: The Key to the Confederate Heartland* (Knoxville: University of Tennessee Press, 1987), 1–10; Avery O. Craven, *The Growth of Southern Nationalism, 1848–1861* (Baton Rouge: Louisiana State University Press, 1953), 21–27; Edward C. Smith, *The Borderland in the Civil War* (New York: Macmillan, 1927), 6–11.

3. Cooling, *Forts Henry and Donelson*, 1–10; Hubbart, *Older Middle West*, 74–89.

4. Lloyd Lewis, *Sherman, Fighting Prophet* (New York: Harcourt, Brace, 1932), 252.

5. Smith, *Borderland in the Civil War*, 2–3, 7–10; Hubbart, *Older Middle West*, 85–111, 154–61; Earl Hess, "The Mississippi River and Secession, 1861: The Northwestern Response," *Old Northwest* (summer 1984): 187–88.

6. Clement A. Evans, ed., *Confederate Military History* (Atlanta: Confederate Publishing Company, 1899), 12:2, 17.

7. Brooks D. Simpson and Jean V. Berlin, eds., *Sherman's Civil War: Selected Correspondence of William T. Sherman, 1860–1865* (Chapel Hill: University of North Carolina Press, 1999), 8.

8. *New Albany Daily Ledger,* February 18, 1861; Hess, "Mississippi River and Secession," 187–201.

9. *Cincinnati Daily Gazette,* January 14, 1861; Hess, "Mississippi River and Secession," 187–201.

10. Simpson and Berlin, *Sherman's Civil War,* 149; Smith, *Borderland in the Civil War,* 2–3, 7–10; Cooling, *Forts Henry and Donelson,* 1–10; Thomas L. Connelly, *Army of the Heartland: The Army of Tennessee, 1861–1862* (Baton Rouge: Louisiana State University Press, 1967), 3–18; Hubbart, *Older Middle West,* 154–61; Hess, "Mississippi River and Secession," 187–201.

11. William L. Barney, *The Passage of the Republic: An Interdisciplinary History of Nineteenth-Century America* (Lexington MA: D. C. Heath, 1987), 20–25; *Cincinnati Daily Commercial,* January 25, 1861; Cooling, *Forts Henry and Donelson,* 1–5.

12. Robert C. Black III, *The Railroads of the Confederacy* (Chapel Hill: University of North Carolina Press, 1952), 4–9; Cooling, *Forts Henry and Donelson,* 3–5.

13. Smith, *Borderland in the Civil War,* 22–27; Black, *Railroads of the Confederacy,* 5–11, 70–72; Hubbart, *Older Middle West,* 154–61.

14. Hubbart, *Older Middle West,* 83–85, 146, 154–61, 223–25; Smith, *Borderland in the Civil War,* 7–9; Cooling, *Forts Henry and Donelson,* 2–3.

15. *Congressional Globe,* 36th Cong., 2d sess., 1861, 49; Barney, *Passage of the Republic,* 200.

16. *De Bow's Review* quoted in William L. Barney, *The Road to Secession* (New York: Praeger Publishers, 1972), 40; Smith, *Borderland in the Civil War,* 26–35; Richard C. Wade, *Slavery in the Cities: The South, 1820–1860* (New York: Oxford University Press, 1964), 273–81.

17. Smith, *Borderland in the Civil War,* 26–35; Barney, *Passage of the Republic,* 200–208.

18. Craven, *Growth of Southern Nationalism,* 8; Cooling, *Forts Henry and Donelson,* xii.

19. Stephen V. Ash, ed., *Secessionists and Other Scoundrels: Selections from Parson Brownlow's Book* (Baton Rouge: Louisiana State University Press, 1999), 82–83.

20. Phillip Shaw Paludan, *"A People's Contest": The Union and the Civil War* (New York: Harper and Row, 1988), 26; Smith, *Borderland in the Civil War,* 134–39, 283–85; E. Merton Coulter, *The Civil War and Readjustment in Kentucky* (Chapel Hill: University of North Carolina Press, 1926), 6–12.

21. U.S. Navy Department, *Official Records of the Union and Confederate Navies in the War of Rebellion,* 30 vols. (Washington DC: Government Printing Office, 1894–

1921), ser. 1, 25:474 (cited hereafter as ORN, all references are to series 1 unless otherwise indicated).

22. Nevins, *War for the Union,* 14–15.

23. Connelly, *Army of the Heartland,* 3–10.

24. U.S. War Department, *The War of the Rebellion: A Compilation of the Official Records of the Union and Confederate Armies,* 128 vols. (Washington DC: Government Printing Office, 1880–1901), ser. 3, 1:70–81 (cited hereafter as OR, all references are to series 1 unless otherwise indicated); William B. Hesseltine, *Lincoln and the War Governors* (Gloucester MA: Peter Smith, 1972), 146–47; Connelly, *Army of the Heartland,* 9–11; Smith, *Borderland in the Civil War,* 263–66.

25. OR, ser. 3, 1:167–70; Hubbart, *Older Middle West,* 166–73; Hesseltine, *Lincoln and the War Governors,* 147–73.

26. Coulter, *Civil War and Readjustment in Kentucky,* 57–80; Cooling, *Forts Henry and Donelson,* 5–6; Smith, *Borderland in the Civil War,* 278–79.

27. Hesseltine, *Lincoln and the War Governors,* 147–74; William D. Foulke, *Life of Oliver P. Morton,* 2 vols. (Indianapolis IN: Bowen-Merrill, 1898–99), 1:110–15; Connelly, *Army of the Heartland,* 25.

28. Joseph A. Frank and George K. Reaves, *"Seeing the Elephant": Raw Recruits at the Battle of Shiloh* (New York: Greenwood Press, 1989), 20; Connelly, *Army of the Heartland,* 3–25; Gerald Prokopowicz, "All for the Regiment: Unit Cohesion and Tactical Stalemate in the Army of the Ohio, 1861–1862" (Ph.D. diss., Harvard University, 1994), 9–82; Paludan, *"A People's Contest,"* 3–30. See also James M. McPherson, *For Cause and Comrades: Why Men Fought in the Civil War* (New York: Oxford University Press, 1997).

29. *Harper's Weekly,* October 12, 1861; Connelly, *Army of the Heartland,* 10–13; Hesseltine, *Lincoln and the War Governors,* 158–61, 210–11.

30. William C. Davis, *Jefferson Davis: The Man and His Hour* (New York: Harper Collins, 1991), 364–80. See also T. Harry Williams, *Lincoln and His Generals* (New York: Alfred A. Knopf, 1952); and Steven E. Woodworth, *Jefferson Davis and His Generals: The Failure of Confederate Command in the West* (Lawrence: University Press of Kansas, 1990).

31. Davis, *Jefferson Davis,* 372–79; Woodworth, *Davis and His Generals,* 33–35.

32. Woodworth, *Davis and His Generals,* 30–36; Connelly, *Army of the Heartland,* 47–50; Davis, *Jefferson Davis,* 376–77; Nathaniel Cheairs Hughes Jr. and Roy P. Stonesifer Jr., *The Life and Wars of Gideon J. Pillow* (Chapel Hill: University of North Carolina Press, 1993), 188–205.

33. William P. Johnston, *The Life of General Albert Sidney Johnston* (New York: D. Appleton, 1878), 291; Charles Roland, *Albert Sidney Johnston: Soldier of Three Republics* (Austin: University of Texas Press, 1964), 249–61; Davis, *Jefferson Davis,* 377.

34. Davis quoted in Davis, *Jefferson Davis,* 378; Roland, *Albert Sidney Johnston,* 249–61.

35. Roy P. Basler, ed., *Collected Works of Abraham Lincoln*, 8 vols. (New Brunswick NJ: Rutgers University Press, 1953–55), 4:532; Phillip Shaw Paludan, *The Presidency of Abraham Lincoln* (Lawrence: University Press of Kansas, 1994), 83; Roland, *Albert Sidney Johnston*, 261–63; Davis, *Jefferson Davis*, 376–80.

36. Basler, *Works of Lincoln*, 4:532; Smith, *Borderland in the Civil War*, 290–91; Richard Current, *Lincoln's Loyalists: Union Soldiers from the Confederacy* (Boston: Northeastern University Press, 1992), 29–30; Daniel W. Crofts, *Reluctant Confederates: Upper South Unionists in the Secession Crisis* (Chapel Hill: University of North Carolina Press, 1989), 270–72, 350–55.

37. OR, 4:257 (see also 52:140); Steven E. Woodworth, "The Indeterminate Quantities: Jefferson Davis, Leonidas Polk, and the End of Kentucky Neutrality, September 1861," *Civil War History* 38 (December 1992): 289–97; Davis, *Jefferson Davis*, 376–78.

38. Woodworth, "Indeterminate Quantities," 289–97.

39. Roland, *Albert Sidney Johnston*, 263–74; Woodworth, "Indeterminate Quantities," 376–78.

40. OR, 4:420–21; Roland, *Albert Sidney Johnston*, 263–74; Connelly, *Army of the Heartland*, 63–65; Nathaniel Cheairs Hughes Jr., *General William J. Hardee: Old Reliable* (Baton Rouge: Louisiana State University Press, 1965), 81–86; Steven E. Woodworth, ed., *Civil War Generals in Defeat* (Lawrence: University Press of Kansas, 1999), 15.

41. John F. Marszalek, *Sherman: A Soldier's Passion for Order* (New York: Free Press, 1993), 156–62. For other biographies of Sherman, see Michael Fellman, *Citizen Sherman: A Life of William Tecumseh Sherman* (New York: Random House, 1995); and Stanley P. Hirshson, *The White Tecumseh: A Biography of William T. Sherman* (New York: John Wiley & Sons, 1997).

42. Jay Monaghan, *The Civil War on the Western Border, 1854–1865* (Boston: Little, Brown, 1955), 185; OR, 3:466–67; Paludan, *Presidency of Lincoln*, 86–87; Wallace J. Schutz and Walter N. Trenerry, *Abandoned by Lincoln: A Military Biography of General John Pope* (Champaign: University of Illinois Press, 1990), 64–73. See also Michael Fellman, *Inside War: The Guerrilla Conflict in Missouri during the American Civil War* (New York: Oxford University Press, 1989).

43. William S. McFeely, *Grant: A Biography* (New York: W. W. Norton, 1981), 91–94; Cooling, *Forts Henry and Donelson*, 16–19. See also Nathaniel C. Hughes Jr., *The Battle of Belmont: Grant Strikes South* (Chapel Hill: University of North Carolina Press, 1991); Geoffrey Perret, *Ulysses S. Grant: Soldier and President* (New York: Random House, 1997), 124–40; and Brooks D. Simpson, *Ulysses S. Grant: Triumph over Adversity, 1822–1865* (New York: Houghton Mifflin, 2000), 76–109.

44. Stephen W. Sears, *George B. McClellan: The Young Napoleon* (New York: Ticknor and Fields, 1988), chapters 1–3; George B. McClellan, *McClellan's Own Story* (New York: Charles L. Webster, 1887), 2–12.

45. *Harper's Weekly*, November 30, 1861; Sears, *George B. McClellan*, 128–39;

Stephen E. Ambrose, *Halleck: Lincoln's Chief of Staff* (Baton Rouge: Louisiana State University Press, 1962), 11–12; Curt Anders, *Henry Halleck's War: A Fresh Look at Lincoln's Controversial General-in-Chief* (Carmel: Guild Press of Indiana, 1999), 34–41.

46. Henry Villard, *Memoirs of Henry Villard, Journalist, and Financier, 1835–1900*, 2 vols. (Boston: Houghton, Mifflin, 1904), 1:211–12; Sears, *George B. McClellan*, 35, 128.

47. OR, 52:184; Basler, *Works of Lincoln*, 5:303.

48. OR, 4: 257; Freeman Cleaves, *Rock of Chickamauga: The Life of General George H. Thomas* (Norman: Oklahoma University Press, 1948), 76–93.

49. Stephen W. Sears, ed., *The Civil War Papers of George B. McClellan: Selected Correspondence, 1860–1865* (New York DaCapo Press, 1992), 71–72; Paludan, *Presidency of Lincoln*, 82–83; Mark Grimsley, *The Hard Hand of War: Union Military Policy toward Southern Civilians, 1861–1865* (New York: Cambridge University Press, 1995), 32–33.

50. Sears, *Papers of McClellan*, 72–75.

51. Sears, *Papers of McClellan*, 75; Grimsley, *Hard Hand of War*, 32–33; Stephen V. Ash, *When the Yankees Came: Conflict and Chaos in the Occupied South, 1861–1865* (Chapel Hill: University of North Carolina Press, 1995), 24–28.

52. Basler, *Works of Lincoln*, 4:506; Grimsley, *Hard Hand of War*, 35; Paludan, *Presidency of Lincoln*, 86–88; Cooling, *Fort Donelson's Legacy*, 38–39; David Donald, *Lincoln* (New York: Simon and Schuster, 1995), 313–17.

53. Grimsley, *Hard Hand of War*, 8–46; Paludan, *Presidency of Lincoln*, 82–88.

54. Emory M. Thomas, *The Confederacy as a Revolutionary Experience* (Englewood NJ: Prentice-Hall, 1971), 45–48; Davis, *Jefferson Davis*, 318; Barney, *Passage of the Republic*, 198–211.

55. Davis, *Jefferson Davis*, 318–75; Thomas, *Confederacy as a Revolutionary Experience*, 45–58.

56. Barney, *Road to Secession*, 11; Barney, *Passage of the Republic*, 198–211; William C. Davis, *A Government of Our Own: The Making of the Confederacy* (New York: Free Press, 1994), chapters 1–3.

57. Ira Berlin et al., eds., *The Destruction of Slavery* (New York: Cambridge University Press, 1985), 249; Cooling, *Forts Henry and Donelson*, 1–4.

58. Charles W. Wills, *Army Life of an Illinois Soldier: Letters and Diary of the Late Charles W. Wills* (Washington DC: Globe Printing, 1906), 121, 32, 76.

59. Cooling, *Forts Henry and Donelson*, 2–10.

2. POLITICS, PLANNING, AND PROCRASTINATION

1. Basler, *Works of Lincoln*, 5:48–49; Paludan, *Presidency of Lincoln*, 84–104; Paludan, *"A People's Contest,"* 87–88; Hans L. Trefousse, *The Radical Republicans: Lincoln's Vanguard for Racial Justice* (New York: Alfred Knopf, 1969), 184–86.

2. Philip S. Foner, ed., *The Life and Writings of Frederick Douglass*, 5 vols. (New York: International Publishers, 1955), 3:198–203; *Congressional Globe*, 37th Cong., 2d sess., 1861, 6–16, 3–32; James Richardson, *A Compilation of the Messages and Papers of the Presidents, 1789–1897*, 10 vols. (Washington DC: Government Printing Office, 1896–99), 6:54; *New York Weekly Tribune*, January 18, 1862; Trefousse, *Radical Republicans*, 184–86.

3. *New York Independent*, January 23, 1862; Bruce Tap, *Over Lincoln's Shoulder: The Committee on the Conduct of the War* (Lawrence: University Press of Kansas, 1998), 16–37; Grimsley, *Hard Hand of War*, 23; Hans L. Trefousse, *Thaddeus Stevens: Nineteenth-Century Egalitarian* (Chapel Hill: University of North Carolina Press, 1997), 113–18.

4. Ash, *When the Yankees Came*, 24–28; Grimsley, *Hard Hand of War*, 8, 23; Paludan, *"A People's Contest,"* 87–88; Berlin et al., *Destruction of Slavery*, 249–51.

5. Berlin et al., *Destruction of Slavery*, 249–51; Louis S. Gerteis, *From Contraband to Freedom: Federal Policy towards Southern Blacks, 1861–1865* (Westport CT: Greenwood Press, 1973), 120; Ash, *When the Yankees Came*, 24–28; Trefousse, *Radical Republicans*, 184–86; T. Harry Williams, "The Committee on the Conduct of the War," *Journal of the American Military Institute* 3 (1939): 139–48; Tap, *Over Lincoln's Shoulder*, 40–41; Grimsley, *Hard Hand of War*, 8, 23; Paludan, *"A People's Contest,"* 87–88; Anders, *Henry Halleck's War*, 57–59.

6. Paludan, *"A People's Contest,"* 87–88; Donald, *Lincoln*, 328–29; Tap, *Over Lincoln's Shoulder*, 18–42. See also James Rawley, *Politics and Union: Northern Politics during the Civil War* (Lincoln: University of Nebraska Press, 1974).

7. Ambrose, *Halleck*, 13–14; Stephen D. Engle, *Don Carlos Buell: Most Promising of All* (Chapel Hill: University of North Carolina Press, 1999), 88–102; Prokopowicz, "All for the Regiment," 116–19; Berlin et al., *Destruction of Slavery*, 247–51.

8. Ambrose, *Halleck*, 13–14; Engle, *Don Carlos Buell*, 100–104; Williams, *Lincoln and His Generals*, 53–61.

9. OR, 7:468, 473–74; Sears, *Papers of McClellan*, 140–41; Ambrose, *Halleck*, 15–17; Engle, *Don Carlos Buell*, 100–104; Williams, *Lincoln and His Generals*, 53–61; Herman Hattaway and Archer Jones, *How the North Won: A Military History of the Civil War* (Champaign: University of Illinois Press, 1983), 61–62.

10. Ambrose, *Halleck*, 17–18; Hattaway and Jones, *How the North Won*, 62.

11. Cooling, *Forts Henry and Donelson*, 65.

12. *New York Herald*, February 26, 1862; Cooling, *Forts Henry and Donelson*, 66–67; Engle, *Don Carlos Buell*, 110–26.

13. Buell to McClellan, November 16, 30, 1862, Buell Papers, Filson Club Historical Society, Louisville KY; William T. Sherman, *Memoirs*, 2 vols. (New York: Appleton, 1875), 1:219–20; Ambrose, *Halleck*, 19; Lewis, *Sherman*, 210; Anders, *Henry Halleck's War*, 48–49.

14. Sears, *George B. McClellan*, 136–39; Donald, *Lincoln*, 328–29; Ambrose, *Halleck*, 20–21; Engle, *Don Carlos Buell*, 127–31.

15. OR, 7:524–25, 927; Donald, *Lincoln*, 329.

16. Howard K. Beale, ed., *The Diary of Edward Bates, 1859–1866* (Washington DC: Government Printing Office, 1933), 217–18; OR, 7:526–28, 927; Paludan, *Presidency of Lincoln*, 100; Donald, *Lincoln*, 329.

17. OR, 7:528–29.

18. OR, 7:532–33.

19. Ambrose, *Halleck*, 20–21.

20. OR, 7:531–32.

21. OR, 7:524, 532–33, 927–28.

22. OR, 7:531.

23. OR, 7:927–28; Hans L. Trefousse, *Andrew Johnson: A Biography* (New York: W. W. Norton, 1989), 148–49.

24. OR, 7:535; Basler, *Works of Lincoln*, 5:91–92; Ambrose, *Halleck*, 20–22; Engle, *Don Carlos Buell*, 135–39.

25. OR, 7:533; Paludan, *Presidency of Lincoln*, 100.

26. OR, 7:533–34; John Y. Simon, ed., *The Papers of Ulysses S. Grant*, 18 vols. (Carbondale: Southern Illinois University Press, 1967–91), 4:3; Cooling, *Forts Henry and Donelson*, 67–70; Ambrose, *Halleck*, 21–23; Simpson, *Ulysses S. Grant*, 108–9.

27. Cooling, *Forts Henry and Donelson*, 70–82.

28. Simon, *Papers of Grant*, 4:60–74; OR, 7:561; Cooling, *Forts Henry and Donelson*, 70–82; Connelly, *Army of the Heartland*, 106; Roland, *Albert Sidney Johnston*, 280–85.

29. Cooling, *Forts Henry and Donelson*, 71–72.

30. Paludan, *Presidency of Lincoln*, 102; Sears, *George B. McClellan*, 141; Henry J. Raymond, *The Life and Public Service of Abraham Lincoln* (New York: Stevens, 1865), 772–77; Beale, *Diary of Bates*, 218–20; Basler, *Works of Lincoln*, 5:98–99; John Niven, *Salmon P. Chase: A Biography* (New York: Oxford University Press, 1995), 278–79; OR, 7:928–29; Trefousse, *Radical Republicans*, 184–86.

31. OR, 7:547.

32. OR, 7:547.

33. *New York Times*, December 21, 1861.

34. Cooling, *Forts Henry and Donelson*, 72.

35. Alexis Cope, *The Fifteenth Ohio Volunteers* (Columbus OH: Edward T. Miller, 1916), 64; Judson W. Bishop, *The Story of a Regiment: Being a Narrative of the Service of the Second Regiment Minnesota Veteran Volunteer Infantry* (St. Paul MN: Published by the Regiment, 1890), 32–47; Henry M. Cist, *The Army of the Cumberland: The Campaigns of the Civil War* (New York: Charles Scribner's Sons, 1882), 15–16; John D. Inskeep Diary, January 19, 1862, John D. Inskeep Papers, Ohio Historical Society, Columbus; Thomas M. Small Diary, January 19, 1862, Thomas M. Small Papers, Indiana Historical Society, Indianapolis; Prokopowicz, "All for the Regiment," 129–59.

36. OR, 7:102; Benjamin P. Thomas and Harold M. Hyman, *Stanton: The Life and Times of Lincoln's Secretary of War* (New York: Alfred Knopf, 1962), 150–55.

37. Stanton quoted in Thomas and Hyman, *Stanton*, 143–50; Paludan, *Presidency of Lincoln*, 105–6.

38. OR, 7:572–79; Ambrose, *Halleck*, 17–25; Peter Cozzens and Robert I. Girardi, *The Military Memoirs of General John Pope* (Chapel Hill: University of North Carolina Press, 1998), 43–47; Stanley Horn, *The Army of Tennessee* (Norman: University of Oklahoma Press, 1955), 36.

39. OR, 8:408–10, 462–63; Kenneth P. Williams, *Lincoln Finds a General* (New York: Macmillan, 1952), 3:179.

40. Cooling, *Forts Henry and Donelson*, 72–73; Ambrose, *Halleck*, 24–25.

41. OR, 7:561–62, 572–73; Simon, *Papers of Grant*, 4:96; Ulysses S. Grant, *Personal Memoirs of U. S. Grant*, 2 vols. (New York: Webster, 1885), 1:287; Cooling, *Forts Henry and Donelson*, 74–75; Ambrose, *Halleck*, 21–25.

42. Grant, *Memoirs*, 1:287.

43. Simon, *Papers of Grant*, 4:99, 103; OR, 7:575; Cooling, *Forts Henry and Donelson*, 75–77.

44. OR, 8:508–11, 7:121, 571–72; Ambrose, *Halleck*, 22–25.

45. Ambrose, *Halleck*, 22–25; OR, 8:508–11, 7:121, 571–72.

46. OR, 7:528–29, 571–79, 8:508–11; Ambrose, *Halleck*, 23–25.

47. OR, 7:574.

48. OR, 7:576, 936–37.

49. OR, 7:578–79, 580–83; Engle, *Don Carlos Buell*, 137–46.

50. Basler, *Works of Lincoln*, 5:115; Donald, *Lincoln*, 332–35; Sears, *George B. McClellan*, 147–52; Williams, *Lincoln Finds a General*, 3:187–88.

51. Connelly, *Army of the Heartland*, 63–83; Peter Franklin Walker, "Command Failure: The Fall of Forts Henry and Donelson," *Tennessee Historical Quarterly* 16 (December 1957): 335–38.

52. Johnston, *Life of Johnston*, 346; Woodworth, *Davis and His Generals*, 54; Horn, *Army of Tennessee*, 59–61; Cooling, *Forts Henry and Donelson*, 83–84; Roland, *Albert Sidney Johnston*, 261–67; Davis, *Jefferson Davis*, 395–96; Woodworth, *Civil War Generals in Defeat*, 15–17.

53. Connelly, *Army of the Heartland*, 78–81; Woodworth, *Davis and His Generals*, 57–58; Roland, *Albert Sidney Johnston*, 265–77; Cooling, *Forts Henry and Donelson*, 44–61; Woodworth, *Civil War Generals in Defeat*, 15–17.

54. Connelly, *Army of the Heartland*, 78–81; Woodworth, *Davis and His Generals*, 57–58; Woodworth, *Civil War Generals in Defeat*, 15–17.

55. Roland, *Albert Sidney Johnston*, 263–77; Robert U. Johnson and Clarence C. Buel, eds., *Battles and Leaders of the Civil War*, 4 vols. (New York: Century, 1887), 1:368–70 (cited hereafter as *Battles and Leaders*).

56. Johnston quoted in Roland, *Albert Sidney Johnston*, 285; *Battles and Leaders* 1:368–70; OR, 7:831–39; Connelly, *Army of the Heartland*, 78–85; Woodworth, *Davis*

and His Generals, 71; Cooling, *Forts Henry and Donelson,* 84–85; Woodworth, *Civil War Generals in Defeat,* 15–18.

57. OR, 7:831–39; Connelly, *Army of the Heartland,* 106; Cooling, *Forts Henry and Donelson,* 84–85; Woodworth, *Civil War Generals in Defeat,* 15–18.

58. Johnston quoted in Roland, *Albert Sidney Johnston,* 276; Davis, *Jefferson Davis,* 395–96; Woodworth, *Davis and His Generals,* 54–60.

59. St. John R. Liddell, "Liddell's Record of the Civil War," *Southern Bivouac* 1 (December 1885), 417–19; Connelly, *Army of the Heartland,* 92–93; Nathaniel Cheairs Hughes Jr., ed., *Liddell's Record* (reprint; Baton Rouge: Louisiana State University, 1997), 41–43; Davis, *Jefferson Davis,* 396–97.

60. Roland, *Albert Sidney Johnston,* 281–82; Cooling, *Forts Henry and Donelson,* 81–82.

61. OR, 7:850–51; Connelly, *Army of the Heartland,* 106.

62. *Battles and Leaders,* 1:368–69; Woodworth, *Davis and His Generals,* 56–57.

63. *Battles and Leaders,* 1:398–99; Hughes, *Gideon J. Pillow,* 206–9.

64. OR, 7:131–35; *Battles and Leaders,* 1:368; Cooling, *Forts Henry and Donelson,* 85–86.

65. OR, 7:576, 931–32; Cooling, *Forts Henry and Donelson,* 73–89

66. OR, 7:931–32; Engle, *Don Carlos Buell,* 154–58.

67. OR, 7:937–38.

68. OR, 7:575, 578–79, 580; Engle, *Don Carlos Buell,* 154–58.

69. OR, 7:583; Ambrose, *Halleck,* 26; Cooling, *Forts Henry and Donelson,* 73–89.

70. OR, 7:583–84; Ambrose, *Halleck,* 27.

71. OR, 7:585–86.

72. Engle, *Don Carlos Buell,* 154–58.

73. Thomas A. Scott to Stanton, February 1–6, 1862; and Scott to Stanton, February 6, 7, 1862, letters designated "Private and Confidential," Edwin M. Stanton Papers, Library of Congress; Thomas and Hyman, *Stanton,* 172–73; John G. Nicolay and John Hay, ed., *Complete Works of Lincoln,* 12 vols. (New York: Francis D. Tandy, 1905), 5:188; Samuel R. Kamm, "The Civil War Career of Thomas A. Scott" (Ph.D. diss., University of Pennsylvania, 1940), 93–96; OR, 7:589.

74. OR, 7:587–88, 844–45; Engle, *Don Carlos Buell,* 154–58.

3. HENRY AND DONELSON

1. James Hamilton, *The Battle of Fort Donelson* (Cranbury NJ: Thomas Yoseloff, 1968), 15–21; McFeely, *Grant,* 97; Simpson, *Ulysses S. Grant,* 110.

2. OR, 7:572–75, 22:522–30; Simon, *Papers of Grant,* 4:138–39; Hamilton, *Fort Donelson,* 20–23; Cooling, *Forts Henry and Donelson,* 89–90.

3. ORN, 4:141–50; Simon, *Papers of Grant,* 4:145–47; Grant, *Memoirs,* 1:288–90; Cooling, *Forts Henry and Donelson,* 89–93; Richard L. Kiper, *Major General*

John Alexander McClernand: Politician in Uniform (Kent OH: Kent State University Press, 1999), 2–17, 65–69.

4. OR, 7:577–81; Simon, *Papers of Grant,* 4:150–51; Grant, *Memoirs,* 1:288–90; Simpson, *Ulysses S. Grant,* 111–12; Kiper, *McClernand,* 69–70; Williams, *Lincoln Finds a General,* 3:200; Henry Walke, *Naval Scenes and Reminiscences of the Civil War* (New York: F. R. Reed, 1877), 55.

5. OR, 7:581, 857–59; *Battles and Leaders,* 1:368–70; Walker, "Command Failure," 338–39.

6. OR, 7:136–47, 843, 857–59; Walker, "Command Failure," 338; *Battles and Leaders,* 1:368–71; Connelly, *Army of the Heartland,* 106–7; Roland, *Albert Sidney Johnston,* 285–86.

7. OR, 7:583–87; Ambrose, *Halleck,* 24–30.

8. OR, 7:136–47, 858–59; *Battles and Leaders,* 1:369–71; Connelly, *Army of the Heartland,* 107; Roland, *Albert Sidney Johnston,* 285–86.

9. OR, 7:585–87.

10. Simon, *Papers of Grant,* 4:153.

11. OR, 7:122, 131–52; *Battles and Leaders,* 1:369–71.

12. OR, 7:122–35, 136–44; Connelly, *Army of the Heartland,* 107; Walker, "Command Failure," 340–41; Cooling, *Forts Henry and Donelson,* 103–6.

13. Tilghman and Foote quoted in Cooling, *Forts Henry and Donelson,* 107–8; OR, 7:122–23, 142–43; ORN, 22:538; *Battles and Leaders,* 1:362–63, 370–72; Walke, *Naval Scenes,* 57; Connelly, *Army of the Heartland,* 107–8; Jay Slagle, *Ironclad Captain: Seth Ledyard Phelps and the U.S. Navy, 1841–1864* (Kent OH: Kent State University Press, 1996), 160–61.

14. Simon, *Papers of Grant,* 4:157–59; OR, 7:124–47; Ambrose, *Halleck,* 26–28; Kiper, *McClernand,* 72–73.

15. OR, 7:590.

16. OR, 7:590; Ambrose, *Halleck,* 27–28.

17. OR, 7:860–64.

18. George W. Johnson to wife, February 15, 1862, George W. Johnson Papers, Filson Club Historical Society, Louisville KY.

19. Woodworth, *Civil War Generals in Defeat,* 16–18; Roland, *Albert Sidney Johnston,* 287–88.

20. OR, 7:860–64; Connelly, *Army of the Heartland,* 108–9; Woodworth, *Davis and His Generals,* 79–80; Roland, *Albert Sidney Johnston,* 287–88.

21. *New York Daily Tribune,* February 8, 1862.

22. ORN, 22:570–74; *Harper's Weekly,* March 1, 1862; Simon, *Papers of Grant,* 4:188.

23. OR, 7:153–56.

24. OR, 7:153–56, 591, 10(2):8; *New York Daily Tribune,* February 13, 1862; *New York Herald,* February 21, 1862; *Harper's Weekly,* March 8, 1862; Simon, *Papers of Grant,* 4:169; Slagle, *Ironclad Captain,* 167–73.

25. Grant, *Memoirs,* 1:173.

26. Lew Wallace to wife, February 7,9, 1862, Lew Wallace Papers, Indiana Historical Society, Indianapolis; OR, 7:124–25; Simon, *Papers of Grant,* 4:183–91; Simpson, *Ulysses S. Grant,* 112–13; Lew Wallace, *Lew Wallace: An Autobiography* (New York: Harper and Brothers, 1906), 1:376–77; *Battles and Leaders,* 1:405; Kiper, *McClernand,* 73; Ambrose, *Halleck,* 28.

27. Simon, *Papers of Grant,* 4:179.

28. OR, 7:593–94.

29. OR, 7:590–91; Engle, *Don Carlos Buell,* 160–62; Ambrose, *Halleck,* 28–29; Cooling, *Forts Henry and Donelson,* 117–19.

30. OR, 7:608–9; Anders, *Henry Halleck's War,* 74–75.

31. OR, 7:608–9; Anders, *Henry Halleck's War,* 74–75; Ambrose, *Halleck,* 27–29; Engle, *Don Carlos Buell,* 161–64; Cooling, *Forts Henry and Donelson,* 118–19; Anders, *Henry Halleck's War,* 74–75.

32. OR, 7:599; Engle, *Don Carlos Buell,* 165; Sears, *George B. McClellan,* 180; Ambrose, *Halleck,* 30.

33. OR, 7:604.

34. OR, 7:601–4; Simon, *Papers of Grant,* 4:191–94; Kiper, *McClernand,* 75–76.

35. OR, 7:130–31; Roland, *Albert Sidney Johnston,* 287–88; T. Harry Williams, P. G. T. *Beauregard: Napoleon in Gray* (Baton Rouge: Louisiana State University Press, 1954), 116–17.

36. OR, 7:861–62; Walker, "Command Failure," 342–43; Roland, *Albert Sidney Johnston,* 289–90; Connelly, *Army of the Heartland,* 111–12; Hughes and Stonesifer, *Gideon J. Pillow,* 210–11.

37. Woodworth, *Civil War Generals in Defeat,* 20; Williams, P. G. T. *Beauregard,* 116–19; Roland, *Albert Sidney Johnston,* 290.

38. Johnson quoted in Roland, *Albert Sidney Johnston,* 290; Cooling, *Forts Henry and Donelson,* 123–27; Williams, P. G. T. *Beauregard,* 116–19; Woodworth, *Davis and His Generals,* 78–79.

39. Connelly, *Army of the Heartland,* 112; Roland, *Albert Sidney Johnston,* 289–90; Hughes and Stonesifer, *Gideon J. Pillow,* 211–13; Woodworth, *Civil War Generals in Defeat,* 20–21.

40. Williams, P. G. T. *Beauregard,* 119.

41. OR, 7:867–71; Hughes and Stonesifer, *Gideon J. Pillow,* 214.

42. Cooling, *Forts Henry and Donelson,* 132–33; Arndt M. Stickles, *Simon Bolivar Buckner: Borderland Knight* (Chapel Hill: University of North Carolina Press, 1940), 130–37; Hughes and Stonesifer, *Gideon J. Pillow,* 213–15.

43. Roland, *Albert Sidney Johnston,* 291; Cooling, *Forts Henry and Donelson,* 133–34; Stickles, *Simon Bolivar Buckner,* 131–41; Walker, "Command Failure," 344–46; Hughes and Stonesifer, *Gideon J. Pillow,* 215–17.

44. OR, 7:131–35, 145–47, 870–71, 52(2):271–74; Hamilton, *Fort Donelson,* 78–81.

45. Grant, *Memoirs*, 1:299; OR, 7:613; ORN, 22:594; Cooling, *Forts Henry and Donelson*, 137–38; Kiper, *McClernand*, 76–77.

46. OR, 52(2):271–72; Grant, *Memoirs*, 1:294; Hamilton, *Fort Donelson*, 83–85; Roland, *Albert Sidney Johnston*, 290–91; Hughes and Stonesifer, *Gideon J. Pillow*, 217–20.

47. ORN, 22:594; Simon, *Papers of Grant*, 4:206–8; Connelly, *Army of the Heartland*, 115–17; Roland, *Albert Sidney Johnston*, 291; Walker, "Command Failure," 347–48; Kiper, *McClernand*, 76–79.

48. OR, 7:183–87, 192–98, 219–24; Connelly, *Army of the Heartland*, 118; Cooling, *Forts Henry and Donelson*, 141–43; Kiper, *McClernand*, 76–79.

49. Simpson, *Ulysses S. Grant*, 113–14; Cooling, *Forts Henry and Donelson*, 139–41; OR, 7:122–24, 159–60, 162–64, 170–82, 258–61, 267–75, 278–93.

50. OR, 7:166–67, 615–16; Simon, *Papers of Grant*, 4:211–13; Grant, *Memoirs*, 1:302; Slagle, *Ironclad Captain*, 177–79.

51. Forrest quoted in John A. Wyeth, *That Devil Forrest: Life of General Nathan Bedford Forrest* (New York: Harper and Brothers, 1959), 38–40; OR, 7:166–67, 394–95; Slagle, *Ironclad Captain*, 178–79; Cooling, *Forts Henry and Donelson*, 155–58; Hamilton, *Fort Donelson*, 134–41.

52. OR, 7:255–56, 394–95, 52(2):274; Slagle, *Ironclad Captain*, 180–81; Connelly, *Army of the Heartland*, 120; Cooling, *Forts Henry and Donelson*, 158–59; Hamilton, *Fort Donelson*, 141–46.

53. Simon, *Papers of Grant*, 4:211.

54. Halleck to Scott, February 12, 1862, Stanton Papers, Library of Congress; OR, 7:580–90; Ambrose, *Halleck*, 29–30; Anders, *Henry Halleck's War*, 74–76.

55. OR, 7:608–9; Ambrose, *Halleck*, 29–30; Cooling, *Forts Henry and Donelson*, 161–62.

56. OR, 7:620; Simon, *Papers of Grant*, 4:196–97; Ambrose, *Halleck*, 30–32; Anders, *Henry Halleck's War*, 74–76.

57. OR, 7:614–17; Simon, *Papers of Grant*, 4:213.

58. OR, 7:880; Williams, *P. G. T. Beauregard*, 120.

59. Roland, *Albert Sidney Johnston*, 290–95.

60. Stickles, *Simon Bolivar Buckner*, 140–41; Hughes and Stonesifer, *Gideon J. Pillow*, 222–24; Cooling, *Forts Henry and Donelson*, 163–65.

61. OR, 7:263, 285–86, 330; Stickles, *Simon Bolivar Buckner*, 140–41; Hamilton, *Fort Donelson*, 157–60; Cooling, *Forts Henry and Donelson*, 164–65; Connelly, *Army of the Heartland*, 121; Hughes and Stonesifer, *Gideon J. Pillow*, 222–24.

62. Hughes and Stonesifer, *Gideon J. Pillow*, 222–25; Cooling, *Forts Henry and Donelson*, 166–76.

63. Grant, *Memoirs*, 1:179, 304–8; Simon, *Papers of Grant*, 4:216; Hamilton, *Fort Donelson*, 163–70; Simpson, *Ulysses S. Grant*, 114–17; Kiper, *McClernand*, 79–85.

64. OR, 7:177–79, 190, 237, 243, 282, 343; ORN, 22:585–86; Connelly, *Army of*

the Heartland, 121; Lew Wallace, *Autobiography,* 1:420; Cooling, *Forts Henry and Donelson,* 169–70; Kiper, *McClernand,* 75–85.

65. OR, 7:177–79, 255, 278–85; Roland, *Albert Sidney Johnston,* 292; Connelly, *Army of the Heartland,* 121–22; Stickles, *Simon Bolivar Buckner,* 143–44; Hamilton, *Fort Donelson,* 167–219; Cooling, *Forts Henry and Donelson,* 173–75; Kiper, *McClernand,* 83–89.

66. Woodworth, *Davis and His Generals,* 82; OR, 7:269, 284, 332–33, 600, 612, 616; Roland, *Albert Sidney Johnston,* 292; Walker, "Command Failure," 352; Cooling, *Forts Henry and Donelson,* 180–82; Hughes and Stonesifer, *Gideon J. Pillow,* 229–31.

67. Grant, *Memoirs,* 1:304–5; *Battles and Leaders,* 1:421–22; OR, 7:177–79, 237, 282; Cooling, *Forts Henry and Donelson,* 183–84.

68. Smith quoted in Cooling, *Forts Henry and Donelson,* 185; OR, 7:178–79; Williams, *Lincoln Finds a General,* 3:245; *Battles and Leaders,* 1:421.

69. OR, 7:163, 170, 179, 221, 233–34, 238; *Battles and Leaders,* 1:421–22.

70. OR, 7:163, 170, 179, 221, 233–34, 238; *Battles and Leaders,* 1:421–22; Cooling, *Forts Henry and Donelson,* 197–98; Kiper, *McClernand,* 86–89.

71. Roland, *Albert Sidney Johnston,* 292; Woodworth, *Davis and His Generals,* 83.

72. Stickles, *Simon Bolivar Buckner,* 144–57; OR, 7:255–56, 275, 296–99, 302, 386; Hughes and Stonesifer, *Gideon J. Pillow,* 222–23.

73. OR, 7:161, 297–99; Simon, *Papers of Grant,* 4:218.

74. OR, 7:160–61, 275, 297–300, 385–86; Horn, *Army of Tennessee,* 94–95; Roland, *Albert Sidney Johnston,* 292–93; Stickles, *Simon Bolivar Buckner,* 144–57; Hughes and Stonesifer, *Gideon J. Pillow,* 234–39.

75. Hughes and Stonesifer, *Gideon J. Pillow,* 234–39; Cooling, *Forts and Henry and Donelson,* 205–22.

76. Stickles, *Simon Bolivar Buckner,* 144–57; OR, 7:160–61, 256, 296–97.

77. OR, 7:160–61, 256, 275, 296–97, 302; Walker, "Command Failure," 354–58; Cooling, *Forts Henry and Donelson,* 209–21; Hamilton, *Fort Donelson,* 303–15; Simpson, *Ulysses S. Grant,* 117–18.

78. OR, 7:303–4; Simon, *Papers of Grant,* 4:223–26; Hamlin Garland, *Ulysses S. Grant: His Life and Character* (New York: Macmillan, 1920), 192; Stickles, *Simon Bolivar Buckner,* 145–71; Cooling, *Forts Henry and Donelson,* 211–16; Simpson, *Ulysses S. Grant,* 117–18.

79. James F. Drish to wife, February 21, 1862, James F. Drish Papers, Illinois State Historical Library, Springfield.

80. Simon, *Papers of Grant,* 4:229.

81. Charles Dana, *Recollections of the Civil War; with the Leaders at Washington and in the Field in the Sixties* (New York: D. Appleton, 1898), 10–14; Helen Nicolay, *Lincoln's Secretary: A Biography of John G. Nicolay* (New York: Longmans, Green, 1949), 131; McFeely, *Grant,* 102; Cooling, *Forts Henry and Donelson,* 223–25.

82. Hattaway and Jones, *How the North Won*, 68–76; Herman Hattaway, *Shades of Blue and Gray: An Introductory Military History of the Civil War* (Columbia: University of Missouri Press, 1997).

83. OR, 7:889.

84. Cooling, *Fort Donelson's Legacy*, 50–53, 60–64; Sutherland, *Guerrillas, Unionists, and Violence*, 120–21.

85. OR, 7:628; Ambrose, *Halleck*, 30–33.

86. OR, 7:627–28.

87. OR, 7:625; Ambrose, *Halleck*, 30–32.

88. John Niven, ed., *Salmon P. Chase Papers*, 3 vols. (Kent OH: Kent State University Press, 1993–), 3:135; OR, 7:624.

89. *New York Herald*, February 19, 1862.

4. MISSED OPPORTUNITIES

1. George W. Johnson to wife, February 15, 1862, George W. Johnson Papers, Kentucky Historical Society, Frankfurt; *Harper's Weekly*, April 12, 15, 1862; Horn, *Army of Tennessee*, 100–101; Roland, *Albert Sidney Johnston*, 298–99; Walter T. Durham, *Nashville: The Occupied City* (Nashville: Tennessee Historical Society, 1985), 14–18; John M. McKee, *The Great Panic, Being Connected with Two Weeks of the War in Tennessee* (Nashville: Johnson and Whiting, 1862), 8–11.

2. *Richmond Enquirer*, February 18, 1862; *Richmond Examiner*, February 19, 1862; Horn, *Army of Tennessee*, 100–104; J. Cutler Andrews, *The South Reports the War* (Princeton NJ: Princeton University Press, 1970), 134; Davis, *Jefferson Davis*, 398–99; Roland, *Albert Sidney Johnston*, 299; James M. McPherson, *Battle Cry of Freedom: The Civil War Era* (New York: Oxford University Press, 1988), 404.

3. Lynda Crist, ed., *The Papers of Jefferson Davis*, 10 vols. (Baton Rouge: Louisiana State University Press, 1995), 8:58–62, 87–89; Johnston, *Life of Johnston*, 496–500; Roland, *Albert Sidney Johnston*, 299–300; Davis, *Jefferson Davis*, 398–400; Hudson Strode, *Jefferson Davis: Confederate President* (New York: Harcourt, Brace, 1959), 221; Cooling, *Fort Donelson's Legacy*, 7–10; Felicity Allen, *Jefferson Davis: Unconquerable Heart* (Columbia: University of Missouri Press, 1999), 300–302.

4. Ephraim D. Adams, *Great Britain and the American Civil War*, 2 vols. (New York: Longmans, Green, 1925), 1:272–73; Howard Jones, *Union in Peril: The Crisis over British Intervention in the Civil War* (Chapel Hill: University of North Carolina Press, 1992), 102–4; McPherson, *Battle Cry of Freedom*, 396–404; *New York Times*, February 19, 20, 1862; Cooling, *Fort Donelson's Legacy*, 15.

5. *Memphis Daily Appeal*, March 8, 1862; Allen, *Jefferson Davis*, 302.

6. McKee, *Great Panic*, 8–24; Cooling, *Fort Donelson's Legacy*, 8; Durham, *Nashville*, 14–18; Hughes, *General William J. Hardee*, 92–95.

7. *Battles and Leaders*, 1:399.

8. Roland, *Albert Sidney Johnston*, 299–302; Davis, *Jefferson Davis*, 398–99.

9. Roland, *Albert Sidney Johnston*, 299–302; Williams, *P. G. T. Beauregard*, 119–20.

10. *Memphis Daily Appeal*, February 20, 1862; F. A. Mitchel, *Ormsby MacKnight Mitchel: Astronomer and General* (New York: Houghton, Mifflin, 1887), 242; McKee, *Great Panic*, 20–28; Durham, *Nashville*, 6–39; Roland, *Albert Sidney Johnston*, 295–302.

11. Andrews, *South Reports the War*, 131–32; Durham, *Nashville*, 6–45; Ash, *When the Yankees Came*, 16–17; McKee, *Great Panic*, 19, 254–55; Hughes and Stonesifer, *Gideon J. Pillow*, 239.

12. Kay Baker Gaston, "A World Overturned: The Civil War Experience of Dr. William A. Cheatham and His Family," *Tennessee Historical Quarterly* 50 (spring 1991): 3–16; McKee, *Great Panic*, 29–30; *Memphis Daily Avalanche*, February 25, 1862; *Indianapolis Daily Journal*, March 4, 1862; OR, 7:425–32; Durham, *Nashville*, 6–45; Stanley Horn, "Nashville during the Civil War," *Tennessee Historical Quarterly* 4 (March 1945): 3–22; Cooling, *Fort Donelson's Legacy*, 19–22.

13. OR, 7:632–33.

14. John Lellyett to Buell, February 13, 1862, Buell Papers, Filson Club Historical Society; OR, 7:636, 639, 641–47; Stanton to Scott, February 21, 1862, Stanton Papers, Library of Congress; Thomas and Hyman, *Stanton*, 175; Kamm, "Thomas A. Scott," 112; Simon, *Papers of Grant*, 4:222–23; Nicolay and Hay, *Complete Works of Lincoln*, 5:307–8.

15. *Harper's Weekly*, February 22, 1862.

16. *New York Herald*, February 21, 1862.

17. OR, 7:423–24; Simon, *Papers of Grant*, 4:252–53; *New York Times*, March 4, 1862. Cooling, *Fort Donelson's Legacy*, 15–19; Stephen V. Ash, *Middle Tennessee Society Transformed, 1860–1870: War and Peace in the Upper South* (Baton Rouge: Louisiana State University Press, 1988), 84–86; Slagle, *Ironclad Captain*, 187.

18. Slagle, *Ironclad Captain*, 187.

19. Slagle, *Ironclad Captain*, 187; *New York Times*, March 4, 1862.

20. OR, 7:647; McClellan to Buell, February 20, 1862, Generals Papers, Record Group 94, National Archives and Records Administration, Washington DC (cited hereafter as RG 94, National Archives); Stanton to Scott, February 21, 1862, Stanton Papers.

21. Stanton to Scott, February 21, 1862, Stanton Papers; Thomas and Hyman, *Stanton*, 172–75.

22. Thomas and Hyman, *Stanton*, 172–75; Kamm, "Thomas A. Scott," 112; Niven, *Salmon P. Chase*, 285.

23. *Harper's Weekly*, March 8, 1862.

24. Eric Foner, *Reconstruction: America's Unfinished Revolution, 1863–1877* (New York: Harper and Row, 1988), 43; Grimsley, *Hard Hand of War*, 7–34; Herman Belz, *Reconstructing the Union: Theory and Practice during the Civil War* (Ithaca NY: Cornell University Press, 1969), 19–28; Cooling, *Fort Donelson's Legacy*, 17–19.

25. Drish to wife, February, 21, 1862, Drish Papers, Illinois State Historical Library; Foner, *Reconstruction*, 4–5; Gerteis, *From Contraband to Freedom*, 11–13; Ash, *When the Yankees Came*, 26–31; Berlin et al., *Destruction of Slavery*, 15–16, 253–54; Randall C. Jimerson, *The Private Civil War: Popular Thought during the Sectional Conflict* (Baton Rouge: Louisiana State University, 1988), 60–65; Leon Litwack, *Been in the Storm So Long: The Aftermath of Slavery* (New York: Alfred Knopf, 1979), chapter 2; James L. Roark, *Masters without Slaves: Southern Planters in the Civil War and Reconstruction* (New York: W. W. Norton, 1977), chapters 2 and 3.

26. Drish to wife, February 21, 1862; Grimsley, *Hard Hand of War*, 7–66; Cooling, *Fort Donelson's Legacy*, 17–19, 38–43; John Cimprich, "Slave Behavior during the Federal Occupation of Tennessee, 1862–1865," *The Historian* 44 (March 1982): 335–47.

27. *Congressional Globe*, 37th Congress, 2d sess., 1862, 6; Trefousse, *Thaddeus Stevens*, 116; Foner, *Reconstruction*, 4–6; James McPherson, *The Struggle for Equality: Abolitionists and the Negro in the Civil War and Reconstruction* (Princeton NJ: Princeton University Press, 1964), 59–82; Cooling, *Fort Donelson's Legacy*, 18–19; Hesseltine, *Lincoln and the War Governors*, 218–60.

28. Foner, *Reconstruction*, 5–8; Ash, *Middle Tennessee Society Transformed*, 113; Richardson, *Messages and Papers of the Presidents*, 6:54.

29. Grant quoted in Brooks D. Simpson, *Let Us Have Peace: Ulysses S. Grant and the Politics of War and Reconstruction, 1861–1868* (Chapel Hill: University of North Carolina Press, 1991), 21; John Cimprich, *Slavery's End in Tennessee, 1861–1865* (Tuscaloosa: University of Alabama Press, 1985), 34–35; OR, 7:669–76, 10(2):30–33; Berlin et al., *Destruction of Slavery*, 194–97, 250–52, 270–74; Simon, *Papers of Grant*, 4:267–70, 285, 290–91; Grimsley, *Hard Hand of War*, 48–52, 61–63; Cooling, *Fort Donelson's Legacy*, 18, 44, 50–51.

30. *Harper's Weekly*, April 12, 1862.

31. Stephen D. Engle, "Don Carlos Buell: Military Philosophy and Command Problems in the West," *Civil War History* 41 (1995): 89–115.

32. Charles R. Mott Jr., ed., "War Journal of a Confederate Officer [W. H. Mott]," *Tennessee Historical Quarterly* 5 (September 1946): 239–40; Ash, *When the Yankees Came*, 18–24.

33. Simon, *Papers of Grant*, 4:284; OR, 7:891; Ash, *When the Yankees Came*, 18–24.

34. OR, 7:424–25; *Cincinnati Commercial*, March 15, 1862; *New York Daily Tribune*, February 26, 1862.

35. Edward Hannaford, *Story of a Regiment: A History of the Campaigns and Association in the Field of the Sixth Regiment Ohio Volunteer Infantry* (Cincinnati: Published by the author), 201–6.

36. *New York Times*, February 21, 1862; Thomas J. Wright, *History of the Eighth Regiment Kentucky Vol. Infantry* (St. Joseph MO: St. Joseph Steam Printing, 1880), 41–43; *National Tribune*, July 14, 1892; Hannaford, *Story of a Regiment*, 201–6; Villard, *Memoirs*, 1:225–27; John Beatty, *The Citizen Soldier: or Memoirs of a Volunteer*

(Cincinnati:Wilstach, Baldwin, 1879), 86–89. See also Henry [?] to Sidney Baker, March 17, 1862, Sidney Baker Papers, Ohio Historical Society, Columbus.

37. OR, 7:424–25, 668–70; Scott to Stanton, March 1, 1862, Stanton Papers; Durham, *Nashville*, 1–3.

38. Thaddeus H. Capron, "War Diary of Thaddeus Capron, 1861–1865," *Journal of the Illinois State Historical Society* 12 (October 1919): 341.

39. Ash, *Middle Tennessee Society Transformed*, 84–85.

40. Grant, *Memoirs*, 1:217; Simon, *Papers of Grant*, 4:344; OR, 7:425, 670–71; Villard, *Memoirs*, 1:230–31; Durham, *Nashville*, 51–52; *New York Daily Tribune*, February 22, 26, 1862; *Frank Leslie's Illustrated Magazine*, March 8, 1862.

41. Simon, *Papers of Grant*, 4:319–21; OR, 10(2):4–5; Daniel, *Shiloh*, 52, 57–58.

42. Villard, *Memoirs*, 1:225–26; *New York Herald*, February 25, 1862; OR, 7:425, 668–71; Durham, *Nashville*, 3–10; Edwin T. Hardison, "In theToils ofWar: Andrew Johnson and the Federal Occupation of Tennessee, 1862–1865" (Ph.D. diss., University Tennessee, 1981), 64–67; *New York Times*, February 26, 27, 1862.

43. Peter Maslowski, "From Reconciliation to Reconstruction: Lincoln, Johnson, and Tennessee," *Tennessee Historical Quarterly* 42 (fall 1983): 281–95; Ash, *When the Yankees Came*, 25–27; Ash, *Middle Tennessee Society Transformed*, 97–98; Grimsley, *Hard Hand of War*, 23–38; Gerteis, *From Contraband to Freedom*, 14–19.

44. OR, 7:669–70; Engle, *Don Carlos Buell*, 184–92; Wright, *Eighth Kentucky*, 44; *Indianapolis Daily Journal*, March 4, 1862; *New York Daily Tribune*, March 8, 18, 1862.

45. James G. Smart, ed., *A Radical View: The "Agate" Dispatches of Whitelaw Reid, 1861–1865*, 2 vols. (Memphis: Memphis State University Press, 1976), 1:115; *New York Daily Tribune*, March 6, 18, 1862; *Memphis Daily Avalanche*, March 18, 1862; Drish to wife, March 3, 1862, Drish Papers; Ash, *When the Yankees Came*, 40–41; Engle, *Don Carlos Buell*, 184–92.

46. OR, 7:671.

47. Scott to Stanton, March 1, 2, 4, 1862, Stanton Papers.

48. Muriel D. MacKenzie, ed., *"Maggie!" Maggie Lindsley's Journal, Nashville, 1864,Washington DC 1865* (Southberry CT: M. D. MacKenzie, 1977), 8.

49. *New York Times*, March 16, 1862.

50. OR, 7:679.

51. MacKenzie, *"Maggie!"* 9; OR, 7:679, 16:633.

52. OR, 16:59–60.

53. Nelson to Chase, February 28, 1862, Salmon P. Chase Papers, Claremont University Microfilm Collection, Claremont, Calif. (cited hereafter as Chase Papers, Claremont); Scott to Stanton, March 1, 4, 6, 1862, Stanton Papers; *New York Daily Tribune*, March 8, 17, 1862.

54. Trefousse, *Andrew Johnson*, 152–57; LeRoy P. Graf, Ralph W. Haskins, and Paul H. Bergeron, eds., *The Papers of Andrew Johnson*, 13 vols. (Knoxville: University ofTennessee Press, 1967–89), 5:177.

55. Nelson to Chase, February 28, 1862, Chase Papers, Claremont; Graf, Haskins, and Bergeron, *Papers of Johnson,* 5:202–4; *Cincinnati Commercial,* March 19, 1862; Trefousse, *Andrew Johnson,* 152–57.

56. Harris quoted in Clifton R. Hall, *Andrew Johnson: Military Governor of Tennessee* (Princeton NJ: Princeton University Press, 1916), 20–22.

57. Joseph Warren Keifer to wife, March 11, 1862, Keifer Papers, Library of Congress; Scott to Stanton, March 4, 1862, Stanton Papers.

58. Engle, *Don Carlos Buell,* 196–205.

59. Ormsby Macknight Mitchel to Chase, March 2, 1862, Chase Papers, Claremont; *Memphis Daily Appeal,* March 8, 1862; Grimsley, *Hard Hand of War,* 64–65.

60. Keifer to wife, March 10, 11, 1862, Keifer Papers.

61. OR, 10(2): 10; Ash, *Middle Tennessee Society Transformed,* 100–101; Peter Maslowski, *Treason Must Be Made Odious: Military Occupation and Wartime Reconstruction in Nashville, Tennessee, 1862–1865* (Millwood NJ: KTO Press, 1978), 53–54, 121–37.

62. Halleck to wife, March 5, 1862, Halleck Papers, Federal Collection, Tennessee State Archives, Nashville.

63. Ambrose, *Halleck,* 35.

64. Larry J. Daniel and Lynn N. Brock, *Island No. 10: Struggle for the Mississippi Valley* (Tuscaloosa: University of Alabama Press, 1996), 21–94; Ambrose, *Halleck,* 36; Cozzens and Girardi, *Memoirs of Pope,* 30–53.

65. OR, 7:679–80.

66. Simon, *Papers of Grant,* 4:319–20; OR, 7:679; Grant, *Memoirs,* 1:166; Daniel and Brock, *Island No. 10,* 21–94; Ambrose, *Halleck,* 36; Daniel, *Shiloh,* 51–53; Simpson, *Ulysses S. Grant,* 122.

67. OR, 10(2):24–25; Williams, *P. G. T. Beauregard,* 123; Daniel and Brock, *Island No. 10,* 45–68; Schutz and Trenerry, *Abandoned by Lincoln,* 77–79; Cozzens and Girardi, *Memoirs of Pope,* 49–51.

68. OR, 10(2):22–23; Ambrose, *Halleck,* 39.

69. Keifer to wife, March 14, 1862, Keifer Papers; Sears, *George B. McClellan,* 164–67.

70. Ambrose, *Halleck,* 40.

71. James G. Wilson, "General Halleck, a Memoir," *Journal of the Military Service Institution of the United States* 36 (1905): 555; Ambrose, *Halleck,* 40.

72. Keifer to wife, March 7, 1862, Keifer Papers.

73. Kenneth M. Stampp, *Indiana Politics during the Civil War* (Bloomington: Indiana University Press, 1949), 123; James G. Blaine, *Twenty Years of Congress from Lincoln to Garfield,* 2 vols. (Norwick CT: Henry Bill Publishing, 1884–86), 1:356–57; Paludan, *"A People's Contest,"* 91–95.

74. Liddell quoted in Daniel, *Shiloh,* 44; Hughes, *Liddell's Record,* 54–55; Connelly, *Army of the Heartland,* 138–40; Cooling, *Fort Donelson's Legacy,* 26–

27, 48–49; Roland, *Albert Sidney Johnston*, 300; Hughes, *General William J. Hardee*, 93.

75. *Richmond Enquirer*, February 19, 1862; Daniel, *Shiloh*, 44–45; Roland, *Albert Sidney Johnston*, 300–301; Connelly, *Army of the Heartland*, 135–38.

76. OR, 6:823–25, 847, 7:890–95; Connelly, *Army of the Heartland*, 138–42; Williams, P. G. T. *Beauregard*, 121–24; Roland, *Albert Sidney Johnston*, 301; Horn, *Army of Tennessee*, 107–8; Woodworth, *Davis and His Generals*, 332; Daniel, *Shiloh*, 47–48; Thomas Connelly and Archer Jones, *The Politics of Command: Factions and Ideas in Confederate Strategy* (Baton Rouge: Louisiana State University Press, 1973), 98–101. One of the great postwar controversies among former Confederate commanders was over who persuaded whom about uniting at Corinth. T. Harry Williams argues perhaps most convincingly that both Johnston and Beauregard came to the same conclusion independently since they both suspected correctly that Grant would move up the river to cut Confederate communications.

77. OR, 10(2):297; Daniel, *Shiloh*, 47–48; Richard McMurry, *Two Great Rebel Armies: An Essay in Confederate Military History* (Chapel Hill: University of North Carolina Press, 1989), 122; Williams, P. G. T. *Beauregard*, 121; Connelly, *Army of the Heartland*, 131, 138–41; Woodworth, *Davis and His Generals*, 95; Alfred Roman, *The Military Operations of General Beauregard in the War between the States, 1861–1865*, 2 vols. (New York: Harper and Brothers, 1883), 1:233, 244.

78. OR, 10(2):304.

79. Connelly, *Army of the Heartland*, 139–40; Williams, P. G. T. *Beauregard*, 121–24; Horn, *Army of Tennessee*, 111–12; Roland, *Albert Sidney Johnston*, 302–3; Davis, *Jefferson Davis*, 400.

80. Williams, P. G. T. *Beauregard*, 121–24; Connelly, *Army of the Heartland*, 140–41; Roland, *Albert Sidney Johnston*, 302–3; Hughes, *General William J. Hardee*, 97–99.

81. Connelly, *Army of the Heartland*, 140–41; Williams, P. G. T. *Beauregard*, 121–24.

82. Gilmer quoted in Roland, *Albert Sidney Johnston*, 303; Connelly, *Army of the Heartland*, 141–42; OR, 10(2):302.

5. TOWARD PITTSBURG LANDING

1. Capron, "War Diary," 340–41; McFeely, *Grant*, 107–9; Grant, *Memoirs*, 1:221; Simon, *Papers of Grant*, 4:344.

2. Simon, *Papers of Grant*, 4:327; Simpson, *Ulysses S. Grant*, 123–25.

3. OR, 7:68–83; Simon, *Papers of Grant*, 4:319–20; McFeely, *Grant*, 107–9.

4. OR, 10(2):2, 6, 17; Simon, *Papers of Grant*, 4:319–20; Ambrose, *Halleck*, 42–43.

5. Ambrose, *Halleck*, 42–43; Daniel, *Shiloh*, 73–75; Engle, *Don Carlos Buell*, 210–15; Anders, *Henry Halleck's War*, 96–98.

6. Simpson and Berlin, *Sherman's Civil War,* 196–98; OR, 10(2):21; Simon, *Papers of Grant,* 4:301–15; Capron, "War Diary," 341–42; Marszalek, *Sherman,* 173; McFeely, *Grant,* 109; Daniel, *Shiloh,* 74–77; Simpson, *Ulysses S. Grant,* 126–27.

7. Isabel Wallace, *Life and Letters of W. H. L. Wallace* (Chicago: R. R. Donnelly and Sons, 1909), 175; Daniel, *Shiloh,* 77–78.

8. Lew Wallace, *Autobiography,* 1:444–45; Daniel, *Shiloh,* 78.

9. OR, 10(1):10–11; Wallace to wife, March 10, 1862, Lew Wallace Papers, Indiana Historical Society; Daniel, *Shiloh,* 79. The spelling "Hayes" in the OR actually should be "Haynes."

10. Capron, "War Diary," 343; OR, 10(1):22–24, 28–29, 83–84; T. J. Lindsey, *Ohio at Shiloh* (Cincinnati: C. J. Krehbiel, 1903), 85–87; James L. McDonough, *Shiloh: In Hell before Night* (Knoxville: University of Tennessee Press, 1977), 44; Daniel, *Shiloh,* 80–82.

11. Grady McWhiney, *Braxton Bragg and Confederate Defeat* (New York: Columbia University Press, 1969), 208–11; Williams, *P. G. T. Beauregard,* 124–25; Connelly, *Army of the Heartland,* 150–51. It was during this time that Beauregard took time out to return a letter to Father James Mullen of St. Patrick's Church in New Orleans. The general had issued a call to Mississippi planters asking them to contribute their plantation bells to be cast into cannon. Father Mullen was apparently apprehensive about offering the bell of his church. Beauregard responded, "Our wives and children have been accustomed to the call, and would miss the tones of 'Church-going bells,' but if there is no alternative we must make the sacrifice." As much as he may have wanted to spare the South's bells, he simply could not. The war was intensifying, and Beauregard needed every available resource to carry on his operations to restore the Confederacy in the West. OR, 10(2):350.

12. OR, 10(2):362, 373, 387; Connelly, *Army of the Heartland,* 148–50; Roland, *Albert Sidney Johnston,* 308–9.

13. Roland, *Albert Sidney Johnston,* 309–10; Daniel, *Shiloh,* 89; Crist, *Papers of Jefferson Davis,* 8:92–94.

14. OR, 10(2):332–41; McWhiney, *Braxton Bragg,* 210–11; Phillip Thomas Tucker, *The Forgotten "Stonewall of the West": Major General John Stevens Bowen* (Macon GA: Mercer University Press, 1997), 99–101; Diane Neal and Thomas W. Kremm, *The Lion of the South: General Thomas C. Hindman* (Macon GA: Mercer University Press, 1993), 102–4; Connelly, *Army of the Heartland,* 146–50.

15. McWhiney, *Braxton Bragg,* 211–13; Roland, *Albert Sidney Johnston,* 311; Williams, *P. G. T. Beauregard,* 125; Connelly, *Army of the Heartland,* 146–51; Daniel, *Shiloh,* 90–91; OR, 10(2):361–62.

16. *Battles and Leaders,* 1:579; Connelly, *Army of the Heartland,* 147–49; Daniel, *Shiloh,* 92.

17. Daniel, *Shiloh,* 93–95; McWhiney, *Braxton Bragg,* 216.

18. Mott, "War Journal of a Confederate Officer," 244.

19. OR, 10(2):370–71, 379; McWhiney, *Braxton Bragg*, 216–17; Connelly, *Army of the Heartland*, 145–50; Hughes, *General William J. Hardee*, 98.

20. Johnson quoted in Roland, *Albert Sidney Johnston*, 311–12; Williams, *P. G. T. Beauregard*, 125; *Battles and Leaders*, 1:578; Davis, *Jefferson Davis*, 402–3.

21. OR, 10(2):370–71; McWhiney, *Braxton Bragg*, 215–18; Williams, *P. G. T. Beauregard*, 125; Roland, *Albert Sidney Johnston*, 313–15; Connelly, *Army of the Heartland*, 145–51; Roman, *Military Operations of Beauregard*, 1:267–68; William C. Davis, *Breckinridge: Statesman, Soldier, Symbol* (Baton Rouge: Louisiana State University Press, 1974), 301–2; Daniel, *Shiloh*, 95–96.

22. OR, 8:282, 10(2): 354, 371; Roland, *Albert Sidney Johnston*, 311–16; Arthur B. Carter, *Major General Earl Van Dorn, C.S.A.* (Knoxville: University of Tennessee Press, 1999), 68–69; Daniel, *Shiloh*, 98–99.

23. Lewis, *Sherman*, 213; OR, 10(1):24–25.

24. Loudon to Hannah, March 23, 1862, DeWitt Clinton Loudon Papers, Ohio Historical Society, Columbus; Lindsey, *Ohio at Shiloh*, 85–87; Lewis, *Sherman*, 213; Daniel, *Shiloh*, 131; Simpson and Berlin, *Sherman's Civil War*, 197–200.

25. Lewis, *Sherman*, 213; Lindsey, *Ohio at Shiloh*, 85–87; Daniel, *Shiloh*, 131; McDonough, *Shiloh*, 4.

26. Simon, *Papers of Grant*, 4:354–55; Simpson, *Ulysses S. Grant*, 123–27; Anders, *Henry Halleck's War*, 94.

27. OR, 10(2):43; Simpson, *Ulysses S. Grant*, 127.

28. Simon, *Papers of Grant*, 4:385–86; Williams, *Lincoln Finds a General*, 3:310–11.

29. Simon, *Papers of Grant*, 4:385–89; OR, 10(2):46–47; McFeely, *Grant*, 109–12; Daniel, *Shiloh*, 104–5.

30. OR, 10(2):41, 50–51; Simon, *Papers of Grant*, 4:386–87; Anders, *Henry Halleck's War*, 94–95.

31. OR, 10(2):33–44, 66.

32. Engle, *Don Carlos Buell*, 210–15.

33. OR, 7:679–80.

34. Bush to Buell, January 16, 1886, Buell Papers, Filson Club; OR, 10(2):44; Halleck to Buell, March 16, 17, 26, 1862; and Buell to Halleck, March 18, 1862, Generals Papers, RG 94, National Archives; Engle, *Don Carlos Buell*, 215–18.

35. OR, 10(1):329–30; Hannaford, *Story of a Regiment*, 231–33; Edgar Kellog, "Recollections of Civil War Service," April 6, 1862, Civil War Miscellaneous Collection, U.S. Army Military History Institute, Carlisle Barracks, Carlisle, Penn. (cited hereafter as USAMHI); Charles C. Briant, *History of the Sixth Regiment Indiana Volunteer Infantry* (Indianapolis: W. B. Burford, 1891), 98–99; Villard, *Memoirs*, 1:238–40.

36. OR, 10(1):329–30.

37. OR, 10(2):84–88, 112–13; Daniel, *Shiloh*, 106.

38. Wallace, *Life and Letters of W. H. L. Wallace*, 178–79; OR, 10(2):87–88; Kiper, *McClernand*, 86–103.

39. For the contribution of foreign-born soldiers to the Union war effort, see William L. Burton, *Melting Pot Soldiers: The Union's Ethnic Regiments* (New York: Fordham University Press, 1998). Nicolay, *Lincoln's Secretary*, 132–33.

40. Frank and Reaves, *"Seeing the Elephant,"* 66–69; Daniel, *Shiloh*, 106–13; Alexander Varian to Father, February 19, 1862; and Varian to Sister, March 27, 1862, Alexander Varian Jr. Papers, Western Reserve Historical Society, Cleveland, Ohio; George Botkin to "Dear Friend," March 19, 1862, Sidney Baker Papers, Ohio Historical Society, Columbus; George Mills, ed., "The Sharp Family Civil War Letters," *Annals of Iowa* (January 1959), 491.

41. Wallace, *Life and Letters of W. H. L. Wallace*, 172.

42. Wisconsin soldier quoted in Frank and Reaves, *"Seeing the Elephant,"* 67–69.

43. Frank and Reaves, *"Seeing the Elephant,"* 66–76; Daniel, *Shiloh*, 106–11.

44. Johnston quoted in Roland, *Albert Sidney Johnston*, 315; OR, 10(2):385.

45. Roland, *Albert Sidney Johnston*, 315; *Battles and Leaders*, 1:579; Daniel, *Shiloh*, 116–17; OR, 10(2):385.

46. *Battles and Leaders*, 1:579; Williams, *P. G. T. Beauregard*, 126; Roland, *Albert Sidney Johnston*, 316; Connelly, *Army of the Heartland*, 150–51; Christopher Losson, *Tennessee's Forgotten Warriors: Frank Cheatham and His Confederate Division* (Knoxville: University of Tennessee Press, 1989), 44–45.

47. *Battles and Leaders*, 1:579–94; Roman, *Military Operations of Beauregard*, 1:270–72; McWhiney, *Braxton Bragg*, 218; Roland, *Albert Sidney Johnston*, 316–18; Daniel, *Shiloh*, 118; OR, 10(2):381–89.

48. OR, 10(1):392–97; Connelly, *Army of the Heartland*, 153; Williams, *P. G. T. Beauregard*, 127; McWhiney, *Braxton Bragg*, 219–21; Losson, *Tennessee's Forgotten Warriors*, 45.

49. Connelly, *Army of the Heartland*, 153–55; Daniel, *Shiloh*, 119–21.

50. Roland, *Albert Sidney Johnston*, 318–19; Williams, *P. G. T. Beauregard*, 129–30; McWhiney, *Braxton Bragg*, 221–23; Hughes, *General William J. Hardee*, 100–102; OR, 10(2):390–94.

51. Williams, *P. G. T. Beauregard*, 130–31; Roland, *Albert Sidney Johnston*, 319–20; Hughes, *General William J. Hardee*, 103.

52. Daniel, *Shiloh*, 126–27; OR, 10(1):464–66, 566–68.

53. Beauregard quoted in Williams, *P. G. T. Beauregard*, 131–32; McWhiney, *Braxton Bragg*, 226–27; Roland, *Albert Sidney Johnston*, 323; Daniel, *Shiloh*, 128.

54. *Battles and Leaders*, 1:555; Roland, *Albert Sidney Johnston*, 324–25; Davis, *Breckinridge*, 303.

55. Interestingly, these remarks passed through the Union camps after the battle. See, for example, George Carrington Diary, April 9, 1862, George Carrington Papers, Chicago Historical Society, Chicago, Ill.; *Battles and Leaders*, 1:555;

Roland, *Albert Sidney Johnston*, 324–25; McWhiney, *Braxton Bragg*, 227; Daniel, *Shiloh*, 129.

56. OR, 10(2):50, 88–91, 257–58; Simon, *Papers of Grant*, 4:397; Marszalek, *Sherman*, 174–76.

57. Loudon to Hannah, April 2, 4, 1862, Loudon Papers; Simpson and Berlin, *Sherman's Civil War*, 199; Marszalek, *Sherman*, 174–76; Daniel, *Shiloh*, 132.

58. Sherman quoted in Marszalek, *Sherman*, 176; Lewis, *Sherman*, 219; OR, 10(2):93–94;Wiley Sword, *Shiloh: Bloody April* (New York:William Morrow, 1974), 124.

59. Loudon to Hannah, April 3, 1862, Loudon Papers.

60. Lewis, *Sherman*, 219; Marszalek, *Sherman*, 176–77; Sword, *Shiloh*, 126–30; McDonough, *Shiloh*, 56.

61. OR, 10(2):87–92; Daniel, *Shiloh*, 137–38.

62. *Battles and Leaders*, 1:466–67; Daniel, *Shiloh*, 139; Simpson, *Ulysses S. Grant*, 129–30.

63. *Battles and Leaders*, 1:467, 491; OR, 10(1):329–31;Wallace, *Life and Letters of W. H. L. Wallace*, 180–81; Simon, *Papers of Grant*, 5:13–14.

64. OR, 10(1):329–31; *Battles and Leaders*, 1:467, 491.

65. Mildred Throne, ed., *The Civil War Diary of Cyrus F. Boyd: Fifteenth Iowa Infantry, 1861–1863* (Iowa City: State Historical Society of Iowa, 1953), 25–27.

66. OR, 10(1):89, 329–31; *Battles and Leaders*, 1:467, 491; Daniel, *Shiloh*, 141; Engle, *Don Carlos Buell*, 218–19.

67. Joseph R. Ruff, "Civil War Experiences of a German Emigrant as Told by the Late Joseph Ruff of Albion," *Michigan History Magazine* 27 (1943), 294; Hannaford, *Story of a Regiment*, 240; OR, 10(1):282, 10(2):94; Lindsey, *Ohio at Shiloh*, 95–97; Daniel, *Shiloh*, 141–42.

68. Jacob Ammen Diary, April 6, 1862, Jacob Ammen Papers, Indiana Historical Society, Indianapolis.

6. BLOODY SHILOH

1. Ruff, "Civil War Experiences," 289–90; OR, 10(1):278, 590–96; Daniel, *Shiloh*, 143–45; Stacy D. Allen, "Shiloh!: The Campaign and First Day's Battle," *Blue and Gray Magazine* 14 (February 1997), 19.

2. "Gen. Albert Sidney Johnston," *Confederate Veteran* 3 (1895): 82; Roland, *Albert Sidney Johnston*, 326.

3. *Battles and Leaders*, 1:556–57.

4. *Battles and Leaders*, 1:557; Roland, *Albert Sidney Johnston*, 326; Williams, *P. G. T. Beauregard*, 134; McWhiney, *Braxton Bragg*, 228.

5. Joseph Rich, *The Battle of Shiloh* (Iowa City: State Historical Society of Iowa, 1911), 529; Charles A. Morton, "A Boy at Shiloh," *Military Order of the*

Loyal Legion of the United States, New York Commandery (1907), 52–69; *National Tribune,* April 17, 1884; OR, 10(1):280–84; Allen, "Shiloh!: The Campaign and First Day's Battle," 19–20; Daniel, *Shiloh,* 147.

6. OR, 10(1):282–85; Daniel, *Shiloh,* 148.

7. *Battles and Leaders,* 1:556–57; Neal and Kremm, *Lion of the South,* 104.

8. *Battles and Leaders,* 1:559–61; Neal and Kremm, *Lion of the South,* 107; Allen, "Shiloh!: The Campaign and First Day's Battle," 18–21.

9. OR, 10(1):278–79; Daniel, *Shiloh,* 153–55; Allen, "Shiloh!: The Campaign and First Day's Battle," 18–21.

10. OR, 10(1):248–49; Marszalek, *Sherman,* 177–78; Craig L. Symonds, *Stonewall of the West: Patrick Cleburne and the Civil War* (Lawrence: University Press of Kansas, 1997), 70–71.

11. Lewis, *Sherman,* 220–21; Marszalek, *Sherman,* 177; Sherman, *Memoirs,* 1:230; OR, 10(1):249; Ruff, "Civil War Experiences," 296–97; Simpson and Berlin, *Sherman's Civil War,* 201.

12. Ruff, "Civil War Experiences," 289–90; OR, 10(1):249; Sherman, *Memoirs,* 1:230; Lewis, *Sherman,* 220–21; Marszalek, *Sherman,* 177–78.

13. Simpson, *Ulysses S. Grant,* 130–31.

14. Samuel B. Franklin, "Memoirs of a Civil War Veteran," April 16, 1862, Samuel B. Franklin Papers, Harrisburg Civil War Round Table Collection, USAMHI; OR, 10(1):184–85; *Battles and Leaders,* 1:467–68, 492–93; Simpson, *Ulysses S. Grant,* 130–31.

15. Lew Wallace, *Autobiography,* 1:461; OR, 10(1):175–84; *Battles and Leaders,* 1:467–68; McDonough, *Shiloh,* 96; Daniel, *Shiloh,* 174–75.

16. OR, 10(1):179, 185, 286–88; Grant, *Memoirs,* 1:225–26; Daniel, *Shiloh,* 175; McDonough, *Shiloh,* 124; Simpson, *Ulysses S. Grant,* 131.

17. OR, 10(1):115–17, 278; Grant, *Memoirs,* 1:231; William T. Sherman, "The Battle of Pittsburgh Landing: A Letter from Sherman," *United States Service Magazine* 3 (January 1865): 2–4; Lewis, *Sherman,* 224; Marszalek, *Sherman,* 178; Daniel, *Shiloh,* 206; McDonough, *Shiloh,* 124–25; Kiper, *McClernand,* 105–7.

18. OR, 10(1):278–79; McDonough, *Shiloh,* 126; Simpson, *Ulysses S. Grant,* 131–32.

19. *Battles and Leaders,* 1:492; OR, 10(2):95; Simpson, *Ulysses S. Grant,* 132; Kiper, *McClernand,* 108–9.

20. *Battles and Leaders,* 1: 492–96; OR, 10(1):292; Simpson, *Ulysses S. Grant,* 132; Engle, *Don Carlos Buell,* 218–23; Daniel, *Shiloh,* 243.

21. Grant, *Memoirs,* 1:345; OR, 10(1):291–92; *Battles and Leaders,* 1:474, 493–95; Engle, *Don Carlos Buell,* 224–27; Daniel, *Shiloh,* 244.

22. McDonough, *Shiloh,* 131; Daniel, *Shiloh,* 176–218; Frank and Reaves, *"Seeing the Elephant,"* 88–101; Throne, *Diary of Cyrus Boyd,* 32.

23. Williams, *P. G. T. Beauregard,* 139; Roland, *Albert Sidney Johnston,* 331–35; McDonough, *Shiloh,* 132–33.

24. McDonough, *Shiloh*, 133–36; Daniel, *Shiloh*, 203–10.

25. McWhiney, *Braxton Bragg*, 231–35.

26. OR, 10(1):204–5, 466

27. OR, 10(1):204–5, 465–66; McWhiney, *Braxton Bragg*, 236–38; Daniel, *Shiloh*, 230–33.

28. OR, 10(1):480–81, 498, 574; McDonough, *Shiloh*, 149–50; McWhiney, *Braxton Bragg*, 236–40; Neal and Kremm, *Lion of the South*, 108; Allen, "Shiloh!: The Campaign and First Day's Battle," 50.

29. Johnston, *Life of Johnston*, 613–15; "Gen. Albert Sidney Johnston," 86; Roland, *Albert Sidney Johnston*, 336–38; Davis, *Breckinridge*, 307; Tucker, *Forgotten "Stonewall,"* 107–11; McDonough, *Shiloh*, 152; Allen, "Shiloh!: The Campaign and First Day's Battle," 52.

30. OR, 10(1):404; Johnston, *Life of Johnston*, 613–15; "Gen. Albert Sidney Johnston," 86; Roland, *Albert Sidney Johnston*, 338; Sword, *Shiloh*, 261–72; William Payne, "On Shiloh," William Payne Papers, Special Collections, United States Military Academy (cited hereafter as USMA).

31. *Battles and Leaders*, 1:468–74; Daniel, *Shiloh*, 235–37; Simpson, *Ulysses S. Grant*, 133.

32. Lew Wallace, *Autobiography*, 1:466–70; OR, 10(1):170–79, 185–86; *Battles and Leaders*, 1:476; Daniel, *Shiloh*, 256–61.

33. Hannaford, *Story of a Regiment*, 241–48; *Battles and Leaders*, 1:491–92; OR, 10(1):291–92; Jacob Ammen to A. B. Martin, April 8, 9, 1862, Jacob Ammen Papers, Special Collections, USMA; Engle, *Don Carlos Buell*, 221–24.

34. OR, 10(1):466; McWhiney, *Braxton Bragg*, 240–41; Daniel, *Shiloh*, 254–56; McDonough, *Shiloh*, 162; Losson, *Tennessee's Forgotten Warriors*, 49–50; Allen, "Shiloh!: The Campaign and First Day's Battle," 54.

35. OR, 10(1):203–5, 279, 533–34, 537–38, 541; McDonough, *Shiloh*, 164; McWhiney, *Braxton Bragg*, 241–43; Allen, "Shiloh!: The Campaign and First Day's Battle," 54–62.

36. OR, 10(1):386–87, 551–55; Williams, *P. G. T. Beauregard*, 141–42; Daniel, *Shiloh*, 250–52.

37. OR, 10(1):213–15, 553–54, 558–622; Williams, *P. G. T. Beauregard*, 141–42; Daniel, *Shiloh*, 264–67.

38. William McCann, *Ambrose Bierce's Civil War* (Chicago: Gateway Editions, 1956), 17; Villard, *Memoirs*, 1:246; Jacob H. Smith, *Personal Reminiscences Three Weeks Prior, during, and 10 Days after the Battle of Shiloh* (Detroit: Winn and Hammond, 1894), 8–11; William Shanks, *Personal Recollections of Distinguished Generals* (New York: Harper and Brothers, 1866), 43; Throne, *Diary of Cyrus Boyd*, 34; Wallace, *Life and Letters of W. H. L. Wallace*, 186–87; Beatty, *Citizen Soldier*, 162.

39. OR, 10(1):384.

40. Williams, *P. G. T. Beauregard*, 143.

41. Throne, *Diary of Cyrus Boyd,* 35.

42. OR, 10(1):582–83; Symonds, *Stonewall of the West,* 74.

43. Grant quoted in Simpson, *Ulysses S. Grant,* 134; Stacy Allen, "Shiloh!: The Second Day's Battle and Aftermath," *Blue and Gray Magazine* 14 (April 1997), 7; OR, 10(1):113–20.

44. Bruce Catton, *Grant Moves South* (Boston: Little, Brown, 1960), 242; Grant, *Memoirs,* 1:354; Marszalek, *Shiloh,* 180; McDonough, *Shiloh,* 183; Simpson, *Ulysses S. Grant,* 134.

45. Sherman, *Memoirs,* 1:246; *Battles and Leaders,* 1:519–20; Thomas Van Horne, *History of the Army of the Cumberland: Its Organization, Campaigns, and Battles,* 3 vols. (Cincinnati: Robert Clarke, 1875), 1:109; Sherman, "Battle of Pittsburgh Landing," 1–4; Lewis, *Sherman,* 228; Fellman, *Citizen Sherman,* 330–32; Simpson and Berlin, *Sherman's Civil War,* 202; Engle, *Don Carlos Buell,* 228.

46. Franklin, "Memoirs of a Civil War Veteran"; McCann, *Bierce's Civil War,* 17; *Battles and Leaders,* 1:474, 519; J. Amos Glover Diary, April 6, 7, 1862, J. Amos Glover Papers, Ohio Historical Society, Columbus; William B. Hazen, *A Narrative of Military Service* (Boston: Ticknor and Fields, 1885), 25.

47. Engle, *Don Carlos Buell,* 228–30.

48. Throne, *Diary of Cyrus Boyd,* 34–39; McDonough, *Shiloh,* 186.

49. McWhiney, *Braxton Bragg,* 247; Davis, *Breckinridge,* 311; McDonough, *Shiloh,* 190; Daniel, *Shiloh,* 262–63.

50. *Battles and Leaders,* 1:602–3.

51. Brian S. Wills, *A Battle from the Start: The Life of Nathan Bedford Forrest* (New York: Harper Collins, 1992), 68–69; Wyeth, *That Devil Forrest,* 63; Hughes, *General William J. Hardee,* 109.

52. OR, 10(1):324, 518, 570; McDonough, *Shiloh,* 196–97; Allen, "Shiloh!: The Second Day's Battle and Aftermath," 16–17.

53. Bragg quoted in McWhiney, *Braxton Bragg,* 246–47; Williams, *P. G. T. Beauregard,* 144; Connelly, *Army of the Heartland,* 168–69.

54. OR, 10(1):411, 440–42, 456, 518–19; *Battles and Leaders,* 1:590–91; Connelly, *Army of the Heartland,* 170–74; Williams, *P. G. T. Beauregard,* 144–45; Losson, *Tennessee's Forgotten Warriors,* 50–51; Allen, "Shiloh!: The Second Day's Battle and Aftermath," 18–19.

55. OR, 10(1):570–72; Symonds, *Stonewall of the West,* 74–77.

56. Barnes Lathrop, "A Confederate Artilleryman at Shiloh," *Civil War History* 7 (December 1962): 378; Davis, *Breckinridge,* 311; McWhiney, *Braxton Bragg,* 247–48 (quote, 248).

57. OR, 10(1):324–25, 341, 349; Engle, *Don Carlos Buell,* 230–32; McDonough, *Shiloh,* 200–201; Allen, "Shiloh!: The Second Day's Battle and Aftermath," 22–23.

58. Hannaford, *Story of a Regiment,* 572–73; Thomas Prickett to Matilda, April 18, 1862, Prickett Papers, Indiana Historical Society, Indianapolis; OR, 10(1): 335–36.

59. *Battles and Leaders*, 1:603; Williams, *P. G. T. Beauregard*, 145; Allen, "Shiloh!: The Second Day's Battle and Aftermath," 27.

60. William C. Davis, ed., *Diary of a Confederate Soldier: John S. Jackman of the Orphan Brigade* (Columbia: University of South Carolina, 1990), 32.

61. William H. Harder Diary, April 7, 1862, private collection in the possession of Emily Stockard, Fort Lauderdale, Fla.; OR, 10(1):388; *Battles and Leaders*, 1:603; Williams, *P. G. T. Beauregard*, 145; Daniel, *Shiloh*, 290–91; McDonough, *Shiloh*, 208.

62. OR, 10(1):263, 268, 10(2):96–97; Simon, *Papers of Grant*, 5:20–21; Wills, *Battle from the Start*, 70; Marszalek, *Sherman*, 180.

63. H. H. Giesy to "Brother, Sister, and Mother," April 9, 1862, H. H. Giesy Papers, Western Kentucky University, Bowling Green.

64. Throne, *Diary of Cyrus Boyd*, 39–42.

65. Engle, *Don Carlos Buell*, 232–39.

66. Nelson to Chase, April 10, 1862, Chase Papers, Claremont.

67. Davis to brother, April 21, 1862, Andrew F. Davis Papers, *Civil War Times Illustrated* Collection, USAMHI.

68. Hambleton Tapp and James C. Klotter, eds., *The Union, the Civil War, and John H. Tuttle: A Kentucky Captain's Account* (Frankfort: Kentucky Historical Society, 1980), 88.

69. Larry J. Daniel, *Soldering in the Army of Tennessee: A Portrait of Life in a Confederate Army* (Chapel Hill: University of North Carolina Press, 1990), 152.

70. Stanton Garner, *The Civil War World of Herman Melville* (Lawrence: University Press of Kansas, 1993), 141–42.

71. Throne, *Diary of Cyrus Boyd*, 42.

72. Buell to wife, April 18, 1862, Buell Papers, Filson Club Historical Society.

73. Louis M. Buford to Charles Buford Jr., April 21, 1862, Charles M. Buford Papers, Library of Congress; Engle, *Don Carlos Buell*, 236.

74. Rousseau to Chase, April 15, 1862, Chase Papers, Claremont; Engle, *Don Carlos Buell*, 235–39.

75. *New York Daily Tribune*, April 16, 1862.

76. J. Cutler Andrews, *The North Reports the War* (Pittsburgh: University of Pittsburg Press, 1955), 176–79.

77. Thomas and Hyman, *Stanton*, 190–91; David Donald, *Charles Sumner and the Rights of Man* (New York: Alfred A. Knopf, 1970), 59; Blaisdell to "Sister and Brother," April 12, 1862, Timothy Blaisdell Papers, Civil War Miscellaneous Papers, USAMHI; Tompkins to wife, April 8, 1862, Charles Tompkins Papers, Duke University, Durham, N.C.

78. Nelson to Chase, April 10, 1862, Chase Papers, Claremont.

79. Lewis, *Sherman*, 211–13, 232–33; Fitzhugh, "On Shiloh," William Payne Papers, Special Collections, USMA; Marszalek, *Sherman*, 172–83; McFeely, *Grant*, 111–13.

80. Ward N. Baker, "Mishawaka and Its Volunteers through the Shiloh Campaign," *Indiana Magazine of History* 58 (June 1962): 134–35; Henry C. Barnett, "Civil War Recollections," *Indiana Magazine of History* 38 (March 1942): 68–69; Louis M. Starr, *Bohemian Brigade: Civil War Newsmen in Action* (New York: Knopf, 1954), 99–100.

81. OR, 10(1):98–99; *New York Daily Tribune,* May 9, 1862; Ambrose, *Halleck,* 45–46.

82. Carrington Diary, April 9, 1862, Carrington Papers, Chicago Historical Society; Daniel, *Shiloh,* 332.

83. Simpson and Berlin, *Sherman's Civil War,* 202; Mark A. DeWolfe Howe, ed., *Home Letters of General Sherman* (New York: Charles Scribner's Sons, 1909), 222–23; Carter, *Van Dorn,* 68–71.

7. A SIEGE FROM BEGINNING TO CLOSE

1. Anders, *Henry Halleck's War,* 102–3; Simon, *Papers of Grant,* 5:20.

2. Simon, *Papers of Grant,* 5:48; Ambrose, *Halleck,* 45–47.

3. Lewis, *Sherman,* 234; Simpson and Berlin, *Sherman's Civil War,* 204.

4. OR, 10(1):98–99.

5. OR, 10(1):98–99; Simpson, *Ulysses S. Grant,* 136–37.

6. Williams, *Lincoln and His Generals,* 85–86.

7. OR, 10(1):99–100; Lewis, *Sherman,* 234–35.

8. Andrews, *South Reports the War,* 153.

9. OR, 7:889; Black, *Railroads of the Confederacy,* 139.

10. Black, *Railroads of the Confederacy,* 139–45.

11. Charles Tompkins Diary, May 5, 1862, Tompkins Papers, Duke University.

12. Ambrose, *Halleck,* 47.

13. *New York Daily Tribune,* May 9, 1862.

14. *New York Daily Tribune,* May 31, 1862.

15. Anders, *Henry Halleck's War,* 103; *New York Daily Tribune,* May 31, 1862; OR, 10(2):107; Ambrose, *Halleck,* 47–48.

16. *Frank Leslie's Illustrated Magazine,* April 26, 1862; Schutz and Trenerry, *Abandoned by Lincoln,* 82–84; Cozzens and Girardi, *Memoirs of Pope,* 63–65.

17. Basler, *Works of Lincoln,* 5:186.

18. Cozzens and Girardi, *Memoirs of Pope,* 63; OR 10(2):138–39, 677; Ambrose, *Halleck,* 47–48; Schutz and Trenerry, *Abandoned by Lincoln,* 82–84.

19. OR 10(2):138–39; Cozzens and Girardi, *Memoirs of Pope,* 64–67; Roy Morris Jr., *The Life and Wars of General Phil Sheridan* (New York: Crown, 1992), 55–57; Ambrose, *Halleck,* 47–48; Kiper, *McClernand,* 116–18.

20. Ambrose, *Halleck,* 48–49.

21. Throne, *Diary of Cyrus Boyd,* 47.

22. Grant, *Memoirs*, 1:370; Lew Wallace, *Autobiography*, 2:575–76; OR 10(2):138–39, 144, 52:245.

23. Simon, *Papers of Grant*, 5:115–16; Simpson, *Ulysses S. Grant*, 140–41; Lewis, *Sherman*, 235–36.

24. Grant, *Memoirs*, 1:376.

25. Simon, *Papers of Grant*, 5:115; OR 10(2):182–83.

26. OR 10(2):144–45; Williams, *Lincoln Finds a General*, 3:410.

27. Mitchel, *Ormsby MacKnight Mitchel*, 270–75; OR 10(2):71–72, 617; Beatty, *Citizen Soldier*, 95–103, 111–14; *Battles and Leaders*, 2:701–16; Frederick D. Williams, ed., *The Wild Life of the Army: Civil War Letters of James A. Garfield* (East Lansing: Michigan State University Press, 1964), 87–91; Grimsley, *Hard Hand of War*, 79–81; Engle, *Don Carlos Buell*, 243–50; Jeffrey R. Hummel, *Emancipating Slaves, Enslaving Free Men: A History of the American Civil War* (Chicago: Open Court, 1996), 182–86.

28. OR 10(2):101, 110–11, 126, 129; Trefousse, *Andrew Johnson*, 157–59; Durham, *Nashville*, 73–80; Engle, *Don Carlos Buell*, 243–50.

29. OR 10(2):128.

30. OR 10(2):129; Trefousse, *Andrew Johnson*, 157–59.

31. OR 10(2):154.

32. OR, 10(1):665.

33. Ambrose, *Halleck*, 49.

34. Lewis Mathewson to "Father and Mother," May 2, 1862, Mathewson Papers, Ohio Historical Society; OR, 10(1):665; Anders, *Henry Halleck's War*, 112–13; Ambrose, *Halleck*, 49; Morris, *Sheridan*, 57; Williams, *Lincoln Finds a General*, 3:411–13.

35. *Memphis Daily Appeal*, April 15, 1862; *New York Daily Tribune*, May 9, 1862; OR, 6:432, 10(2):465; Williams, *P. G. T. Beauregard*, 150–51; Connelly, *Army of the Heartland*, 174–75.

36. Williams, *P. G. T. Beauregard*, 150–51; Connelly, *Army of the Heartland*, 175–76.

37. Williams, *P. G. T. Beauregard*, 150–51; Connelly, *Army of the Heartland*, 175–76; McWhiney, *Braxton Bragg*, 256.

38. OR 10(2):484–91, 502–7, 517–21, 523–41; Cozzens and Girardi, *Memoirs of Pope*, 85; Williams, *Lincoln Finds a General*, 3:411.

39. OR, 10(1):665, 10(2):166, 172, 176, 177; Andrews, *South Reports the Civil War*, 155; Cozzens and Girardi, *Memoirs of Pope*, 66–67; Schutz and Trenerry, *Abandoned by Lincoln*, 85; Williams, *P. G. T. Beauregard*, 151.

40. Capron, "War Diary," 350; C. Mitchell to Will, May 18, 1862, William Mitchell Papers, Ohio Historical Society.

41. Mathewson to "Father and Mother," May 12, 15, 1862, Mathewson Papers.

42. Basler, *Works of Lincoln*, 5:210; C. Mitchell to Will, May 18, 1862; Ambrose, *Halleck*, 49–51; Williams, *Lincoln Finds a General*, 3:412–18.

43. OR 10(2):196–99; Cozzens and Girardi, *Memoirs of Pope*, 67–68; Engle, *Don Carlos Buell*, 244–45.

44. Cozzens and Girardi, *Memoirs of Pope*, 67–68; Ambrose, *Halleck*, 50.

45. *New York World*, June 13, 1862, *Cincinnati Commercial*, May 24, 1862; Bernard A. Weisberger, *Reporters for the Union* (Boston: Little, Brown, 1953), 96–97; Ambrose, *Halleck*, 50–51; Andrews, *North Reports the Civil War*, 182–85.

46. OR, 10(1):666–67.

47. Williams, *Wild Life of the Army*, 105; Throne, *Diary of Cyrus Boyd*, 46–51; Loudon to Hannah, April 24, May 2, 3, 15, 1862, Loudon Papers, Ohio Historical Society; David H. Thomas to "Father and Mother," May 28, 1862, David H. Thomas Papers, Ohio Historical Society; Thomas Prickett to Matilda, May 25, 1862, Prickett Papers, Indiana Historical Society.

48. OR 10(2):173–77; Engle, *Don Carlos Buell*, 246–54.

49. Daniel, *Soldering in the Army of Tennessee*, 127; OR, 10(1):778.

50. Bell I. Wiley, *The Life of Johnny Reb: The Common Soldier of the Confederacy* (1943; reprint, Baton Rouge: Louisiana State University Press, 1970), 247; Daniel, *Soldering in the Army of Tennessee*, 69–70; Andrews, *South Reports the War*, 154; OR, 10(1):771.

51. Daniel, *Soldering in the Army of Tennessee*, 69–70; OR, 10(1):776; Williams, *P. G. T. Beauregard*, 152; McWhiney, *Braxton Bragg*, 256–57.

52. OR 10(2):529–30; Williams, *P. G. T. Beauregard*, 152–53; Connelly, *Army of the Heartland*, 176.

53. Andrews, *South Reports the War*, 155–57; Williams, *P. G. T. Beauregard*, 153; Connelly, *Army of the Heartland*, 176–77.

54. OR 10(2):544–47; Williams, *P. G. T. Beauregard*, 153–54; Connelly, *Army of the Heartland*, 177; McWhiney, *Braxton Bragg*, 257.

55. OR, 10(1):557, 562, 773; Williams, *P. G. T. Beauregard*, 154; McWhiney, *Braxton Bragg*, 257–58; Connelly, *Army of the Heartland*, 177.

56. Ephraim Holloway to wife, May 25, 1862, Ephraim Holloway Papers, Ohio Historical Society; OR, 10(1):667; Ambrose, *Halleck*, 52.

57. Hannaford, *Story of a Regiment*, 303–8; Cope, *Fifteenth Ohio*, 152–53; James B. Shaw, *History of the Tenth Regiment Indiana Volunteer Infantry* (Lafayette IN: n.p., 1912), 167–69; Villard, *Memoirs*, 1:274–78; Henry S. Osburn Diary, May 29, 1862, Henry Osburn Papers, Ohio Historical Society; Ambrose, *Halleck*, 52–53.

58. Lew Wallace, *Autobiography*, 2:581.

59. *Memphis Daily Appeal*, June 11, 1862; OR, 10(1):771.

60. Cozzens and Girardi, *Memoirs of Pope*, 67–70.

61. OR, 10(1):668; Ambrose, *Halleck*, 53.

62. OR, 10(1):669.

63. Schutz and Trenerry, *Abandoned by Lincoln*, 88; OR, 10(1):669.

64. OR, 10(1):771–73; *Chicago Tribune*, June 2, 1862; Ambrose, *Halleck*, 53.

65. OR, 10(1):771–73.

66. Lewis Mathewson to "Father and Mother," June 6, 1862, Mathewson Papers.

67. OR, 10(1):668–71; Ambrose, *Halleck,* 53–54.

68. OR, 10(1):762, 10(2):546, 17(2): 594–95; Williams, *P. G. T. Beauregard,* 154–55.

69. Beauregard quoted in Davis, *Jefferson Davis,* 406; Woodworth, *Davis and His Generals,* 105.

8. THE PROMISE OF SUMMER

1. Williams, *P. G. T. Beauregard,* 156–58; Andrews, *South Reports the War,* 146–48, 156–57; Davis, *Jefferson Davis,* 406–7.

2. Connelly, *Army of the Heartland,* 178–79; Williams, *P. G. T. Beauregard,* 156–58.

3. Grimsley, *Hard Hand of War,* 70–82; Paludan, *"A People's Contest,"* 75–76.

4. Sherman quoted in Marszalek, *Sherman,* 186.

5. Sherman quoted in Marszalek, *Sherman,* 186; Simpson and Berlin, *Sherman's Civil War,* 232–39.

6. Marszalek, *Sherman,* 186–89.

7. Crist, *Papers of Jefferson Davis,* 8:148–49; Charles P. Roland, *An American Iliad: The Story of the Civil War* (New York: McGraw-Hill, 1991), 103–4; Thomas, *Confederacy as a Revolutionary Experience,* 61–62; Albert B. Moore, *Conscription and Conflict in the Confederacy* (New York: Macmillan, 1924), 56–71; Davis, *Jefferson Davis,* 450–52; Paul Escott, *After Secession: Jefferson Davis and the Failure of Confederate Nationalism* (Baton Rouge: Louisiana State University Press, 1978), 88.

8. Thomas, *Confederacy as a Revolutionary Experience,* 61–62; Davis, *Jefferson Davis,* 450–52; Escott, *After Secession,* 88; Richard E. Beringer et al., *Why the South Lost the Civil War* (Athens: University of Georgia Press, 1986), 205–25.

9. Beringer et al., *Why the South Lost,* 205–25.

10. Beringer et al., *Why the South Lost,* 205–25.

11. Grimsley, *Hard Hand of War,* 47–52, 67–82; Weisberger, *Reporters for the Union,* 152–54; Engle, *Don Carlos Buell,* 196–203, 273–74.

12. Grimsley, *Hard Hand of War,* 47–52, 67–82; Cooling, *Fort Donelson's Legacy,* 60, 75.

13. Beatty, *Citizen Soldier,* 124–37.

14. Beatty, *Citizen Soldier,* 136–37.

15. Beatty, *Citizen Soldier,* 138–39; Keifer to wife, May 3, 1862, Keifer Papers, Library of Congress; Cope, *Fifteenth Ohio,* 170; Grimsley, *Hard Hand of War,* 80–85.

16. Williams, *Wild Life of the Army,* 89; Berlin et al., *Destruction of Slavery,* 250–56; Grimsley, *Hard Hand of War,* 80–85; Engle, *Don Carlos Buell,* 266–68.

17. Williams, *Wild Life of the Army,* 89–90.

18. Ash, *Middle Tennessee Society Transformed,* 106–8; Ash, *When the Yankees Came,* 38–42; Jimerson, *Private Civil War,* 60–65. See also Roark, *Masters without Slaves,* chapters 2 and 3; and Litwack, *Been in the Storm So Long,* chapter 2.

19. Berlin et al., *Destruction of Slavery,* 20–27; Jimerson, *Private Civil War,* 60–85; Engle, *Don Carlos Buell,* 185–99.

20. Beatty, *Citizen Soldier,* 117; Ash, *Middle Tennessee Society Transformed,* 107–8.

21. Ash, *Middle Tennessee Society Transformed,* 107–8.

22. Beatty, *Citizen Soldier,* 140; Hannaford, *Story of a Regiment,* 227; Ash, *Middle Tennessee Society Transformed,* 106–7; Berlin et al., *Destruction of Slavery,* 20–27.

23. OR, 10(1):6–7; Beatty, *Citizen Soldier,* 112–23; Ash, *Middle Tennessee Society Transformed,* 108–11; Berlin et al., *Destruction of Slavery,* 22–27.

24. Berlin et al., *Destruction of Slavery,* 22, 250–58; Paludan, *Presidency of Lincoln,* 125–28; Paludan, *"A People's Contest,"* 80.

25. Williams, *Wild Life of the Army,* 89–90.

26. Engle, *Don Carlos Buell,* 244–50.

27. Ready quoted in Ash, *When the Yankees Came,* 38.

28. Ash, *When the Yankees Came,* 38–42.

29. Grimsley, *Hard Hand of War,* 80–81.

30. Simpson and Berlin, *Sherman's Civil War,* 231; Grant, *Memoirs,* 1:368–69; Simpson, *Ulysses S. Grant,* 144–45.

31. Simon, *Papers of Grant,* 5:146.

32. Simon, *Papers of Grant,* 5:146; Simpson, *Let Us Have Peace,* 24–25; Simpson, *Ulysses S. Grant,* 144–45.

33. Grimsley, *Hard Hand of War,* 80–84.

34. Mitchel to Chase, June 19, 1862, Chase Papers, Claremont.

35. Williams, *Wild Life of the Army,* 90.

36. Keifer to wife, March 22, 1862, Keifer Papers.

37. Ash, *When the Yankees Came,* 53–56; Berlin et al., *Destruction of Slavery,* 20–38.

38. John Fox to wife, May 1, 1862, John Fox Papers, Ohio Historical Society; Jimerson, *Private Civil War,* 85.

39. John Easton to "Family," May 30, 1862, John Easton Papers, Ohio Historical Society; Berlin et al., *Destruction of Slavery,* 250–58; Grimsley, *Hard Hand of War,* 50–61.

40. Ambrose, *Halleck,* 56–57.

41. Ambrose, *Halleck,* 56–57.

42. Williams, *P. G. T. Beauregard,* 158–60; Connelly, *Army of the Heartland,* 178–83.

43. OR, 10(1):671, 10(2):248, 278.

44. Simon, *Papers of Grant,* 5:136.

45. Simon, *Papers of Grant,* 5:138.

46. Lewis, *Sherman*, 235–36.

47. OR, 10(2):248, 252, 278, 16(2):62; Ambrose, *Halleck*, 55–57; Schutz and Trenerry, *Abandoned by Lincoln*, 88–89.

48. *Memphis Daily Avalanche*, June 6, 1862; OR, 10(1):906–11; Andrews, *South Reports the War*, 158–59.

49. Andrews, *South Reports the War*, 158–59; OR, 10(1):906–11.

50. OR, 10(1):906–91; Andrews, *South Reports the War*, 158–59; Cooling, *Fort Donelson's Legacy*, 59.

51. Williams, *P. G. T. Beauregard*, 156–57.

52. OR, 10(2):407, 529–30, 546, 17(2):594–95, 52(2):300; Woodworth, *Davis and His Generals*, 104.

53. Jefferson Davis quoted in Davis, *Jefferson Davis*, 406; Woodworth, *Davis and His Generals*, 105.

54. OR, 10(2):403, 404–5, 407, 529–30, 546, 17(2):2, 599–601; Williams, *P. G. T. Beauregard*, 156–57; McWhiney, *Braxton Bragg*, 260–61; Davis, *Jefferson Davis*, 406–7; Woodworth, *Davis and His Generals*, 106–8; Roman, *Military Operations of Beauregard*, 1:395–96; Connelly, *Army of the Heartland*, 179–81.

55. Beauregard quoted in Williams, *P. G. T. Beauregard*, 160–61; Catton, *Terrible Swift Sword*, 294; Davis, *Jefferson Davis*, 408; Woodworth, *Davis and His Generals*, 106–7.

56. Andrews, *South Reports the War*, 232; Davis, *Jefferson Davis*, 406–8; McWhiney, *Braxton Bragg*, 260–61; OR, 17(2):599, 601, 614.

57. Engle, *Don Carlos Buell*, 257–85.

58. Simon, *Papers of Grant*, 5:142–43; Sutherland, *Guerrillas, Unionists, and Violence*, 113–50.

59. Grimsley, *Hard Hand of War*, 67–72; Hummel, *Emancipating Slaves, Enslaving Free Men*, 185.

60. Simon, *Papers of Grant*, 5:134.

61. Force, *From Fort Henry to Corinth*, 191.

Bibliographical Essay

This study of the Civil War in the West in early 1862 derives more on the author's interpretation of material already known to most students of the campaigns than on the discovery and use of new sources. It is informed primarily by the works of scholars who have analyzed not only the military operations from Fort Henry to Corinth but also the political and social implications of the war in the region. The notes document the primary-source material from which quotes are taken as well as the most prominent secondary works relevant to these particular campaigns.

Among the most valuable of all manuscript collections dealing with these campaigns can be found in the most obvious national repositories such as the United States Army Military History Institute and the Library of Congress. The archives and historical societies representing those states involved in this study are also extremely important for their manuscript holdings. Additionally, one should consult the private collections in the Chicago Historical Society, the Filson Club Historical Society, the Western Reserve Historical Society, and the Huntington Library as well as in the Southern Historical Collection at the University of North Carolina at Chapel Hill. Indispensable to serious consideration of the war are the official documents found in the National Archives in Washington, D.C., which contains the largest collection of Civil War governmental records, both Federal and Confederate. A fragment of those records were published by the U.S. government as *War of Rebellion: A Compilation of the Official Records of the Union and Confederate Armies* (1881–1902) and *Official Records of the Union and Confederate Navies in the War of Rebellion* (1894–1927).

It is impossible to cover the plethora of contemporary army regimental histories, campaign narratives, and personal memoirs that cover the western war such as Manning F. Force, *Fort Henry to Corinth* (1882), in more detail. Still, many contemporary accounts of the campaigns in early 1862 come from unofficial observers and reporters whose influence on the initial interpretation of the war has been far reaching. Some of the more relevant works that provide keen insights and valuable perspectives on the Union side include: John Beatty, *The Citizen*

Soldier (1879); Frederick Williams, ed., *The Wild Life of the Army: Civil War Letters of James A. Garfield* (1964); and Edwin Hannaford, *The Story of a Regiment: A History of the Campaigns and Association in the Field of the Sixth Regiment Ohio Volunteer Infantry* (1868). Accounts by journalists such as Henry Villard (*Memoirs of Henry Villard* [1904]) and William Shanks (*Personal Recollections of Distinguished Generals* [1866]) should also be consulted. On the Confederate side one should include Nathaniel Cheairs Hughes, ed., *Liddell's Record* (1866; reprint, 1985).

Many public leaders as well as private citizens involved in the battles have left recollections, memoirs, and other personal accounts. The memoirs of William T. Sherman (1875) and the *Personal Memoirs of U. S. Grant* (1885) are both representative examples of the postwar attempt to refashion contemporary accounts of the campaigns and battles in which they participated. The collected and published works of politicians and commanders are equally useful, including John Simon, ed., *The Papers of Ulysses S. Grant* (1967–); Lynda Crist, ed., *Papers of Jefferson Davis* (1971–); John Niven, ed., *Salmon P. Chase Papers* (1993–); Peter Cozzens and Robert Girardi, eds., *The Military Memoirs of General John Pope* (1998); Leroy Graf, Ralph Haskins, and Paul Bergeron, eds., *The Papers of Andrew Johnson* (1967–); Roy P. Basler, ed., *The Collected Works of Lincoln* (1953–55); and Brooks D. Simpson and Jean V. Berlin, eds., *Sherman's Civil War: Selected Correspondence of William T. Sherman, 1860–1865* (1999).

Additionally, the essays published by editors Robert Johnson and Clarence Buel in *Battles and Leaders of the Civil War* (1887–88) as well as those in the *Southern Historical Society Papers* (1876–1959) and the *Confederate Veteran* (1893–1932) provide some later assessments of the campaigns and battles by participants and others. The various published papers of military historical societies such as the *Papers of the Military Society of Massachusetts* (1896–1918) and *The Military Order of the Loyal Legion of the United States* (1887–1915) are also informative.

Though frequently excluded in such essays, a few unpublished dissertations should not be overlooked. The most prominent on Shiloh is Edward O. Cunningham's "Shiloh and the Western Campaign of 1862" (Louisiana State University, 1966). Gerald Prokopowicz, "All for the Regiment: Unit Cohesion and Tactical Stalemate in the Army of the Ohio, 1861–1862" (Harvard University, 1994), is an excellent analysis of the Army of the Ohio. Also useful and perceptive is Samuel Kamm's dissertation on Edwin Stanton's assistant secretary of war, "The Civil War Career of Thomas A. Scott" (University of Pennsylvania, 1940). The best account of the Federal occupation of Tennessee remains Edwin T. Hardison, "In the Toils of War: Andrew Johnson and the Federal Occupation of Tennessee, 1862–1865" (University of Tennessee, 1981).

Campaign studies, battle narratives, and unit histories abound on these campaigns. Among the more prominent include Thomas Van Horne, *History of the Army of the Cumberland* (1875); Henry M. Cist, *The Army of the Cumberland* (1885); Stanley Horn, *The Army of Tennessee* (1941); and Thomas Connelly, *Army of the*

Heartland: The Army of Tennessee, 1861–1862 (1967). One should also consult Larry Daniel, *Soldering in the Army of Tennessee* (1991). The first scholarly assessment, though not the best, of the battle of Fort Donelson is James T. Hamilton, *The Battle of Fort Donelson* (1968). Though not a battle narrative, Joseph Frank and George Reaves's study, *"Seeing the Elephant": Raw Recruits at the Battle of Shiloh* (1989), is an excellent examination of the combat experience at the battle of Shiloh. James McDonough's *Shiloh: In Hell before Night* (1977) and Wiley Sword's *Shiloh: Bloody April* (1974) are excellent analyses of the battle. While both emphasize the possibility of Confederate victory on the first day and the failure to capitalize during the second, McDonough highlights the failure of Beauregard, whereas Sword places much of the blame on Johnston.

Biographies continue to surface in Civil War scholarship, particularly on the Confederate commanders and politicians involved in the campaigns. The best account to date on Jefferson Davis is William C. Davis's *Jefferson Davis: The Man and His Hour* (1991), though Felicity Allen's *Jefferson Davis: Unconquerable Heart* (1999) has appeared. The following continue to endure as the best analyses on the Confederate high command in the West: Grady McWhiney, *Braxton Bragg and Confederate Defeat* (1969); T. Harry Williams, *P.G.T. Beauregard: Napoleon in Gray* (1954); Charles Roland, *Albert Sidney Johnston: Soldier of Three Republics* (1964); Brian Steel Wills, *A Battle from the Start: The Life of Nathan Bedford Forrest* (1992); Joseph Parks, *General Leonidas Polk, C.S.A.: The Fighting Bishop* (1962); Arndt Stickles, *Simon Bolivar Buckner: Borderland Knight* (1940); Arthur B. Carter, *The Tarnished Cavalier: Major General Earl Van Dorn, C.S.A.* (1999); and Nathaniel Cheairs Hughes, *General William J. Hardee: Old Reliable* (1965). In 1993 Nathaniel Cheairs Hughes and Roy Stonesifer produced a long-overdue work on Gideon Pillow, *The Life and Wars of Gideon J. Pillow* (1993). In 1990, as a Confederate companion to T. Harry Williams's *Lincoln and His Generals* (1952), Steven Woodworth published *Jefferson Davis and His Generals: The Failure of Confederate Command in the West*. Woodworth's emphases throughout his study concern personalities, Davis's varied relationships with other commanders, and the struggle between political and military authorities in dealing with the challenges of the West. His recent work, *Civil War Generals in Defeat* (1998), extends some of these themes and explores commanders, both North and South, who by their losses provided valuable lessons for Union and Confederate political leaders in shaping war aims.

The lives of Union commanders who participated in the campaigns from Fort Henry to Corinth have only recently received the attention of scholars. For all his prominence in the war, Henry W. Halleck has been the subject of only one modern biography, and even that is outdated. Still, Stephen Ambrose, *Halleck: Lincoln's Chief of Staff* (1962), is quite useful, though recently Curt Anders has added to the literature on Halleck with his *Henry Halleck's War: A Fresh Look at Lincoln's Controversial Commander-in-Chief* (1999). Not surprisingly, both William T. Sherman and Ulysses S. Grant have received considerably more consideration than any other Union commanders in the war, except perhaps George B. McClellan. The most thoughtful and thorough treatment of Sherman is John Marszalek's 1993 work, *Sherman: A Soldier's Passion for Order.* William McFeely's *Grant: A Biography* (1981) portrays the general as an ordinary commander with no particularly distinguishing qualities, but who was able to be an effective leader (a theme Geoffrey Perret also explores in his work, *Ulysses S. Grant: Soldier and President* [1997]). In *Let Us Have Peace: Ulysses S. Grant and the Politics of War and Reconstruction, 1861–1868* (1991), Brooks Simpson depicts Grant as a commander who understood the political implications of the war, which made him most effective. Simpson builds on this earlier portrayal of Grant in his recent work, *Ulysses S. Grant: Triumph over Adversity, 1822–1865* (2000), the first installment of a planned two-volume biography. Stephen Sears, in *George B. McClellan: The Young Napoleon* (1988), reveals that as general in chief of the armies, McClellan certainly appreciated the political significance of the war in the West in early 1862 but failed to do anything about the command relationship between Halleck and Don Carlos Buell or to promote an aggressive offensive in the West. Stephen Engle's *Don Carlos Buell: "Most Promising of All"* (1999) analyzes the relationship between the Union commanders in the West as well as the effects of Federal occupation in Tennessee. Like Halleck, Pope has been accorded minimal attention by modern biographers. In 1990 Wallace Schutz and Walter Trenerry produced a brief account of Pope's military career in *Abandoned by Lincoln: A Military Biography of General John Pope,* and recently Peter Cozzens has contributed to our understanding of the commander in his *General John Pope: A Life for the Nation* (2000). John McClernand's Civil War career has seen the light of day in Richard L. Kiper's *Major General John Alexander McClernand: Politician in Uniform* (1999). In addition to military biographies, the works chronicling the lives of Edwin M. Stanton and Andrew Johnson need to be consulted for their roles in the war in the West during early 1862; see Thomas Benjamin and Harold Hyman, *Stanton: The Life and Times of Lincoln's Secretary of War* (1962), and Hans L. Trefousse, *Andrew Johnson* (1989).

Besides general histories of the war, scholars have treated the campaigns and battles of western Tennessee in 1862 in the context of combined military operations. Rowena Reed's *Combined Operations in the Civil War* (1958) is an excellent example of such a study. More recently, however, scholars have brought these campaigns into their proper social and political context. Benjamin Franklin Cooling has led the way with two excellent and long-needed works: *Forts Henry and Donelson: The Key to the Confederate Heartland* (1987) and *Fort Donelson's Legacy: War and Society in Kentucky and Tennessee, 1862–1863* (1997). Larry Daniel has added to this new conceptualization of seeing battles in the broadest context— for example, arguing that the battle of Shiloh changed the attitudes of Federal military and civilian leaders about the political implications of the war—in his most recent work, *Shiloh: The Battle that Changed the Civil War.* Stephen V. Ash has added to our understanding of the social complexity of the region that came under Federal occupation as a result of the twin rivers campaign and the capture of Corinth in *Middle Tennessee Society Transformed, 1860–1870* (1988). Important insights can also be drawn from Ash's *When the Yankees Came: Conflict and Chaos in the Occupied South, 1861–1865* (1995), which is an excellent study of the Federal occupation of the South. Peter Maslowski, *Treason Must Be Made Odious: Military Occupation and Wartime Reconstruction in Nashville, Tennessee, 1862–1865* (1978), and Walter T. Durham, *Nashville: The Occupied City* (1985), deal exclusively with the Union occupation in Nashville, while Mark Grimsley's *The Hard Hand of War: Union Military Policy toward Southern Civilians, 1861–1865* (1995) is a valuable analysis of the evolution of Federal policy against Southerners, arguing that Northern leaders ultimately combined deliberate severity with an equally deliberate attempt at restraint. Too, Ira Berlin et al., eds., *Freedom: A Documentary History of Emancipation, 1861–1867* (1985); Ira Berlin et al., eds., *The Destruction of Slavery* (1985); and Jeffrey Rogers Hummel, *Emancipating Slaves, Enslaving Free Men: A History of the American Civil War* (1996), should not be overlooked in considering the effect of these campaigns on the institution of slavery.

Index

McDowell, John A., 135
McPherson, James B., 155
McWhiney, Grady, 149
Melville, Herman, 162
Michie, James, 132
Miller, Madison, 141
Mill Springs, 38
Mitchel, Ormsby M., 104, 126, 172,
    191, 192, 195, 196, 197
Montgomery, James, 201
Moore, David, 140
Morgan, George, 126
Morrison, William, 70
Morton, Oliver P., 10, 13, 174, 180
Mott, W. H., 96
Munch, Emil, 141

Nashville TN, 2, 6, 16, 85, 89, 97, 98,
    100, 101, 103, 104, 106, 107, 109
Negley, James S., 126
Nelson, William, 16, 97, 102, 127, 137,
    143, 145, 151, 154, 159, 162, 164
Nevins, Allan, 1
New Madrid MO, 39, 123
Nicolay, John, 81

Oglesby, Richard, 70

Peabody, Everett, 138, 140, 141, 142
Phelps, Seth L., 61, 91
Pickens, Francis, 202–3
Pillow, Gideon, xxi, 14, 15, 17, 49, 65,
    66, 67, 68, 71, 74, 76, 77, 79, 80, 89,
    108
Pittsburg Landing TN, 116, 121, 124,
    125, 128, 130, 131, 137, 143, 147
Polk, Leonidas, xxi, 14, 15, 16, 17, 18,
    36, 44, 45, 46, 48, 56, 60, 64, 65,
    66, 80, 105, 109, 118, 119, 120, 121,
    122, 131, 132, 133, 134, 157, 158, 159
Pope, John, 19, 39, 105, 106, 169, 170,
    176, 177, 183, 184, 201

Porter, William D., 32
Potter, M. D., 84
Powell, James E., 138, 139
Prentiss, Benjamin, 128, 135, 140, 141,
    142, 146, 148, 152, 157, 168
Prickett, Thomas, 160, 180
Pryor, Roger, 73
Pugh, Richard, 162

Randall, Alexander, 10
Rawlins, John A., 125
Republicans, 27, 28, 43, 94, 95, 107,
    108, 193
Ricker, Elbridge, 118
Roland, Charles, 79
Rousseau, Lovell, 163
Rowley, William, 151
Ruff, Joseph, 139, 142
Ruggles, Daniel, 109, 118, 133, 152
Rumsey, John W., 136

Savannah TN, 127
Scott, Thomas A., 52, 56, 72, 92, 101,
    102, 103, 104, 173
Shanks, William, 154
Sharp, John, 129
Shaver, R. G., 140
Sheridan, Philip, 170, 174
Sherman, William T., 3, 8, 9, 18, 19,
    30, 64, 72, 115, 116, 118, 124, 125,
    134, 135, 136, 142, 145, 154, 156,
    157, 161, 162, 165, 167, 171, 179,
    188, 189, 196, 197, 200
Shiloh TN, 124, 139, 140, 142, 168
Smith, Charles F., 32, 36, 38, 40, 53,
    57, 62, 70, 74, 78, 80, 91, 98, 105,
    113, 114, 117, 124, 128, 137, 143
Smith, George, 91
Smith, Edmund Kirby, 110, 199
Stanton, Edwin M., 39, 50, 52, 92,
    101, 106, 129, 172, 184, 196
Statham, William, 120, 150

In the Great Campaigns of the Civil War series

Six Armies in Tennessee
The Chickamauga and Chattanooga Campaigns
By Steven E. Woodworth

Fredericksburg and Chancellorsville
The Dare Mark Campaign
By Daniel E. Sutherland

Banners to the Breeze
The Kentucky Campaign, Corinth, and Stones River
By Earl J. Hess

The Chessboard of War
Sherman and Hood in the Autumn Campaigns of 1864
By Anne J. Bailey

Atlanta 1864
Last Chance for the Confederacy
By Richard M. McMurry

Struggle for the Heartland
The Campaigns from Fort Henry to Corinth
Stephen D. Engle